A Study in Dissent

The Warren–Gerry Correspondence

1776-1792

A Study in Dissent

The Warren–Gerry Correspondence

1776-1792

. .

Edited with Introduction and Commentary by

C. Harvey Gardiner

Carbondale and Edwardsville
Southern Illinois University Press

Feffer & Simons, Inc.
London and Amsterdam

To Philip D. Sang

a philanthropic collector

CONTENTS

. .

1778

1779

EDITORIAL APPARATUS
AND METHOD

. .

Inter-letter Commentary

Varying amounts of historical summation accompany these letters. That inter-letter commentary is intended to tie the individual letters together by treating the intervening activities of the correspondents, thereby attaining maximum continuity and unity.

The commentary is not competitive with the letters, nor does it summarize them. Rather it is offered as a support for the letters, in the revelation of the personalities and problems. Because they are in a supporting role, the inter-letter comments have been compressed and, the better to insure that relationship, set in a type size that readily distinguishes them from the correspondence.

Editorial Practices

Whenever possible, in the texts of the letters, abbreviations and contractions, some of which are irregular as well as inconsistent, are expanded silently. This includes the ampersand and the thorn. However, the form "&c." is retained, as is the abbreviation for Esquire. In the docketing, on the other hand, all abbreviations have been retained. Superscript has been lowered.

Terminal punctuation remains as found, with one exception— question marks have been introduced where needed. To facilitate reader comprehension, internal punctuation, including apostrophes and commas—the latter in enumerations, has been supplied. When dashes or exaggerated spacing between sentences appear to indicate paragraphing, paragraphing is introduced.

Grammar and spelling, except for the abbreviations and contractions which are silently expanded, remain as found in the materials employed. The original capitalization has also been retained, except that initial lower case letters on words opening sentences have been capitalized.

Textual Devices

[. . .]   Word or words missing and not conjecturable.

[roman]   Conjectural reading of missing or illegible material. A question mark follows when the reading is doubtful.

[*italics*]   Editorial insertion in the text.

⟨roman⟩   Material crossed out by the writer in the manuscript.

Symbols Used to Describe Manuscripts

ADS   Autograph Document Signed

AL   Autograph Letter

ALS   Autograph Letter Signed

LC   Letter Book Copy

LS   Letter Signed

Provenance of Texts

An effort has been made to offer an exhaustive, but not definitive, statement of the availability of the letters employed. The sequence of citation, for any individual item, is as follows: from manuscript to printed and from the complete to the excerpt. In every instance, however, the text listed first is the one used in this project.

The following collections of manuscripts have been utilized:

Boston Public Library, Rare Book Department
    Mellen Chamberlain Collection

Harvard University, The Houghton Library
    Frederick M. Dearborn Collection

Library of Congress, Manuscript Division
    Elbridge Gerry Papers

Massachusetts Historical Society
    Elbridge Gerry 1772–1882 (gift of S. E. Morison)

Gerry II Papers
Russell W. Knight–Gerry Collection
Mercy Warren Letterbook
Mercy Warren Papers

The New-York Historical Society
Miscellaneous Manuscripts, Gen. James Warren

The New York Public Library, Manuscript Division
Gerry-Townsend Papers

The Historical Society of Pennsylvania
George M. Conarroe Collection, American Authors Series
Frank M. Etting Collection, American Authors Series

Southern Illinois University Library, Carbondale
Elbridge Gerry Collection of Elsie O. and Philip D. Sang, River
Forest, Illinois

Justin G. Turner, Los Angeles, California
Elbridge Gerry Collection

Biographical Notes

Unless otherwise indicated, the brief biographical notes by which
individuals mentioned in the correspondence are identified have been
derived from the *Dictionary of American Biography*, *Appletons' Cyclopaedia of
American Biography*, and the *Biographical Directory of the American Congress*,
1774–1961.

Appreciation Voiced

Director Stephen T. Riley and his staff at the Massachusetts Historical
Society once again have extended their unlimited support and assistance
to a scholarly project deeply dependent upon the manuscript riches of the
Society's collections. Those kindnesses are most gratefully acknowledged.
Other indispensable assists came from John Alden, Keeper of Rare Books
at the Boston Public Library, from Librarian W. H. Bond and the late
William A. Jackson of The Houghton Library at Harvard University,
from Librarian Robert O. Dougan of the Huntington Library, from
Director James J. Heslin and Wilmer R. Leech, Curator of Manuscripts
of The New-York Historical Society, from Robert W. Hill, Keeper of
Manuscripts at The New York Public Library, and from Director

Nicholas B. Wainwright and the late R. N. Williams 2d of The Historical Society of Pennsylvania.

Three private collectors have been especially helpful: Philip D. Sang of River Forest, Illinois, Russell W. Knight of Marblehead, Massachusetts, and Justin G. Turner of Los Angeles, California. All epitomize the collector concerned with scholarship.

In addition to generous individuals and cooperative institutions, correspondence that concluded many fruitless searches came from archivists and librarians from coast to coast.

A special word of appreciation is extended to Nelson Gardiner, my son, whose widening awareness of bibliography and biography admirably served this project.

Short Titles and Abbreviations

This alphabetical list includes only those works cited frequently.

AC

> *The Debates and Proceedings in the Congress of the United States; with an Appendix, Containing Important State Papers and Public Documents, and All the Laws of a Public Nature*, Washington 1834——

Adams FC

> Lyman H. Butterfield *et al* (eds.), *Adams Family Correspondence*, Cambridge, 1963——

Anthony, *First Lady*

> Katherine Anthony, *First Lady of the Revolution: the Life of Mercy Otis Warren*, Garden City, 1958.

Austin, *EG*

> James T. Austin, *The Life of Elbridge Gerry*, 2 vols., Boston, 1828–29.

Burnett, *CC*

> Edmund Cody Burnett, *The Continental Congress*, New York, 1941.

Commager and Morris, *'Seventy-Six*

> Henry Steele Commager and Richard B. Morris (eds.), *The Spirit of 'Seventy-Six; The Story of the American Revolution as Told by Participants*, 2 vols., Indianapolis, 1958.

D&A–JA

> L. H. Butterfield *et al* (eds.), *Diary and Autobiography of John Adams*, 4 vols., Cambridge, 1961.

DFC

Gaillard Hunt and James Brown Scott (eds.), *The Debates in the Federal Convention of 1787 which Framed the Constitution of the United States of America*, New York, 1920.

Farrand, *Records*

Max Farrand (ed.), *The Records of the Federal Convention of 1787*, 4 vols., revd. edn., New Haven, 1937.

Force, *AA*

Peter Force (ed.), *American Archives*, 4th ser., 6 vols., Washington, 1837–46.

Ford, *Essays*

Paul Leicester Ford (ed.), *Essays on the Constitution of the United States*, Brooklyn, 1892.

Ford, *Pamphlets*

Paul Leicester Ford (ed.), *Pamphlets on the Constitution of the United States . . .*, Brooklyn, 1888.

JCC

Journals of the Continental Congress, 1774–1789, 34 vols., Washington, 1904–37.

LCC

Edmund C. Burnett (ed.), *Letters of Members of the Continental Congress*, 8 vols., Washington, 1921–36.

Mass., *A&R*

Massachusetts. *Acts and Resolves of Massachusetts* (with variants thereof), Boston, 1890——

NEHGR

The New-England Historical and Genealogical Register

Syrett, *P-AH*

Harold C. Syrett *et al* (eds.), *The Papers of Alexander Hamilton*, New York, 1961——

W-A Ltrs.

Warren-Adams Letters; being chiefly a Correspondence among John Adams, Samuel Adams, and James Warren, 2 vols., Boston, 1917–25, constitute volumes 72 and 73 of the Massachusetts Historical Society *Collections*.

WARREN–GERRY: *A Chronology*

· ·

1775 July 19 to 1776 May 10
EG represented the town of Marblehead in the Massachusetts House of Representatives

1775 July 19 to 1776 May 10
JW represented the town of Plymouth and served as Speaker of the Massachusetts House of Representatives

1775 July 27
JW unanimously elected paymaster general by the Continental Congress

1775 November 10
JW, as Speaker of the Massachusetts House of Representatives, signed the resolve which named the Massachusetts delegation to the Continental Congress

1776 January 18
EG elected to the Continental Congress, to serve until January 1, 1777

1776 January 25
EG started for Philadelphia, via Framingham, Worcester, Brookfield, and Springfield

1776 February 9 to July 16
EG attended the Continental Congress in Philadelphia

1776 March 30
JW submitted his resignation as paymaster general of the Continental Army

1776 April 18
JW's resignation from the office of paymaster general of the army
was received by the Congress and referred to committee

1776 April 19
By resolution JW's resignation was accepted

1776 May 8
JW named one of three major generals of militia by the House of
Representatives of Massachusetts but declined the appointment,
Azor Orne succeeding him

1776 May 29 to 1777 May 10
JW represented the town of Plymouth and served as Speaker of
the Massachusetts House of Representatives

1776 May 29 to 1777 May 10
EG elected to represent Marblehead in the Massachusetts House
of Representatives

1776 June 19
JW appointed the second major general of Massachusetts militia

1776 July 16
EG left Philadelphia for Massachusetts, visiting General Joseph
Trumbull in New York en route

1776 mid-year [?]
JW declined appointment as justice of the Supreme Judicial Court
of Massachusetts

1776 August 17
EG started for Philadelphia, visiting Gov. Jonathan Trumbull of
Connecticut en route

1776 September 2 to December 31
EG attended the Continental Congress in Philadelphia and
Baltimore

1776 early autumn
JW declined an opportunity to lead Massachusetts troops in the
field

1776 October 29
       JW became President of the nine-man Board of War created by
       Massachusetts

1776 December 10
       EG elected to the Continental Congress, to serve until January 1,
       1778

1777 January 1 to December 31
       EG attended the Continental Congress in Baltimore, Philadelphia,
       Lancaster and York

1777 May 6
       JW named to the three-man Navy Board of the Eastern Depart-
       ment by the Continental Congress

1777 May 28 to 1778 May 1
       JW represented the town of Plymouth and served as Speaker of the
       Massachusetts House of Representatives

1777 summer [?]
       JW resigned his commission as major general of Massachusetts
       militia

1777 December 4
       EG elected to the Continental Congress, to serve the calendar year
       1778

1778 January 1 to December 31
       EG attended the Continental Congress in York and Philadelphia

1778 May
       JW failed to win re-election to the Massachusetts House of Repre-
       sentatives

1778 July 9
       EG signed the Articles of Confederation

1778 October 15
       EG elected to the Continental Congress, to serve the calendar year
       1779

1779 January 1 to December 31
       EG attended the Continental Congress in Philadelphia

1779 May 26 to 1780 May 17
      JW represented the town of Plymouth in the Massachusetts House
      of Representatives

1779 November 18
      EG elected to the Continental Congress

1779
      MW's play *The Motley Assembly: A Farce* was published in Boston

1780 January 1 to February 17
      EG attended the Continental Congress in Philadelphia

1780 May 31 to October 4
      JW represented the town of Plymouth in the Massachusetts House
      of Representatives

1780 October 4
      EG elected to the Continental Congress but did not attend

1780 October 31
      EG declined election to Senate by Essex County and accepted seat
      in the House of Representatives as representative of Marblehead

1780 October
      JW chosen lieutenant governor by the General Court but he
      declined the post

1780 October 25 to 1781, spring
      JW represented the town of Plymouth in the Massachusetts House
      of Representatives

1781 January
      JW purchased Milton Hill, the estate of former governor Thomas
      Hutchinson

1781 January
      EG elected to membership in the American Academy of Arts and
      Sciences

1781 June
      JW, MW and family moved to Milton Hill

1781 June
      EG elected to the Continental Congress but did not attend

1782 May 30
EG formally notified that he had been elected senator by Essex County, which post he declined on June 1

1782 June 6
EG elected to the Continental Congress, to serve until November 5, 1783, but did not attend

1782 autumn
EG and JW named to the Massachusetts delegation to Congress, for the year beginning November 1, 1782, but neither attended

1783 May 23
Death of MW's brother James Otis, "The Patriot"

1783 June 27
EG elected to the Continental Congress

1783 August 14
EG took his seat in Congress, in Princeton

1783 August 14 to November
EG attended the Continental Congress in Princeton

1783 December 13–31
EG attended the Continental Congress in Annapolis

1784 January 1 to June 3
EG attended the Continental Congress in Annapolis

1784 May 20–24
EG absent from seat of Congress, with committee charged with reporting on Potomac site for national capital

1784 June 17
EG elected to the Continental Congress

1784 December 6–24
EG attended the Continental Congress in Trenton

1785 January 13 to March 1
EG attended the Continental Congress in New York City

1785 May
      JW lost race for governorship

1785 July 12 to November 4
      EG attended the Continental Congress in New York City

1786 January 12
      EG married Ann Thompson of New York City

1786 June 17
      EG, one of four, named to represent Massachusetts at the meeting
      scheduled to discuss trade regulation at Annapolis. He declined to
      attend

1787 March 1
      EG's first child, Catherine, born

1787 March 10
      EG, one of five, named to represent Massachusetts at the conven-
      tion in Philadelphia to revise the Articles of Confederation

1787 April 25
      EG appointed Justice of Peace, Middlesex County, by Governor
      James Bowdoin

1787 May 29
      EG took his seat in the convention in Philadelphia

1787 May 30 to 1788, spring
      JW represented the town of Milton and served as Speaker of the
      Massachusetts House of Representatives

1787 late July to early August
      EG spent the period that the convention was not in session with his
      family in New York City

1787 August 10
      EG resumed his seat in the Philadelphia convention

1787 December
      JW and EG failed to win election to the Massachusetts ratifying
      convention

1787 December 27 to 1788 January *passim*
      JW's series of letters signed "Helvidius Priscus" appeared in the
      Independent Chronicle (Boston)

1787 December 29 to 1788 February 6 *passim*
JW's series of letters signed "A Republican Federalist" appeared in the *Massachusetts Centinel* (Boston)

1788 January 14
Massachusetts Convention invited EG to take a seat and answer questions of fact respecting the passing of the Constitution

1788 January 18–22
EG, seated with the Convention, answered questions regarding the passing of the Constitution

1788

MW's pamphlet *Observations On the New Constitution, and on the Federal and State Conventions* published in Boston and circulated widely

1788 late
EG's second child, a son, born

1789 January 29
EG elected to the U.S. House of Representatives

1789 March 4 to September 29
EG attended first session of the First Congress

1789 autumn
EG's second child, first son, died

1790 January 4 to August 12
EG attended the second session of the First Congress

1790 March 25
JW went to New York to settle his Navy Board accounts of 1776–81

1790 early summer
EG's third child born

1790

MW's volume *Poems, Dramatic and Miscellaneous* published in Boston. Among contents were "The Sack of Rome: a Tragedy" and "The Ladies of Castille: a Tragedy."

1790 December 6 to 1791 March 3
EG attended the third session of the First Congress

1791 early
EG's daughter Eliza born

1791 March 4
Winslow Warren named a second lieutenant in the 2nd Regiment of the U.S. Army

1791 spring
Winslow Warren served sentence in debtors' prison in Boston

1791 October 24 to 1792 May 8
EG attended first session of the Second Congress

1791 November 4
2nd Lieut. Winslow Warren killed in ambush by Indians

1791 December 22
EG's daughter Ann born

1792 May 30
JW served on Governor Hancock's council for the term beginning this day

1792 November 5 to 1793 March 2
EG attended the second session of the Second Congress

INTRODUCTION

· ·

THIS IS a perspective, a limited perspective. The focus embraces three persons, two problems, and a single short interval of time. The individuals are James and Mercy Warren and Elbridge Gerry; the problems are those of political outlook attending both the transition of Massachusetts from colony to state and the erection of a national government. The period is that between 1776 and 1792, from a moment before the Declaration of Independence to one after the inauguration of the government based on the Constitution. The focus on the personalities, the problems, and the period results in yet another perspective, a perspective on dissent.

Massachusetts nurtured them, and all three, James and Mercy Warren and Elbridge Gerry, were revolutionaries. When action, increasingly the action of armed conflict, changed the nature and dimension of colonial American protest, a difference developed among these rebels which set Gerry apart from the Warrens. For all the years between 1776 and 1792, the Warrens, despite their awareness of the wider world and the bigger struggle, immersed themselves in and identified themselves primarily with the affairs of Massachusetts. Even when an occasional office enabled James Warren to contribute locally to the national cause, he did so as one to whom the Plymouth-Boston axis was most important, as one whose enthusiasms diminished, and whose vision dimmed when thrust beyond the boundaries of the Bay State.

While the Warrens labored unstintingly on behalf of American freedom at the state level, within Massachusetts, Elbridge Gerry adopted as the arena of his political activity the nascent national scene. Even when an occasional office kept Gerry within Massachusetts, for short periods, the man from Marblehead primarily identified himself with the search for solutions to national problems.

James Warren

Born in Plymouth in 1726 and graduated from Harvard in 1745, James Warren was descended from Richard Warren of the "Mayflower."[1] A farmer-merchant in the area of his birth, sandy-haired James married Mercy Otis in 1754. Their five sons, James, Winslow, Charles, Henry and George, were born in Plymouth between 1757 and 1766.

Meanwhile James Warren had embarked on a political career. After serving as sheriff of Plymouth County, he entered the lower house of the Massachusetts legislature, where he served regularly from 1766 until the years of the Revolution. A vigorous member and spokesman of the patriot cause, he was confidant and friend of both John and Samuel Adams. A stanch believer in organization, Warren helped to establish and served on numerous revolutionary committees, including committees of correspondence.

On the eve of the outbreak of hostilities Warren's hopes and fears welled up in his correspondence. Shortly after the Boston Tea Party, he wrote John Adams from Plymouth, "Have for some time thought it necessary that the People should strike some bold stroke, and try the Issue."[2] Six months later, in mid-1774, John Adams, named to the First Continental Congress, was told by James, "if I was enquired of, what I thought should be done with the Claim of Exemption from Parliamentary Legislation, as well as Taxation, and some other Grand Questions that have been agitated here, I should answer that it was proper, practicable, expedient, wise, just, good, and necessary, that they should be held up in their full extent in the Congress at Philadelphia, and that means should be devised to support them."

Shortly before Christmas, 1774, Warren wrote John Adams, "I have been extreamly engaged since my return, as a Citizen and Soldier. Civil and military matters engage my whole Attention and engross all my Time. To execute the Resolves of the Congress, to settle my military matters, and prevent the feuds and dissentions that generally arise from the Folly of some, and the Ambition of others, is my whole Business, and has superceded the delightful Study of Agriculture, and scarce left a

---

1. Aside from the short sketches of his career by Clifford K. Shipton in *Sibley's Harvard Graduates* (13 vols., Cambridge, 1873–1965), 11:584–606, and G. Philip Bauer in the *Dictionary of American Biography*, 19:478–79, James Warren has suffered neglect. Doctoral research currently underway at Clark University may fulfill Warren's need for a biographer.

2. This and the immediately succeeding quotations are from the *Warren-Adams Letters* (2 vols., Boston, 1917–25), 1:23, 27–28, 35, 45, 46, 47, 50, 78, 97.

Trace in my mind of Tull's fine Phylosophical System of Vegetation. If those matters continue, I may as well beat my plow shares into Swords, and pruning Hooks into Spears." A few weeks later, more adamant than original, he declared, "now is the Time, the exact Crisis, to determine the point, and the sooner the better, before the Tories here can compleat their efforts to disunite and embarrass."

To Mercy, whom he longed to see, James Warren wrote from Concord on April 6, 1775, "This Town is full of Cannon, ammunition, stores, etc., and the Army long for them and they want nothing but strength to Induce an attempt on them. The people are ready and determine to defend this Country Inch by Inch." On the nineteenth, at Lexington and Concord, the first inches of that military defense were measured out.

A resolute and persevering man, James Warren needed to draw upon his inner strengths in 1775. From Watertown, where he was serving in the Provincial Congress, he wrote John Adams in May, "I am almost discouraged. However as I was born to struggle with difficulties, [I] shall endeavour to answer the End of my Creation as well as I can. The principal Objects of our Attention have been the regulation and officering of the Army, and arming the men, and devising ways and means to support the enormous Expence incurred under our present Situation." A few weeks later the impatient rebel raged, "There is a degree of Timidity and slowness in our movements which my Soul abominates."

When John Adams reported his failure to win a significant Continental military appointment for Warren, James, in honesty and humility, replied, "I am content to move in a small sphere." That sphere, throughout the war—indeed throughout his life, was Massachusetts.

In July, 1775, Warren became Speaker of the new Assembly in his beloved colony. Soon he confided to John Adams, "Our Assembly are drudging on in the old way, shackled with forms and plagued with the concurrence and consent of several branches. A question was started and warmly contested whether our Constitution consisted of two or three branches." In the earliest moments of the transition of Massachusetts from colony to state, Warren played a leading role.

Mercy Warren

Born Mercy Otis in West Barnstable on Cape Cod in 1728, Mercy Warren was early immersed in literature and politics. Compensating for her lack of formal schooling was the access she enjoyed to the library of the

Reverend Jonathan Russell. Native intelligence, wide reading, a phenomenal memory, and unflinching honesty were ingredients, early and late, in this remarkable woman. The political awareness that led her lawyer father to a seat in the General Court in the 1750's and her lawyer brother James to Patriot immortality because of the Writs of Assistance so permeated the Otis household as to be a fact of life in the maturing of Mercy.[3]

Her marriage to James Warren in 1754 was one of deep mutual love and compatible political outlook. In time, despite the demands of a household that included the rearing of their five sons, Mercy's love of political liberty and forceful literary expression dictated certain intellectual endeavors.

In the spring of 1772—by which time her father had served as Speaker of the General Court, her brother had been clubbed unmercifully, and her husband had become a tower of liberal strength, Mercy's dramatic tirade *The Adulateur* was leveled at Governor Hutchinson and his supporters.

The Defeat, another propaganda blast from Mercy's partisan pen, appeared in mid-1773. Likewise aimed at the Hutchinson administration, *The Defeat* contributed to the climate of opinion that led to the Boston Tea Party.

The dark-haired lady with the broad brow made a third contribution to Revolutionary literature in January, 1775. *The Group* aimed its satiric barbs at the intolerable implementers of the Massachusetts Government Act of 1774. James Warren, having urged his wife to write the piece, sent it to John Adams at the Continental Congress. Soon it was available to readers in Philadelphia and New York as well as Boston.

Mercy continued to meditate and write, at times at the side of James in the bustle of the Boston area, at times with her brood and her embroidery in the solitude of Plymouth. The degree to which she interested herself in politics, and the means she employed for expressing herself were, for her day, more masculine than feminine. Quite naturally it followed that many of her admirers and correspondents were prominent masculine revolutionaries of the period.

---

3. Mercy Warren's biographers, a trio of women, include: Alice Brown, *Mercy Warren* (New York, 1896); Maud Macdonald Hutcheson, "Mercy Warren, 1728–1814," *The William and Mary Quarterly*, X (July, 1953), 378–402; and Katharine Anthony, *First Lady of the Revolution: The Life of Mercy Otis Warren* (New York, 1958). Of these the Hutcheson article is the best. Also helpful is G. Philip Bauer's article on Mercy Warren in the *Dictionary of American Biography*, 19: 484–85.

In January, 1775, in a letter to John Adams, she asserted, "let me add my fervent Wishes that you and the other Gentlemen of the ensuing Congress may be endowed with Wisdom and Resolution equal to the Difficulties of the Day, and if you attempt to repair the shattered Constitution, or to erect a new one, may it be constructed with such symmetry of Features, such Vigour of Nerves, and such strength of sinew, that it may never be in the power of Ambition or Tyranny to shake the durable Fabrick."[4]

Seventy-five days after the initiation of hostilities, while with James in Watertown, Mercy wrote their mutual friend John Adams, "I shall not attempt to give you a description of the ten fold difficulties that surround us. You have doubtless had it from better hands. Yet I cannot forbear to drop a tear over the inhabitants of our capital, most of them sent naked from the city to seek a retreat in the villages, and to cast themselves on the charity of the first hospitable hand that will receive them. Those who are left behind are exposed to the daily insults of a foe lost to that sense of honour, freedom and valour, once the characteristic of Britons, and even of the generosity and humanity which has long been the boast of all civilized nations. And while the plagues of famine, pestilence and tyranny reign within the walls, the sword is lifted without, and the artillery of war continually thundering in our ears."

Destiny nominated no woman to play a more meaningful role than did Mercy Warren in the promotion and prosecution of the American Revolution. Quite appropriately she has been termed "First Lady of the Revolution."

Elbridge Gerry

Son of a shipmaster-merchant of Marblehead, Elbridge Gerry was born in 1744 in that port town.[5] A member of the class of 1762 at Harvard, Elbridge returned to Marblehead and joined his father and brothers in the mercantile business that tied their commercial interests to both Europe and the Caribbean.

---

4. This and the succeeding quotation are from *Warren-Adams Letters*, 1:38–39, 71.

5. To date Elbridge Gerry's biographers have produced the following: James T. Austin, *The Life of Elbridge Gerry* (2 vols., Boston, 1828–29); the unsatisfying effort of his son-in-law; and S. E. Morison's "Elbridge Gerry, Gentleman-Democrat," *New England Quarterly*, II (January, 1929), 6–33, a provocative article which resulted from Morison's research for the shorter account of Gerry's career written for the *Dictionary of American Biography*, 7:222–27. Professor George A. Billias's study of Gerry is awaited by students of the Revolution.

In 1772, even as he joined James Warren—who was eighteen years his senior, in the General Court, he fell under the influence of the patriotic fervor of dynamic Samuel Adams. In December, egged on by the word and action of Adams' committee of correspondence in Boston, Elbridge, his father and a brother became members of the Marblehead Committee of Correspondence.

"Touching the part which they are to act," Gerry wrote Samuel Adams, "it is as follows, to constantly employ their thots in inventing, when one Method fails, another Method for having our Greivances redressed; to communicate their Sentiments to the grand Committee at Boston and Collect their Opinion; to receive proposals for Opposition of that Committee or any other in the province to lay the same before the Town when Concurred by the several Committees and to continue this Method undauntedly untill some succeed and our Oppression is removed."[6]

Returned to the General Court in 1773, Gerry was named to the Massachusetts Committee of Safety. Indeed he was serving in that capacity when, on the evening of April 18, 1775, he departed from a tavern between Cambridge and Lexington in his nightclothes to escape an inquisitive detachment of British troops. Spare of frame, dapper and pleasant of manner, his long nose forming a "T" with his broad forehead, Gerry was a complex human dynamo.

After the opening military engagements, the native of Marblehead doubled his war against tyranny by assuming the chairmanship of the Committee of Supply, a post for which his mercantile experience singularly fitted him. Before spring gave way to summer Gerry, along with Warren, had endorsed the colonial need for seapower.

To love of country and a burning desire for its independence, Gerry joined unchallengeable integrity and perseverance. Although he spoke hesitantly, even laboriously, his ideas were couched in confidence and clear thinking. Unlike the ornateness of Mercy Warren's writing, Gerry's speech was devoid of elegance. Unlike James Warren, Elbridge, an equally firm friend of republican government, did not cloud his vision of national needs and procedures with provincial outlook born of love for Marblehead and Massachusetts.

Of the three patriots, James and Mercy Warren and Elbridge Gerry,

---

6. Elbridge Gerry to [Samuel Adams], copy, Marblehead, November 26, 17[72], Elbridge Gerry Collection of Elsie O. and Philip D. Sang, on deposit at Southern Illinois University Library, Carbondale.

the last-named was the most complex personality, the individual who proved most adaptable and resourceful, the person who best reconciled ideals to realities, in the moments of change that saw a colony become a state and a group of states, a national government.

C. HARVEY GARDINER

"The Oaks"
Murphysboro, Illinois
February 1, 1968

The James Warren residence at Milton Hill (formerly owned by
Governor Hutchinson). *Courtesy of the Massachusetts Historical Society.*

First page of James Warren's autograph letter of November 9, 1779 to Elbridge Gerry. *Courtesy of Collection of Elsie O. and Philip D. Sang, Southern Illinois University.*

James Warren. Portrait by John Singleton Copley. *Courtesy, Museum of Fine Arts, Boston. Bequest of Winslow Warren.*

First page of Elbridge Gerry's autograph letter of December 12, 1777 to James Warren. *Courtesy of Collection of Elsie O. and Philip D. Sang, Southern Illinois University.*

Elbridge Gerry. *Courtesy of Russell W. Knight, Marblehead, Massachusetts.*

Second page of Mercy Otis Warren's autograph letter of March 24, 1791 to Elbridge Gerry. *Courtesy of the Massachusetts Historical Society.*

M Warren

Mercy Warren. Portrait by John Singleton Copley. *Courtesy, Museum of Fine Arts, Boston. Bequest of Winslow Warren.*

The Elbridge Gerry residence (popularly known as Elmwood).
Courtesy of the Harvard University Archives.

A Study in Dissent

Massachusetts to Elbridge Gerry *et al*

. .

In Council, January 18, 1776

Whereas John Hancock, Samuel Adams, John Adams, Robert Treat Paine, and Elbridge Gerry Esqrs. have been chosen by joint Ballot of the two houses of Assembly to represent the Colony of Massachusetts Bay in New England in the American Congress untill the first day of January 1777[1]

Resolved that they or any one or more of them are hereby fully Impowered with the delegates from the other American Colonies to concert, direct, and order such further measures as shall to them appear best calculated for the Establishment of Right and Liberty to the American Colonies upon a Basis permanent and secure against the power and arts of the British Administration, And guarded against any future Encroachments of their enemies with power to adjourn to such times and places as shall appear most conducive to the publick safety and advantage

Read and accepted, sent down for Concurrence

John Lowell,[2] Deputy Secretary, pro. tem.

In the House of Representatives January 18, 1776

Read and concurred. And the Secretary is hereby directed as soon as may be to signify to each of those Gentlemen their Appointment with an attested Copy of this Order.

Sent up for Concurrence

In Council January 18, 1776   J. Warren, Speaker

Read and concurred

John Lowell, Deputy Secretary, pro. tem.

ADS, Gerry II Papers, Massachusetts Historical Society; and *JCC*, 4:122.

1. In this five-man delegation, EG was the only individual without prior service in the Continental Congress. John Hancock (1737–93) had served in the Congress of

3

1775; and Samuel Adams (1722–1803), John Adams (1735–1826), and Robert Treat Paine (1731–1814) had all served there in both 1774 and 1775. Dissension attended the naming of EG as a replacement for Thomas Cushing (1725–88) in the Congress. *See W-A Ltrs.*, 1:211–12; and *D&A-JA*, 2:227n.

  2. John Lowell (1743–1802), a lawyer, soon saw service in the militia, the state legislature, and the Continental Congress.

§

EG set out on his journey southward on January 25, in company with John Adams. Arriving in Philadelphia on February 8, EG took his seat the following day.[1]

Meanwhile, in the opening weeks of 1776, JW and MW continued to relish the acclaim accorded MW's political satire *The Group: A Farce* (Boston, 1775) which had been published shortly before the Battle of Lexington. Fortifying the patriotic fervor of the Warrens were the lines of Thomas Paine's (1737–1809) *Common Sense*, an early copy of which had been forwarded to them by Samuel Adams.[2]

EG's first committee appointment came on February 17, when he was named to a five-man standing committee charged with "superintending the treasury." The committee was "to examine the accounts of the treasurer...; to consider of ways and means for supplying gold and silver for the support of the army in Canada; to employ and instruct proper persons for liquidating the public accounts...; to superintend the emissions of bills of credit; [and] to obtain from the different Assemblies and Conventions of the United Colonies, accounts of the number of inhabitants in each colony." EG's early identification with the Canadian campaign pleased many of his constituents, but none more than Joseph Hawley (1723–88).[3]

A second committee appointment, that of February 23, made EG, along with two others, the recipient of sundry papers related to the brig "Nancy." The most significant prize taken in 1775, the 250-ton "Nancy," out of London and loaded with ordnance supplies, had been seized on November 28, 1775 by the "Lee," Captain John Manley (1734–93), in Massachusetts Bay. Its cargo consisted of thousands of cartridge boxes, muskets, bayonets, scabbards and ramrods, tones of musket shot, bags of flints for various types of guns, a 13-inch brass mortar and hundreds of shells. General Washington was delighted and military and civilian morale soared noticeably but the "Nancy" also created and accentuated problems. On February 27, the three-man committee made a report which merely assigned jurisdiction for the case.[4]

1. *D&A–JA*, 2:227–28; and *JCC*, 4:122.

2. Anthony, *First Lady*, 91–94; and *W-A Ltrs.*, 1:204n, 208–9.

3. *JCC*, 4:156–57; and J. Hawley to EG, Watertown, February 18, 1776, EG Collection of Elsie O. and Philip D. Sang, on deposit at Southern Illinois University Library, Carbondale.

4. *JCC*, 3:424, 4:169, 174 and 5:454; and William Bell Clark, *George Washington's Navy; being an Account of His Excellency's Fleet in New England Waters* (Baton Rouge, 1960), 60–222 *passim*.

Elbridge Gerry to James Warren

. .

Philadelphia, March 6, 1776.

Dear Sir:

An express goes off in a few hours for the camp, and affords just time to hint a few things, which I beg you will communicate to the honourable House.[1]

It is of great importance that your Militia should be well armed and equipped; and powder is essentially necessary. Without it, what will be the distresses of the sea-coast frontiers, and how can they defend themselves? I have heard of my vessel in the service of the Colony,[2] and am apprehensive of her being detained at *St. Antonio*, in *Spain*. I saw a letter from the master to the commander of a ship arrived in this place, and find that Captain *Johnson* was waiting for his crew, which had been despatched from *Bilboa* by Messrs. *Guad***[3] ten days before, and ought to have arrived in two or three days at most. He was very uneasy, and intended to get another crew if his own did not arrive soon; and I have since heard a rumour that the vessel is detained, which there is reason to fear. She had on board four hundred and thirty barrels of powder, or, in other words, twenty-one tons and a half; and, should she arrive, will clear for the Colony seven thousand five hundred pounds lawful, estimating the powder at five shillings per pound, which is low. But this is a trifling consideration compared with other advantages. Five tons were ordered to

Cambridge about a week since from the *Jerseys*; since which, twenty-seven tons and a half have arrived here, with about five tons of saltpetre, and three hundred stand of arms. Ten tons of this powder is also ordered to the camp at *Cambridge*; but this will not equip your Militia. Pray let a petition be immediately preferred for the return of the powder which we have lent the Continent, and I apprehend it can be obtained—I mean the powder collected from the towns in the *Massachusetts*. Mr. *Hunt*[4] can furnish a list of the most of them. I would beg one thing further, that you will not suffer any of your stocks of ammunition to be carried out of the Colony, or into the camp, without pressing necessity, or the desire of Congress. News is just arrived of five tons more powder imported into *North-Carolina*, and each Colony looks out for itself, as the times require it.

The Congress have this day preferred General *Thomas*, and make him a Major-General. He is ordered to proceed, without delay, to *Canada*; and General *Lee* is to go to the Southern Colonies.[5]

We[6] are obliged to the honourable House for the Journals and Acts of Assembly lately sent here, and hope that the other Journals will be forwarded when ready, and that one or more persons will be appointed to transmit weekly the doings of the Assembly, as great advantages will result to the Colony from this step. The file of letters, memorandum, and day-books of the Committee of Supplies, are much wanted in adjusting the Colony accounts I understand they are left with Deacon *Cheever*.[7]

I cannot help inculcating the necessity of attending to powder, and carefully preserving it; for, should the enemy remove, and the Army follow them, our Colony may be destitute of this article; and what a situation will it then be in? One thing further I will beg leave to hint: the Assembly, some time since, passed a resolve relative to fire-arms; and I cannot learn that any great number have been yet manufactured. Is it not necessary to inquire into the cause of it, and appoint a Committee to contract with individuals, who manufacture for a certain number in a convenient time? The Southern Colonies give a higher encouragement than we have offered; and it may be of great importance to follow their example. This the Assembly will decide.

Pray give my best respects to Major *Hawley*, Colonel *Orne*, Messrs. *Sullivan*, *Cooper*, *Freeman*,[8] and all our other friends, believing me to be sincerely, sir, your friend and very humble servant,

Elbridge Gerry.

To the Honourable James Warren.
P. S. Pray forward the enclosed letters.

Force, *AA*, 4th ser., 5:84–85.

1. JW was then Speaker of the Massachusetts House of Representatives.

2. No detailed view of EG's shipping interests in this period is possible.

3. Possibly this incomplete name masquerades José Gardoqui and Sons.

4. Probably Squire John Hunt of Watertown.

5. Canada drew the attention of Congress throughout 1776. Massachusetts, meanwhile, was one of three colonies from which Washington had requested a regiment each for service in Canada. See *JCC*, 4:99, 151–52, 157, 175, 180–81, 186.

6. The plural embraces the full Massachusetts delegation. As JW, addressing his letters to EG, or John or Samuel Adams, often meant to convey news and views to the entire delegation, so it was that EG and others often wrote in an equivalently collective sense. Incidentally, all five delegates from Massachusetts were then living in the same house, with Mrs. Yard in Second Street. See *D&A–JA*, 2:237.

7. Deacon David Cheever then represented the town of Charlestown in the Massachusetts House of Representatives. On March 14 he was named to the three-man committee charged with complying with this request; see Force, *AA*, 4th ser., 5:1239.

8. Joseph Hawley, a Northampton lawyer whose activities as selectman and member of the General Court led a biographer (E. Francis Brown, *Joseph Hawley*, *Colonial Radical*, New York, 1931) to describe him as the "Patrick Henry of Massachusetts," served in the Provincial Congress in 1775–76. In that period he corresponded frequently with EG. Samuel Adams termed Hawley a man of "stern Virtue and Spirit." (*W-A Letrs.*, 1:173).

Azor Orne (1731–96), a successful merchant of Marblehead in prerevolutionary days, had demonstrated his attachment to the patriot cause in many ways, in the Essex Convention, in the Provincial Congress, and on various committees which promoted the revolution militarily. Early in 1776 he became one of three major generals of the Massachusetts militia. For many years, after the adoption of the state constitution of 1780, he served in the state senate and council, refusing offers of higher office.

James Sullivan (1744–1808), a wealthy lawyer whose published writings on contemporary issues carried considerable weight, was a significant local leader for more than three decades—in the Provincial Congress and General Court in the mid-1770's, in a variety of executive, judicial and legislative posts in the 1780's, in the office of state attorney general for eighteen years before and beyond the turn of century, and finally (1807–8) as governor of Massachusetts.

William Cooper, Secretary of the Committee of Safety in 1775 and a member of the committee charged with inventorying Boston property deserted by Tories, filled JW's post as Speaker of the Massachusetts House of Representatives for a time in 1776.

Nathaniel Freeman (1741–1827), a lawyer whose Revolutionary years counted membership in the Provincial Congress (1775) and the Massachusetts legislature (1778–80) and some military service, served much later (1795–99) in the U.S. Congress.

James Warren to Elbridge Gerry

. .

Plymouth, March 7th: 1776

My Dear Sir

I am greatly obliged to you for your favour of the 6th of February[1] which found me at Home sick and Confined, but had the Intended Effect it really made my Heart Glad. The want of powder you and I have often bitterly Lamented and if the pleasure of haveing it is to be in proportion to the pain we have felt for the want of it, we may have a right to rejoice on ⟨the⟩ its arrival ⟨of it⟩. I wish I could in return give you an account of the arrival of the Brigantine from Bilboa, but I hear nothing of her lately. I am in a poor situation to give you Intelligence from our Colony. I left Watertown before the Court rose sick, and have been Confined to my House ever since I got home. The Accounts I have had from the Army are very Imperfect. I only learn that they begun to act the second part of Burgoyne's farce, the Blockade of Boston, on Saturday last, and after Canonadeing and Bombarding the Town till Monday Night took possession of Do[r]chester Hill without any opposition, where our Army have strongly Entrenched themselves, since which I don't hear or Understand there has been much fireing. Why there should be a suspension I can't tell without the stock runs low, especially as several Regiments of the Neighbouring Militia were called in, which

Indicated to me an Intention to strike some Capital and decisive stroke.

I admire the Steps you have taken with regard to Canada. Your Committee and your General are very Judiciously Chosen, and I dare say will answer your Expectations. I wish the fatigue may not be too great for Dr. Franklin at his time of life. When are we to Expect measures more Capital? Is this Spring and Summer and the precious Moments thereof to be spent in treating and Negotiateing with the Agents of the British Administration from whence we can derive nothing but Insecurity, disunion, poverty, and oppression, or shall it be spent in Treating with foreign Embassadors, settleing an Extensive and Lucrative Commerce from which we may derive Union, Security, Riches, and Freedom? Your Principles, Sentiments, and Love for your Country will lead you to regret the time spent in the first and to wish to be Employed in the last. You have to Encounter all the subtlety and arts high and low of the 39 Commissioners, and at the same time the Moderation, the Timidity, the Interests, and prejudices of many among us. If the Union of the Colonies is not Injured by this measure of Administration I think we shall have little to fear from them in future.

I thank you for forwarding us a Pamphlet which has made so much Noise to the Southward. It is really a most Excellent thing. I admire every part of it. Surely there never was a Book in which were to be found a Title and subject more strongly connected by nature and Reason. It has done most Eminent Service. It has Convinced, Converted and Confirmed in every place, and has prepared us for the Grand decisive measure my Soul has longed for.[2]

We hear the Fleet has been gone sometime, I am very anxious to hear from them. Do mention it, and the Success they meet with in your Next. No prizes taken here lately. Our Armed Vessels are Building with all Expedition. I hope we shall have 5 or 6 of our 16 Gun Sloops at Sea by the first of May. When I get to Watertown I shall perhaps be able to Collect some Intelligence either Important or Amuseing. When that will be can't so much as

Conjecture. I wish you Every possible Happiness, and among Others a very Good Wife, which I can assure you is the greatest in this Life.[3] I am very Sincerely Your Friend

J. W.

Elbridge Gerry Esqr.

ALS, Russell W. Knight—Gerry collection, Massachusetts Historical Society.

1. This letter by EG has not been located.
2. Apparently a reference to Thomas Paine's *Common Sense*, which had been published in January, 1776.
3. At this time EG still had ten years of bachelorhood ahead of him.

§

Early in February JW had returned to Plymouth. There, while illness confined him to his house for three weeks, he kept eye and ear open to distant happenings. To a letter from John Adams concerning the Canadian plans, JW replied, "I am glad you have taken these steps; but they don't satisfy me. I want to see more capital ones adopted." It was a season when JW desired "a brisk foreign trade, that will both make us rich and safe;" when he entertained doubts about the efficacy of the Massachusetts bounty which was intended to bait the enlistment of two battalions of men; and when he noted increasing prospects of the British evacuation of Boston. Even earlier it had been MW's "wish that the acquisition of Boston and Quebec may make the opening of the year '76 an era of Glory to the arms of America."[1]

Massachusetts was further identified with the Canadian campaign when, on March 8, EG and two others were "appointed to enquire and report the best ways and means of supplying the army in Canada with provisions and necessaries."[2]

Another committee appointment involving EG came five days later with the designation of the seven-man body which was "to enquire and report the best ways and means of raising the necessary supplies to defray the expences of the war for the present year, over and above the emission of bills of credit." A week later, on March 20, the aforementioned three-man committee reported on ways and means of supplying the army in Canada.[3]

1. *W-A Ltrs.*, 1:206, 209–11.
2. *JCC*, 4:192.
3. *Ibid.*, 200, 221, 236.

Elbridge Gerry to James Warren

.   .

Philadelphia, March 26, 1776

Dear Sir

I received with great Pleasure your Favour of the 7th Instant, and two Days ago the agreable News of the Reduction of Boston[1] reached this place, on which happy Event give me Leave to congratulate You.

What an Occurrence is this to be known in Europe? How are parliamentary pretensions to be reconciled to Facts? "Eight or ten thousand british Troops are sufficient to pervade America" and yet that Number of their best Veterans, posted in Boston— a Peninsula fortified by Nature—defended by Works which are the product of two Years' Industry—surrounded by navigable Waters and supported by Ships of War—and Commanded by their best Generals—have done what? Wonders? no, but what is truly wonderful they are driven out of Boston by about the thirtieth Part of the Power of America, scattered in Lines of nearly fifteen Miles Extent and unable to bring more than four thousand Men to Action at a Time. ⟨well let⟩ Surely the invincible Veterans laboured under some great Disadvantages from Want of Provisions, military Stores, &c which the Americans were amply supplyed with? Directly the Reverse is the Fact. They had Ammunition, Muskets and Accoutrements for every Man, and a peice of Ordnance for every ten or fifteen, while the Americans were almost destitute of any and after twelve Months Collection had only a sufficiency of the former to tune their Cannon about six or eight Days and accomplish this Business. I am at a Loss to know how Great Britain is to recover from this Disgrace, and reestablish her Fame and the Glory of her Arms in Europe. I am certain that her Conquests in America never will do it. The Congress have voted Thanks to the General, and all the officers and Soldiers of Army for their Valour on this Occasion and ordered a Medal of Gold with a suitable Device to be

presented the former.[2] I hope however that this will not abate
your Exertions to obtain by your own Manufactures sufficient
Resources of military Stores, for on this and the Discipline of your
Militia depend your Liberty.[3] I am also glad to find that Care is
taking ⟨that⟩ to prevent the spreading of the small pox and that
such Troops only as have had the Distemper are sent into the
Town; surely it ought immediately to be cleansed and all Intercourse stopped for the present.

You are desirous to know whether Capital Measures are to be
expected? Give me Leave to refer You to Colonel Orne for what
is done relative to privateering, and I hope soon that all your
Ports will be opened and a free Trade allowed to all Nations,[4] but
the latter is not yet done—⟨but⟩ all this does not satisfie your
soreing independent Faculties and I hope nothing less will accomplish it than a Determination of America to hold her Rank
in the Creation and give Law to herself. I doubt not that this will
soon take place, and am certain that New England will never be
satisfied with less since not only the Government of Great Britain
but the Collective Body of the people are corrupt and totally
destitute of Virtue. I sincerely wish that You would originate
Instructions expressed with decent Firmness (your natural Style)
and give your Sentiments as a Court in Favour of Independency;
I Am certain It would turn many doubtful Minds and produce a
Reversion of the contrary Instructions adopted by some assemblies. To accomplish such a Reversion the Committee of
Inspection of this City have preferred to the Assembly a petition
for that purpose; and, since some timid Minds are terrified at the
Word Independency It may be well to give the Thing another
Name.

America has gone such Lengths that she cannot recede, and I
am persuaded that a few Weeks or Months will convince her of
the Fact; but the Fruit must have ⟨some better⟩ Time to ripen
a little in the southern Colonies, notwithstanding in New England, the Hot Bed of Sedition as North[5] impudently Called
Boston, It has come to Maturity. Would it not be good Policy for
the New England Governments to think on this Matter and

adopt similar Measures? Perhaps a Circular Letter and the publication of your Instructions would accomplish it.

We have been so unfortunate as to loose Governor Ward;[6] he dyed this Morning of the small pox which he took the natural Way—he was a firm Friend to America.

Four Battalions of Your Army at Cambridge are ordered to Canada, and the Commissioners with Baron de Woedke,[7] who is a continental Brigadier, are gone this Morning.

The Destination of the Fleet is only known to the Marine Committee, "the Lords of the Admiralty," and nothing has transpired relative to them since their sailing.

I thank You for a Recommendation to Matrimony, and am certain You have had the best Experience in the Garden of pleasure. When providence shall kindly place me in a Soil so happy, I will endeavour to follow your worthy Example and do it equal Justice in the Cultivation.

Your Information relative to the Militia and the armed Vessels was very acceptable, the more so as our Friends in general supposing We have the powers of Divination, neglect to relate Things of Importance as they occur in your Government—and as to the Commissioners I am [*at*] a Loss to determine whether they deserve to be received.[8]

Is it not curious that the British ministry should know so little of our feelings or character that after seizing our property, burning our towns and destroying their inhabitants, they should make an act to interdict our trade, and suppose that towns, counties and colonies will bury in oblivion all former abuses, and subscribe themselves slaves in order to be rescued from the severities of this commercial tyranny? This is an instance of the wisdom and policy of the British ministry! Have they not yet ascertained that we know our rights, or at least that we think we know them? Have they not learned that we can defend them too? I remain your friend,

E. Gerry

ALS, EG Papers, Library of Congress; and excerpts in Austin, *EG*, 1:171–75; Force, *AA*, 4th ser., 5:506–7; and *LCC*, 1:409–10.

1. The British evacuation of Boston on March 17 had been reported to the Continental Congress by Washington. See *JCC*, 4:234; and Commager and Morris, *'Seventy-Six*, 1:173–83.

2. John Adams, having urged that a medal be struck, headed the committee which designed it; see *JCC*, 4:234.

3. Treating specific places and measures, John Adams also urged upon JW the consideration of military matters; see *W-A Ltrs.*, 1:216–17.

4. This hope then derived, in part, from the resolution of Congress, dated March 23, in support of privateering. See *JCC*, 4:229–32; and *W-A Ltrs.*, 1:213.

5. Sir Frederick North (1732–92), in the course of debate in the House of Commons on the Boston Port Bill, had observed on March 14, 1774, "the present disorders [*the Boston Tea Party and related activities*] originated in Boston." See Commager and Morris, *'Seventy-Six*, 1:11.

6. Governor of Rhode Island for five years in the 1760's, Samuel Ward (1725–76) had served in the Continental Congress from 1774 until his death.

7. Baron Frederick William de Woedtke.

8. The foregoing major fragment of this letter is derived from the manuscript in the Library of Congress; that which follows is taken from Austin.

§

With the coming of spring, John Adams shared with JW his ideas on the fortification of Boston harbor and, at the same time, urged the Speaker of the Massachusetts House to appoint a committee to look for sulphur. For his part, JW, returned to Watertown after recovering from his recent illness, reported, "Here I find the world topsy turvy . . . the enemies army fled and our own marching into other colonies." Although but recently appointed to the post of paymaster general of the Continental Army, he felt constrained to resign that post because of the imminent prospect of being called upon to follow the army in its movements. To President John Hancock of the Continental Congress, to whom he tendered his resignation on March 30, he wrote, "as I have ever made the publick good my ruling principle, I flatter myself, from the connection and interest I have here, it may be more in my power to render some small services to the publick here than in another part of the Continent." To clinch the matter, JW signified his readiness to render his accounts.[1]

EG, like the Congress at large, was occupied at this time with a number of miscellaneous and general activities. The relation between the efforts of the colonies becoming states and the nation verging on independence shone through in John Adams' cry to JW, "For God's sake and the Land's sake send along your Troops."[2]

1. *W-A Ltrs.*, 1:216–19; and Force, *AA*, 4th ser., 5:551.
2. *JCC*, 4:238–63; and *W-A Ltrs.*, 1:221.

Elbridge Gerry to James Warren

. .

Philadelphia, April 6, 1776.

Dear Sir:

I have just time to send you by the post a newspaper, in which is inserted the resolves of Congress for opening of American Ports to all nations except such as are subject to the King of Great Britain. It is a matter of importance that these resolves should be published in all the papers, and sent to every part of Europe and the West-Indies not inimical to the Colonies.[1] I doubt not the Committee of Correspondence, or other suitable persons, will be desired by the honourable Court to attend to such a measure, and cause the same to be republished in the foreign papers.

I hope by the next post to send some blank commissions and instructions for letters of marque, and the resolves of Congress relative thereto, they being now in the press.[2]

I remain, sir, respectfully, your very humble servant,

Elbridge Gerry

To the Honourable James Warren, Esq., or, in his absence, William Cooper, Esq., Speaker of the honourable House of Representatives, Massachusetts-Bay.

Massachusetts Archives, CXCIV, 324, Force, *AA*, 4th ser., 5:802, and *LCC*, 1:415–16.

1. These resolutions of April 6 (*JCC*, 4:257–59) appeared in the *Pennsylvania Ledger* that same day and in the *Pennsylvania Journal* and the *Pennsylvania Gazette* on April 10.

2. The form of the commission was submitted to Congress on April 2 and the instructions followed the next day. A resolution of April 3 provided for the sending of "Blank commissions for private ships of war and letters of marque and reprisal" to the appropriate authorities in the separate colonies; see *JCC*, 4:247–48, 251, 253–54.

§

For EG, in early April, there were no additional committee appointments, no reports, no vigorous expressions of opinion.

In Massachusetts JW, his resignation as paymaster general of the army en route to the Continental Congress, continued immersed in public affairs. "We are forming," he wrote John Adams, ". . . a fee bill that will drive every man of interest and ability out of office. I dread the consequences of the leveling spirit, encouraged and drove to such lengths as it is." Warped though his judgment was by pessimism on that score, JW was equally capable of the opposite, optimistic extreme, as when he told Adams, regarding the subject of independence, "All are united in this question."[1]

1. *W-A Ltrs.*, 1:217–19.

James Warren to Elbridge Gerry

·   ·

Watertown, April 15, 1776

My Dear Sir

I have the pleasure of your favour of the 26th March, and for some time past have been prevented writeing to you by the hurry and Confusion of affairs here. The removal of the army, and the Consequent Steps necessary for us to take have required perticular Attention in the General Assembly and in the Paymaster's Office.[1] I observed in Colonel Orne's Letter the penalty annexed to not writeing. I hoped however for another by the last Post. I was disappointed. My Friends, however, are kind. Major Hawley shew me a Letter he had received containing much Important Intelligence.

The Evacuation of Boston by the King's Troops seems to be the winding up of a Campaign in the same stile ⟨with⟩ in which it was begun and carried on. The whole must leave a Stain on the British arms which Hirelings will never be able to wipe off, and Impartial Historians will record to the Eternal disgrace of Britain and her administration.

All our Troops are gone Except five Regiments. They may be

said to be picked ones, for they are the poorest in the army if we take into account the Numbers they Consist of. There is but one of them much more than half full, and that is filled in great part by Boys, and are the most undisciplined, profligate Crew that ever were Collected. The Regiments are Hutchinson's, Whitcomb's, Glover's, Sargent's, and Phinney's.[2] Glover's is at Beverly, the rest are at Boston and the Neighbourhood, all under the Command of General Ward,[3] who is ordered to fortify Boston and its Harbour, and is under the direction of our General Court. Fort Hill[4] is the principal place pitched on in Boston to be fortified, and you will be surprised when I tell you that very little is done there Yet and Nothing any where else. You will start at this and Condemn us all in a Lump as stupidly Indolent, and we are Indeed all to Blame. We are now, however, in a way. We have had a Committee for some time to fortify the Harbour of Boston. Their design is to begin with Noddles Island and Do[r]chester[5] but not a shovel full of Earth is yet moved. The Committee were on Fryday last Impowered to purchase and sink Hulks between Castle Rocks and the middle Ground. This I believe they are about, but it is not yet Executed. ⟨We⟩ The Committee have applyed to General Ward for men to move the Guns from Castle Island,[6] and to fortify Noddles Island &c. but he can spare none at all, haveing no more than enough for the necessary Guards and none or next to none for fatigue duty on Fort Hill, where are not yet more, perhaps, than 5 or 6 Cannon mounted. We have therefore ordered a Regiment of 728 Men to be raised Immediately, and till that is done all but what is doing on Fort Hill is at a stand, Except the sinking [*of*] the Hulks. There are left in the Harbour one Man-of-War of 40 or 50 Guns and at Times a number of other vessels, Tenders &c. These Interrupt the Trade, and prevent Vessels from Comeing into Boston, tho' a few run the venture and succeed. From this Station their Cruisers make Excursions, to the plague and Interruption of Business in other ports. It is the opinion of many People here that ⟨that⟩ this knot of Pirates may easily be driven from their present Station. Tryal has been made in our House for another Regiment to fortify the

Islands below, and Effect this Business, but as yet without Success. I Wish for it as I would be ready on all occasions to push every advantage. I hear General Ward has wrote for leave to resign. He is very unwell. You know he has not had his health for some time.[7] I hope you will Continue here a Considerable Force and give us a Spirited active General. We may then do something.

The General deserves the Respect and honour you have Confered on him. You can form no Conception of the Appearance of Cambridge and the Vicinity of Boston. It resembles a desert. I have not been into Boston, being afraid of the Small Pox. There is danger of its spreading. I wish, however, it could be stopped this once more. Independency is a Hobgoblin that frights more People than raw head and Bloody Bones. Had we been more used to it in our Childhood, we might before now have outgrown it. There is something fascinateing in the Name or the same people that tremble at it would not be so easily reconciled to your resolves for seizing British Property or opening your Ports to the Trade of foreign Nations. These are indeed Cousin Germans if not the thing itself. If we must walk and advance by slow Gradations, I must be Content, but I always prefered bolder Steps. I like the quick much better than the Slow Step. I have thought much on your proposals for Instructions. Nothing of that kind has yet been moved. Whenever it is, it must be well Executed. You know we want hands. I shan't loose sight of it.

We are at present Engaged in forming several Acts, a Fee Bill (I think a miserable low Business Calculated only to gratifie the Capricious unruly Temper of Berkshire and Hampshire,[8] who are under no Government but Committees), an amendment of the Act for armed Vessels, a Confession Bill, a darling of the good Majors, and a Bill for disuseing the King's Name in all Acts, Commissions, and Law processes. This is thought by some to be of the Hobgoblin Species, but it will rise to be an Act unless stifled in its Birth by the Upper House, that Monster in Politics where two Branches in three are merged into one.[9] What are Mankind, surely strange Creatures or they would never submit to such Solecisms for the sake of the Forms of an old rotten Charter which

Freedom and Common Sense should have Scattered to the winds many Years ago. But I believe it will get through. We have lately had a Controversy with the Honourable Board about the 16th Year of the Reign &c. They at last gave it up, and upon the same principles may pass this Bill. You have no doubt heard of Manl[e]y's prize with Bill Jackson, and the famous Crean Brush.[10] They are in Boston Goal [*gaol*], and the last in Irons, since which three Cohasset Boats have taken a very fine prize a Snow[11] cheifly laden with rum, and sent her to Plymouth, and the Boats at Martha's Vineyard a Schooner with rum, sugar, Coffee &c. This is all in the prize way. It is Indeed too late to think of any further Connection with a State that ⟨is⟩ has not only treated us with unparrelled Barbarity and Injury, but is tottering to the foundation with its own weakness and wickedness, must fall soon and plunge into ruin whatever is Connected with it. The Lord deliver us from them is my prayer.

You will please to Consider the necessity of sending money here to support your Troops. There is none on hand. I sent with the General 60,000 dollars. It is neither reputable or good policy to have your Treasury Empty, whoever is to Conduct it. The Manufactory of Saltpetre goes on with a rapidity that will drain our Treasury. I am very happy in your old Lodgings. A Number of very good Ladies set by Mrs. Orne, Mrs. Warren, Miss Husits, all desire their Compliments to Mr. Gerry. Give mine to Colonel Hancock, and the Mr. Adams' [*Adamses*]. I wrote to Mr. John Adams a little while ago and Expect Mr. S. Adams home every day. I Lament the [death of Go]vernour Ward.[12] He was one am[ong the] Noblest works of God. I believe you [will] be heartily tired ⟨bef⟩ by that time you get here, and dread another page. I will therefore Conclude, and am Your Assured Sincere Friend and Servant

⟨J. War⟩

Elbridge Gerry Esqr.

Please to deliver Mr. Adams the Inclosed Letters. Shall write him by the next post.

ALS, Gerry-Townsend Papers, Manuscript Division, The New York Public Library.

1. William Winthrop had been employed to accompany the army to New York in the role of paymaster.

2. Israel Hutchinson (1728–1811), a participant in the battles of Ticonderoga and Lake George in the French and Indian War and a company commander at Lexington, commanded the Twenty-seventh Regiment during the siege of Boston. Subsequently he was with Washington in the retreat through New Jersey.

John Whitcomb (1720–1812), a colonel of Massachusetts troops at Crown Point (1755), emerged from retirement at the request of the soldiers and assumed command of a regiment at the beginning of the Revolution. Successively a brigadier and a major general in mid-1776, he soon resumed his retirement.

John Glover (1732–97) had known prior military service with the Massachusetts militia. Subsequently he participated in the retreat from Long Island, the crossing of the Delaware at Trenton, and the sentencing of Major Andre. He was a close friend of EG, with whom he had shared numerous commercial adventures. For a detailed study, see George Athan Billias, *General John Glover and His Marblehead Mariners* (New York, 1960).

Paul Dudley Sargent (1745–1828), son of a militia colonel, commanded a regiment during the siege of Boston, suffered a wound at Bunker Hill, and fought at Harlem, White Plains, Trenton, and Princeton.

Edmund Phinney (1723–1809).

3. Artemas Ward (1727–1800), a veteran of the French and Indian War, had risen to commander-in-chief of the forces of Massachusetts. Both before and after the Battle of Bunker Hill, EG and JW had desired that someone supersede Ward. A detailed and adulatory estimate of Ward is in Charles Martyn's *The Life of Artemas Ward: the First Commander-in-chief of the American Revolution* (New York, 1921), 154–64.

4. Fort Hill, due east of the Common and at the edge of the harbor, lay several hundred yards south of Long Wharf. In early post-Civil War years Fort Hill was leveled. See Justin Winsor (ed.), *The Memorial History of Boston . . . .* (4 vols., Boston, 1882–83), 3: map facing iv, and 272.

5. Athwart the mouth of the Mystick River, Noddles Island lay northeast of downtown Boston and almost due east of Charlestown. Dorchester, on the other hand, lay south of Boston, on the mainland.

6. This small island, lying southeast of Boston, was a short distance due east of Dorchester Neck.

7. "General Ward's health had declined to a somewhat alarming extent during the first months of 1776," asserts biographer Martyn (*Life of Artemas Ward*, 216).

8. Both the economic interests and the political outlook of these counties of western Massachusetts were quite unlike those of the more populous and commercially-oriented coastal districts.

9. The role of the executive in the selection of the upper house of the legislature so related the latter to the outlook of the executive as to draw JW's fire.

10. After his capture of the "Nancy," Manley had become commodore of Washington's fleet, on January 1, 1776, hoisting his pennant on the schooner "Hancock." In mid-1777 he lost that ship and became a prisoner of the British. Highlights of his career are in Gardner W. Allen, *A Naval History of the American Revolution* (2 vols., New York, 1962).

11. A square-rigged vessel, the snow differed but slightly from a brig.

12. Samuel Ward, EG's recently deceased colleague in the Continental Congress, had served repeatedly as governor of Rhode Island between 1762 and 1767.

§

The second half of April was crowded with longings. After telling MW, "The Ladies I think are the greatest Politicians," John Adams, in pursuit of the public virtue requisite as a foundation stone of a republic, longed for the "positive Passion for the public good, the public Interest, Honour, Power and Glory . . . in the Minds of the People." Prodding JW, the same writer insisted, "Why don't your Honours of the General Court, if you are so unanimous in this, give positive Instructions to your own Delegates, to promote Independency." A week later a related theme crept into Adams' letter to JW, "There must be a Decency, and Respect, and Veneration introduced for Persons in Authority, of every Rank, or We are undone. In a popular Government, this is the only Way of supporting order."[1]

In Watertown, meanwhile, JW's longings included the fortifications of Boston, the raising of a regiment of 728 men, a replacement for General Ward, and the close of the General Court, which latter circumstance would permit him "to see my little farm, etc." Writing from Braintree about the role of women in government, Abigail Adams, longing for the powerful pen MW wielded as she composed yet another book, declared, "I think I will get you to join me in a petition to Congress."[2]

In Philadelphia, on April 18, JW's letter of resignation was laid before Congress, read and referred to a committee. The following day it was resolved "That the resignation of James Warren, as pay master general of the army, be accepted . . . and that he be informed . . . to whom he is to render his accounts and vouchers." A week later, President Hancock notified JW of the acceptance of his resignation. Three days earlier General Ward's resignation had been accepted by the same Congress. Several of JW's longings had been fulfilled.[3]

1. *W-A Ltrs.*, 1:222, 228, 234.
2. *Ibid.*, 221–38 *passim*.
3. *JCC*, 4:291, 296, 300; and Force, *AA*, 4th ser., 5:1086.

Elbridge Gerry to James Warren

. .

Philadelphia, May 1, 1776.

My dear Sir,

I am exceedingly desirous that measures of defence should be first attended to, and have place of every other undertaking, and shall be most happy to hear that the capital and its valuable harbour is well fortified, and something done for the other seaports; that your powder mills are at work; that manufactures of lead and sulphur are attended to, and preparation made for casting cannon;[1] that the committees of correspondence throughout the colony are ordered to make returns of the manufactures of fire-arms, employed or unemployed, and that measures are taken to erect public works; that the established forces, whether continental or colonial, are well armed, equipped and ready for action. When this is done, and I think with a little assiduity it may be accomplished, the colony will be in a situation to receive the enemy; and they being informed thereof, as they generally are of our weakness or strength, will carefully avoid another visit.

I think it may be demonstrated that the eastern district alone is able of itself to declare independency. The colony of South Carolina have behaved nobly in taking up government, choosing a governour, &c.;[2] and the convention of North Carolina have unanimously voted to follow their example.[3]

Virginia is always to be depended upon; and so fine a spirit prevails among them, that unless you send some of your cool patriots among them, they may be for declaring independency before congress is ready.[4]

I am glad you approve the proposal for instructions, and can with pleasure inform you that North Carolina has taken off from their delegates the restriction relative to this matter, and as I am informed, has left them at liberty to vote for a final separation from Great Britain.[5] Your friend as ever,

E. Gerry

Austin, *EG*, 1:177–78; Force, *AA*, 4th ser., 5:1163; and excerpts, *LCC*, 1:438.

1. Many of these themes had drawn JW's attention in his letter of the previous day to John Adams (*W-A Ltrs.*, 1:237–38).

2. Ten days earlier John Adams had written JW, "The News from South Carolina has aroused and animated all the Continent. It has Spread a visible Joy." (*Ibid.*, 232).

3. The proceedings of the North Carolina provincial congress, April 4–May 14, are in Force, *AA*, 4th ser., 5:1315–68, with the resolution of April 12 on pages 859–60.

4. The proceedings of the Virginia convention, May 6–July 5, are in Force, *AA*, 4th ser., 6:1509–1616. On May 15 the convention unanimously resolved "That the Delegates appointed to represent this Colony in General Congress be instructed to propose to that respectable body to declare the United Colonies free and independent States." (p. 1524).

5. See EG to JW, May 28, 1776 and JW to EG, June 12, 1776, pp. 28, 31–33 hereinafter.

§

During the early weeks of May three major military problems—finances, recruitment, and supplies—absorbed the attention of the delegates in Philadelphia. On May 6, in the wake of a resolution calling for $10,000,000 for the conduct of the war, a committee of seven, of whom EG was one, was created "to devise ways and means for raising the ten millions."[1] EG was made a member, on May 8, of the three-man committee charged with devising ways and means of recapturing Moses Kirkland, who had been jailed incommunicado in Philadelphia since March. The following day the report of the committee instructed to find means of raising $10,000,000 led to a resolution that half that sum be emitted in bills of credit. To meet the manpower needs in Massachusetts, the Congress resolved, on the fourteenth, that the five battalions presently there be recruited to full strength. Two days later another resolution ordered the raising of an additional battalion, preferably on the basis of two-year service, in Massachusetts.[2]

In Massachusetts, writing to the truckmaster to the Penobscot Indians, JW remarked, "it may be attended with ill consequences to have these Indians uneasy." On May 8 the Massachusetts House of Representatives chose three major generals of militia: John Hancock, JW, and Benjamin Lincoln (1733–1810). When JW declined the appointment, Azor Orne was named in his place.[3]

At this time JW, in addition to sidestepping the militia appointment, was divesting himself of $40,000 in funds related to his late paymaster generalship. Considerable confusion attended the transfer of that office, its records and funds to his successor, William Palfrey (1741–80) of Boston, whose appointment dated from late April. Complaining on the score of men, arms, ammunition and tents, JW insisted, "We are in a worse situation than twelve months ago." If his report on military affairs depressed John Adams, the latter reciprocated when he wrote, "This Day has brought us the Dismals from Canada—Defeated most ignominiously." Politically, however, Adams struck another note—"Every Post and every Day rolls in upon Us. Independence like a Torrent." Massachusetts was contributing its share of that torrent.[4]

1. *JCC*, 4:329–30.
2. *Ibid.*, 239, 242, 246, 265, 284, 337, 339, 355, 360.
3. Force, *AA*, 4th ser., 5:1193–94, 1218.
4. Force, *AA*, 4th ser., 5:1190 and 1691; and *W-A Ltrs.*, 1:239, 240, 247, 249.

James Warren to Elbridge Gerry

. .

Plymouth, May 20th: 1776.

Dear Sir

Your favour of the 1st of May with the Papers Inclosed has reached me here tho' not soon enough to return an answer by the last Post. I am much obliged to you for them, and the agreable Intelligence you give me from the Carolina. This Spirit in the Southern Colonies will I hope accelerate the Motions of the whole. The Cool Patriots you mention will certainly rejoice to see so good a work going on, if it should even hurry a little your august Body.

If I again belong to the Assembly, or Indeed if I do not I will take Care that the several useful hints you have given be properly attended to.

I hope your Advices from Canada will be better than your fears. I dare say we shall have and hold it.

I believe the Court have risen without attending to the Correction of their Journals.

I am at present somewhat out of the way for Collecting Intelligence[1] and must write you very short or loose my Opportunity of forwarding this to the Post Office. I must not however omit mentioning the Grand Prize taken and Carried into Boston tho' I presume you will have it by other hands before this reaches you. The takeing of this Ship is a fresh Instance of the kindness of Providence to us. I am Confidently assured that they have landed more than 70 Tons of powder, and a great variety of other Articles much wanted at this time. This is a Grand Event in our favour. It comes very opportunely to us, and may defeat some of their plans.

With regard to my Continuing to pay the Troops here I am much Obliged to you for your Enquiry and have no kind of Objection if it be not dependant upon and under the Controul of my *worthy* Successor.[2] My Opinion is that as you have divided the Colonies into military districts, the office of Paymaster General should be annihilated and a Paymaster appointed to Each. I hear General [. . .] is to succeed General Ward. How long are we to be punished thus for our folly and Indiscretion the winter before last? If sincere repentance would atone for them, surely he would not be the man. I can add no more but that I am with my regards to Mr. Adams, with great Esteem Your Friend &c.

J. Warren

ALS, photographic copy, EG Papers, Library of Congress.

1. The General Court having adjourned on May 10, JW had hastened home to his wife and sons. Any time JW shifted from such centers of activity as Boston and Watertown to out of the way Plymouth, his reduced capacity to gather news justified this complaint. On May 20 the freeholders of Watertown reported their election of two delegates to the General Court and their unanimous endorsement of independence; see Force, *AA*, 4th ser., 6:532–33.

2. William Palfrey.

Elbridge Gerry to James Warren

. .

Philadelphia, May 20, 1776.
My dear Sir

I enclose you a Virginia paper just come in, by which you will see the spirit of another county in that colony, exhibited in their instructions for independency.[1]

In this colony (Pennsylvania) the spirit of the people is great, if a judgement is to be formed by appearances. They are well convinced of the injury their assembly has done to the continent by their instructions to their delegates.[2] It was these instructions which induced the middle colonies and some of the southern to backward every measure which had the appearance of independency: to them is owing the delay of congress in agitating questions of the greatest importance, which long ere now must have terminated in a separation from Great Britain: to them is owing the disadvantages we now experience for want of a full supply of every necessary for carrying on the war. Alliances might have been formed, and a diversion been given to the enemy's arms in Europe or the West Indies, had these instructions never appeared. But they have had their effect; and while we endeavour to recover the continent from the ill consequences of such feeble politics, we ought to show the cause of such miserable policy. It appears to me that the eyes of every unbeliever are now open; that all are sensible of the perfidy of Great Britain, and are convinced there is no medium between unqualified submission and actual independency. The colonies are determined on the latter. A final declaration is approaching with great rapidity.[3] May the all-wise Disposer of events so direct our affairs that they may terminate in the salvation of these afflicted colonies.

Amidst all our difficulties you would be highly diverted to see the situation of our "moderate gentlemen." They have been more apprehensive of evils than any others, as we have frequently observed, and they have now the mortification to find that their

measures for avoiding have but served to increase them. I sometimes think that Providence permitted them to clog the affairs of
the colonies, that they may become in some degree desperate,
and thus introduce into the circle of determined men those timid
beings, whose constitution never admits of their defending freedom on the noblest principles, and are afterwards obliged to meet
danger by the same motives that induced them to shun it. They
are coming over to us, but I am sorry their counter influence so
long prevented us from adopting the only means by which we
could supply ourselves with the necessaries for defence.

Excerpt, Austin, *EG*, 1:178–80; same excerpt, Force, *AA*, 4th ser., 6:517; and shorter
excerpt, *LCC*, 1:459–60.

1. Probably the instructions of April 23 for the delegates of Charlotte County in the
Virginia Convention, the text of which is in Force, *AA*, 4th ser., 5:1034.

2. Urged to seek redress of grievances, the Pennsylvania delegation was further
instructed to "dissent from and utterly reject any propositions . . . that may cause or
lead to a separation from our Mother Country, or a change of the form of this Government." The full instructions, dated November 9, 1775, are in Force, *AA*, 4th ser.,
3:1792–93. For detailed descriptions of the Philadelphia town meeting of May 20, the
day the Pennsylvania Assembly gathered to consider the repeal of these instructions,
see *W-A Ltrs.*, 1:250–51 and Force, *AA*, 4th ser., 6:517–20.

3. Reiterating his hopes of May 1 (*q.v.*), EG also corroborated the optimism of
John Adams of this same date, i.e. May 20; see *W-A Ltrs.*, 1:249.

§

Soon to return to Watertown for the first session of a new General
Court, in which he again would represent the town of Plymouth and
serve as Speaker of the House, JW spent the fourth week of May in his
beloved coastal community. In compliance with an order of the General
Court, he purchased a sloop "to observe the motions of the enemy and
give intelligence." The command of the "Swift," the sloop for which JW
and three others furnished bond, was given to John Wigglesworth, whose
principal duty was to gather intelligence related to British manpower
and movements in the Halifax area.[1]

In late May EG joined the three-man committee constituted to
consider the issues posed in storekeeper Charles Miller's letter to Commissary General Joseph Trumbull (1737–78). Within forty-eight hours
that committee submitted, in EG's hand, the resolution which instructed
Trumbull relative to provisions in Massachusetts.[2]

1. Force, *AA*, 4th ser., 6:553; Mass., *A&R*, 19:424, 437; and Gardner Weld Allen, *Massachusetts Privateers of the Revolution* (Cambridge, 1927), 58–59, 294, this last work constituting volume 77 of the Massachusetts Historical Society *Collections*.
2. *JCC*, 4:367–98 *passim*.

Elbridge Gerry to James Warren

. .

Philadelphia, May 28, 1776.

My dear Sir,

Some days since I enclosed to our worthy friend Major Hawley sundry newspapers containing intelligence of importance, but not so agreeable in its nature as the enclosed papers announce relative to our sister colonies Virginia and North Carolina. Their conventions have unanimously declared for independency, and have in this respect exceeded their sister colonies in a most noble and decisive measure. I hope it will be forthwith communicated to your honourable assembly,[1] and hope to see my native colony following this laudable example. Your's very truly,

Elbridge Gerry

Austin, *EG*, 1:180–81; and Force, *AA*, 4th ser., 6:606.

1. The following day, Wednesday, May 29, the first session of the new General Court opened in Massachusetts.

§

The Continental Congress, in late May and early June, was wrestling with a multitude of problems related to the war—among others the ratio of troops to be used in opposition to the enemy, a carefully prepared appeal to the citizenry for added support of the revolution, lead production, tightened regulation of the price of salt, the possible employment of 2,000 Indians in the campaign in Canada, penalties for those supplying the enemy with intelligence or provisions, and the disposition of certain militia units. The resolution of the last-mentioned matter found Massachusetts called upon to furnish 3,000 (four battalions) of the 6,000 militiamen needed to reinforce the army in Canada and 2,000 of the 13,800 militiamen required to reinforce the army at New York.[1]

EG, in addition to his duties in Philadelphia, continued to write and receive letters couched with concern. To Massachusetts-based militiaman Joseph Palmer (1716–88) EG voiced his conviction that the colonies soon would "declare themselves as their Interest and Safety have long required, entirely separated from the prostituted Government of G. Britain." "The principal object of our attention at this important Time," he continued, "I think should be the Manufacturing Arms, Lead and Clothing, obtaining Flints."[2]

1. *LCC*, 1:479; and *JCC*, 4:398–416 and 5:417–29.
2. E. Porter to EG, Chamblee, May 31, 1776, EG Collection of Elsie O. and Philip D. Sang, on deposit at Southern Illinois University Library, Carbondale; Henry B. Carrington, *Battles of the American Revolution 1775–1781; a Military History* (6th ed., New York, 1904), 164–69, and *LCC*, 1:468.

Elbridge Gerry to James Warren

· ·

Philadelphia, June 11, 1776.
My dear Sir,

Yesterday after a long debate the question of independence was postponed until the first July,[1] in order to give the assemblies of the middle colonies an opportunity to take off their restrictions and let their delegates unite in the measure.[2] In the interim will go on plans for confederation and foreign alliance.

If these slow people had hearkened to reason in time, this work would have long ere now been completed, and the disadvantage arising from the want of such measures been wholly avoided; but Providence has undoubtedly wise ends in coupling together the vigorous and the indolent; the first are retarded, but the latter are urged on, and both come together to the goal.

To the obstructions in council are owing in part our military misfortunes, which, however, we must use as fresh incitements to greater exertions. Your sincere friend,

E. Gerry

Austin, *EG*, 1:191–92; Force, *AA*, 4th ser., 6:813–14; and excerpt, *LCC*, 1:484.

  1. *JCC*, 6:428–29.
  2. The action by Delaware is recorded in Force, *AA*, 4th ser., 6:883–84.

§

As May gave way to June, Massachusetts was holding elections. Scanning the results, JW considered the new House abler than its predecessor. Reading pamphlets and thinking about the political structure of Massachusetts of the future, he wondered, "Whether it is best there should be a perfect similarity in the form and spirit of the several governments in the colonies, provided they are all independant of Britain, is a question I am not determined on. For some reasons it may be best for us there should be a difference." When, however, his mind ranged over a list of prospective chief executives for Massachusetts, the Speaker again phrased his admiration for John Adams, "I could pitch on a much more suitable person than either of the three you mention, by going as far as Philadelphia, tho' what we should do without him there I can't tell."[1]

That spring, JW thought, promised a good season for crops and a fine time for seizing prizes, but a dreary period for enlistments in the under-manned battalions of Massachusetts. "The army here are in distress for want of money," he informed John Adams. "I have run the venture at the solicitations of General Ward to pay several sums since I had notice that my resignation was accepted. I hope the publick advantage and the General's solicitations will justify my conduct." Almost simultaneously Ward, holding more prisoners than he could quarter in the Boston jail, asked the civil authorities, through JW, for some disposition of them. Foremost on the agenda of the Massachusetts legislature were military affairs: harbor fortifications to be expanded at Boston and initiated at Plymouth, salt peter and powder production, and men to fill four new companies of troops.[2]

James Sullivan, then at Biddeford, reminded JW that the Indians of the Bay of Fundy region required attention, lest they be drawn to the British side. John Adams sent JW a treatise on fire ships and Commissary General Joseph Trumbull, taking steps to supply provisions to the New England troops destined for Canada, instructed Captain Farnsworth to call upon JW "to be informed the route the troops from your Colony will take."[3]

1. *W-A Ltrs.*, 1:252–53.
2. *Ibid.*, 253–54; and Force, *AA*, 4th ser., 6:801 and 5th ser., 1:265–72.
3. *Ibid.*, 4th ser., 6:712, 816; and *W-A Ltrs.*, 1:255–56.

James Warren to Elbridge Gerry

.   .   .

Watertown, June 12, 1776.

My dear Sir,

I received your obliging and friendly letter of the 28th May and the papers enclosed, and should have acknowledged it before this, if it had been in my power. I have endeavoured to use to the best purposes the intelligence you gave me, and to animate your native country to follow the laudable example of the south. Their spirit is in your taste, and I can in imagination see you enjoy it. You have no doubt seen in the papers a short resolve, passed at the close of the last session, for the purpose of getting the sense of the whole country by the instructions given to their members, on the subject of independence.[1] The members have severally been called on by the house, and more than one half of them are instructed fully in favour of it, and not one against it. Many more are expecting similar instructions to follow them, and near or perhaps all would have had them if the resolve had reached them in season; thus it appears to me the sentiments of our colony are more united on this great question than they ever were on any other; perhaps ninety-nine in a hundred would engage, with their lives and fortunes, to support congress in the measure.[2] You seem to intend to avoid too great a shock; there is little left to do but the form and ceremony, but even that is important. Your resolves for trade and captures, and your late resolve for assuming government, the preamble of which is extremely grand,[3] make the substance of the thing. I am glad to find you so determined in the defence of the continent, and making such preparations for it. I expect a warm summer in many parts of it, and to have our share here. I wish we were in a better preparation for it. We want powder, we want arms, and we have great difficulties in raising men. A regiment ordered more than two months ago to be raised under colonel Whitney, yet wants more than a hundred men. Another under Marshal, and one to consist of seven companies of the train, under Crafts make but slow progress.[4] Marshal has not near half filled his regiment, though the enlisting orders were given out six weeks ago. We have now passed in the house a resolve for encouraging the raising the two continental battalions here, by a bounty of twenty dollars for those who shall enlist for two, and ten for those who shall enlist for one year. Great doubts and hesitations we have had about this step, and finally took it, because we could not see any difference in the consequences, whether the bounty was given to colonial or continental regiments, and the men will not come without; and they must come or we must be lost.[5] How to steer between Scilly and Charybdis has been our difficulty. The resentment of congress on one hand, and destruction from our enemies on the other, have been weighed in the balance; we have risked the first to avoid the last. When do you send a general here to succeed Ward? He is impatient, and so is the country. When do you send somebody here with money to pay your troops? I have ventured at the earnest solicitations of general Ward, and on the advice of many gentlemen, to proceed in paying the army as far as the money in my hands would go, and so have really acted as paymaster to this time, as you had made no disposition of the money and no provision for the payment of it here. The money is now gone, and the soldiers are mutining for pay, and every department stagnated. You cannot conceive how your affairs here are injured by these means. The prize you mention is indeed a great affair; the several prizes since are very important, but the loss of the "Yankee Hero" is a damper.[6] What must be done with the West-India prizes? They must be made legal; British property must not escape under the cover of West-India property, which if real will be converted into British as soon as it arrives. I fear the manning of your fleet will go heavily. Why may not the sailors we have taken be obliged to do duty here, as they make ours do on board their's? Will it be saucy to enquire, why you passed such a resolve relative to Church,[7] or if some of your late appointments (I don't mean of major or brigade generals) are judicious? I never expected the people would reward, or be grateful to their benefactors the patriots, but I always supposed if there must be lucrative or honorary places, that congress would confer them on the most distinguished and deserving. When I see you I will explain, if explanation is wanted. I think the French will soon interrupt the system of Britain; every thing appears to me like it, and the intelligence you give confirms it. We have very little news since the last post. A number of transports with troops are arrived below, supposed to be highlanders; the court seem to bend all their attention to defence; we have this session no fee bills, confession or incongealable bills. Did you receive a letter I wrote you from Plymouth? I fear some of my letters to you and Mr. Adams miscarry. We have had rumours for some time of battles in Canada, in which we have been alternately conquerors and conquered. We have had our fears from these rumours. We have, this minute, intelligence from Canada, by which we believe that our arms there have finally been successful, and gained a considerable advantage; but I must conclude this long scroll, and am sincerely Yours, &c.

James Warren.

Austin, *EG*, 1:181–85; and Force, *AA*, 4th ser., 6:829–30.

1. Dated May 10, this read, "Resolved, as the opinion of this House, That the inhabitants of each Town in this Colony ought, in full meeting warned for that purpose, to advise the person or persons who shall be chosen to represent them in the next General Court whether that, if the honourable Congress should, for the safety of the said Colonies, declare them independent of the Kingdom of Great Britain, they, the said inhabitants, will solemnly engage, with their lives and fortunes, to support them in the measure." See Force, *AA*, 4th ser., 6:420.

2. The percentage advanced by JW in favor of independence, although buoyed by his own optimism, was not wishful thinking. He knew, for example, of the unanimous backing of the resolution by such towns as Watertown, Walpole, Malden, New Salem, and Brunswick as well as the favoring action of Boston, Medway, Newburyport, Pittsfield, Stockbridge, Taunton, and many other communities. See Force, *AA*, 4th ser., 6:532, 533, 540, 556–58, 602–3, 649, 698–706.

3. Drawn up by John Adams, this preamble was considered by the Continental

Congress on May 15 and ordered published. Prefacing the copy which Adams incorporated in his letter to JW that day was the remark, "This Day the Congress has passed the most important Resolution that ever was taken in America." See *JCC*, 4:357–58; and *W-A Ltrs.*, 1:245–46.

4. Josiah Whitney (1731–1806) had served in 1755 in the first expedition against Crown Point and had fought at Concord on April 19, 1775. His new regiment was expected to fortify the town and harbor of Boston.

Thomas Marshall (1718–1800), a merchant-tailor with a decade of military experience to his credit, acquitted himself commendably at Saratoga in 1777.

Thomas Crafts, Jr. of Leominster was a protege of John Adams; see *W-A Ltrs.*, 1:186–87, 248.

5. Uncertain as recently as June 2 concerning the advisability of a bounty, JW then had asked John Adams, "Can you advise as to give them a bounty by way of encouragement, or should you disapprove of it?" (*ibid.*, 253) Before Adams could reply, Massachusetts had taken action.

6. Commissioned a privateer on February 20, 1776, the "Yankee Hero," of about 120 tons, was owned by five merchants, one of whom, James Tracy, served as commander. Cruising successfully out of Newburyport, its captures included "a large Ship from and own'd in London, laden with Coal, Cheese and Porter, bound for the Ministerial Assassins at Boston." On June 7 Tracy had taken the twelve-gun privateer out with only one-third of its normal complement. Mistaking the frigate "Milford" for a merchantman, Tracy engaged the man-of-war in an unequal contest amid shifting winds. In the two-hour action four Americans were killed and thirteen wounded, the commander himself sustaining serious wounds. The victorious frigate took the "Yankee Hero" to Halifax. See Force, *AA*, 4th ser., 6:748; and Allen, *Naval History*, 1:73, 149–52.

7. Arrested and jailed in the autumn of 1775 for corresponding with the enemy, Dr. Benjamin Church's detention and health had been the subject of numerous petitions to the Congress. On May 14, in the action referred to by JW, the Congress had resolved to remove Church from the jail in Norwich, Connecticut and transfer him to Boston and release him on bail preparatory to trial. Commenting on that decision, John Adams wrote Benjamin Kent, "Nobody knows what to do with him. There is no law to try him upon, and no court to try him." See *JCC*, 3:294, 334 and 4:61, 65, 350–52; and *LCC*, 1:502.

§

That trio of wartime needs, men, money and materiel, busied the political leaders in Watertown, Massachusetts. They provided for the casting of cannon and the distribution of powder to towns. Their military appointments included the designation, on June 19, of JW as the second major general of Massachusetts militia. During the fourth week of the month they resolved, in response to the wishes of the Continental Congress, to raise 5,000 men for service in Canada and New York.[1]

On the thirteenth the Continental Congress created the five-man Board of War and Ordnance. Problems related to wounded and disabled servicemen, the procurement of good powder, harmonious relations with the Indians, and the exchange of prisoners also received attention.

Military matters notwithstanding, major attention focused on July 1 and the issue of independence. Almost every letter penned by John Adams teemed with it.

EG, meanwhile, kept abreast of activities in Massachusetts as well as Philadelphia. From faithful Joseph Hawley and Samuel Freeman, both then sitting in the Massachusetts House, came information, encouragement, and inquiries.[2]

Cognizant of the woes attending the duties of Commissary General Joseph Trumbull, EG repeatedly wrote that official. On June 25 EG congratulated General Horatio Gates (1728/29–1806), upon his appointment to the Canadian command, although like the other delegates from Massachusetts, he would have preferred the general in that colony "Discipline is the last, but not the least, important object of attention," he wrote Gates, "and I shall be glad of your explicit sentiments on the same. I cannot conceive why we may not, by setting out right, soon make soldiers equal to any that the world affords. For surely men inspired with the principles of liberty, and enthusiastically engaged in its defence, afford as good materials as can anywhere be found for this purpose."[3]

1. Force, *AA*, 5th ser., 1:274–91; and Mass., *A&R*, 19:442, 450, 451, 456, 458, 462–67.

2. *LCC*, 1:488, 491–504 *passim*, *JCC*, 5:436–80 *passim*, Force, *AA*, 4th ser., 6:844–45; and S. Freeman to EG, Watertown, June 16, 1776, EG Collection of Elsie O. and Philip D. Sang, on deposit at Southern Illinois University Library, Carbondale.

3. *LCC*, 1:498, 504–6.

Elbridge Gerry to James Warren

. .

Philadelphia, June 25, 1776.
My dear Sir,

I am favoured with your very agreeable letter of 10th June,[1] and am in hopes congress will soon render it unnecessary to take further measures preparatory to the declaration of independence. New-Jersey has appointed five new delegates,[2] and instructed them to vote in favour of the question, and it appears to me there is not even a doubt of any colony on the continent except New-York and Maryland. These will not impede us a moment. I do not affirm that either of these are of the neuter gender, but on the other hand am persuaded the people are in favour of a total and final separation, and will support the measure, even if the conventions and delegates of those colonies vote against it.

Since my first arrival in this city the New-England delegates have been in a continual war with the advocates of proprietary interests in congress and this colony. These are they who are most in the way of the measures we have proposed, but I think the contest is pretty nearly at an end, and am persuaded that the people of this and the middle colonies have a clearer view of their interest, and will use their endeavours to eradicate the ministerial influence of governours, proprietors and jacobites, and that they now more confide in the politics of the New-England colonies than they ever did in those of their hitherto unequal governments. Your's as ever,

E. Gerry.

Austin, *EG*, 1:193–94; Force, *AA*, 4th ser., 6:1067; and *LCC*, 1:508.

1. Apparently the letter referred to is that of June 12.
2. Elected on June 22, the new delegation from New Jersey consisted of Abraham Clark, John Hart, Francis Hopkinson, Richard Stockton, and John Witherspoon. See *JCC*, 5:489–90; and *LCC*, 1:xlix–lii.

§

The end of June and the beginning of July found the legislators in Massachusetts occupied with many matters: beacons for several coastal communities; balloting for field officers of one battalion after another; supplies—principally cannon—for numerous towns; designation of the route by which the men of Massachusetts were to proceed toward Canada; appropriations to pay officers and soldiers, delegates, selectmen and post-riders; and the procurement of flour, teams, firearms, coats, blankets, shoes, and other necessaries.[1]

The alarming news out of Canada induced Meshech Weare (1713–86), President of the Council of New Hampshire, to write JW, "I am directed to make application to your General Court for the loan of a few cannon and thirty or forty barrels of gunpowder." While neighbors sought assistance, Massachusetts was finding it difficult to marshal her own forces.[2]

In Philadelphia, meanwhile, countless issues commanded attention—John Adams and his Board of War regularly held both morning and evening sessions—but independence was the transcending theme. A draft of the Declaration of Independence was read on June 28, the day that EG was appointed to a committee to consider a petition presented by one Christopher Champlin. From Portsmouth, EG's mail included the latest hopes and fears of John Wendell. Planning to outnumber the enemy two-to-one, Wendell wanted all the troops "to be Continental, and only One Currency throughout the whole Continent, which would serve to Unite us, still more."[3]

1. Mass., *A&R*, 19:470–503; and Force, *AA*, 5th ser., 1:292–309.
2. *Ibid.*, 4th ser., 6:1138 and 5th ser., 1:1.
3. *LCC*, 1:512, 514, 521; *JCC*, 5:491–502; and J. Wendell to EG, Portsmouth, July 2, 1776, EG Collection of Elsie O. and Philip D. Sang, on deposit at Southern Illinois University Library, Carbondale.

Elbridge Gerry to James Warren

. .

Philadelphia 2d July 1776

Dear Sir

I have only Time to inform you that yesterday was agitated in Congress the great Question of Independancy, and as the Facts are as well known at the Coffee House of the City as in Congress I may go on to inform you that in a Committee of the whole House it was carryed by nine Colonies.[1]

I remain Sir with due Regards your assured Friend and humble Servant

Elbridge Gerry

Colonel Warren

Austin, *EG*, 1:between 196 and 197; Force, *AA*, 4th ser., 6:1212; and *LCC*, 1:526.

1. Francis Lightfoot Lee (1734–97), writing to his brother, phrased the action of the Congress differently when he declared, "This day the resolve for independency

was consider'd and agreed to, in Comtee of the whole—two dissentients S. Carolina and Pensylvania. N. York did not vote, not being empowered." See *ibid.*, 1:519.

§

The opening days of July, the forthcoming Declaration of Independence was read, agreed to, engrossed, signed, and ordered printed.[1]

Elsewhere many matters, chiefly military, called for and received attention. In Watertown, the Massachusetts legislators looked favorably on the New Hampshire request for cannon. Reflecting upon the recent debacle in Canada, the Massachusetts Council urged that Thursday, July 31 be set apart "to be observed as a day of solemn Humiliation and Prayer." Meanwhile, to improve the future prospect, action was taken regarding powder, enlistments and pay.[2]

From New York, Commissary General Joseph Trumbull informed EG of the confusion to the north—of British landings and of his own problems with General Schuyler. "These Clashing Commands," he insisted, "I fear will ruin every thing that way."[3]

1. *JCC*, 5:507–23.
2. Force, *AA*, 5th ser., 1:309–15.
3. Jos. Trumbull to EG, New York, July 5, 1776, EG Collection of Elsie O. and Philip D. Sang, on deposit at Southern Illinois University Library, Carbondale; and *ibid.*, EG Papers, Library of Congress.

Elbridge Gerry to James Warren

· ·

Philadelphia, July 5, 1776.
Dear Sir,

I have the pleasure to inform you that a determined resolution of the delegates from some of the colonies to push the question of independency has had a most happy effect, and after a day's debate all the colonies excepting New-York, whose delegates are not empowered to give either an affirmative or negative voice, united in a declaration long sought for, solicited and necessary, the declaration of independency.

New-York will most probably on Monday next, when its convention meets for forming a constitution, join in the measure, and then it will be entitled the unanimous declaration of the thirteen United States of America.

I enclose you a copy of the declaration for yourself, and another for major Hawley, and offer you my sincere congratulations on the occasion, and I pray that we may never want the divine aid, or the spirit and the means to defend it. Yours, &c.

Elbridge Gerry.

Austin, *EG*, 1:202–3; Force, *AA*, 5th ser., 1:14; and excerpt, *LCC*, 2:1.

§

In Philadelphia the Board of War reported concerning the commissary department and the Congress added new members to both the committee on Indian affairs and that inquiring into the collapsed Canadian campaign. On July 6, the Board of Treasury laid an account from JW before the Continental Congress. That same day it was "Ordered, That Mr. Warren pay the balance remaining in his hands to Ebenezer Hancock, Esqr. deputy pay master general for the eastern department."[1]

Undisclosed private business had caused JW to leave Watertown for Plymouth shortly after mid-May. For at least three weeks, JW was with his family.

1. *JCC*, 5:523–25.

James Warren to Elbridge Gerry

·   ·

Plymouth, July the 7th: 1776

My Dear Sir.

I Left the Court to attend to some private affairs three weeks ago, with a design to return in a week if the Court did not rise as I supposed it would. It was then the prevailing Sentiment that when the Committee went out to raise the 5000 Men for Canada and York, it would be best to have a recess. We had as I thought taken every necessary step ⟨and left⟩ in the House and left Nothing but the Concurrence of the Board and the Execution of the measures agreed on, and I suspected no difficulty in either of them. But it seems the Board did not Concur, and the whole proceedings have since undergone a revision and alteration I think for the worse. The Committee are now out, and I hope the men will be forwarded without any further delay. I am sick of this slow way of doing Business. We have been three weeks performing what should have been only the work of three days oweing not so much to the Interested views of different parts of the Colony, as to the Uncertainty ⟨of Ind⟩ and mutability of Judgment in some Persons whose Sentiments however fixed one day may be very different the next. When I was prepared to return I was Informed the Court was certainly to rise in a day or two, and so have been kept along to this time tho' I believe they never rose till Yesterday. Since I have been at home I have had the great pleasure of your several Obligeing and friendly favours of the 11th, 15th and 25th of June.[1] It gives me great pleasure to Observe the Change of ⟨them⟩ measures in some of the Southern Colonies which have hitherto Clogged your proceedings and prevented that policy which would have Effectually ⟨have⟩ served us, and reduced our Enemies. But I hope Providence has so ordered all Events that even this will some how or other terminate to our Advantage. I am glad to see that you have now hopes that such kind of opposition is at an End. As to the affairs of Canada, I am Inclined to think there must have been some Inattention, if not Mismanagement there. It seems to me as if Congress had not been well Informed of the Situation of things there. Bad Success has attended every step since the takeing [*of*] St. Johns, and our Army has at least abandoned the Country and retreated at least as far as the Isle of Noix after suffering ⟨incredible⟩ Excessively from War, Pestilence, and famine and looseing two very valuable General officers.[2] I can't however Blame General Thomas' Conduct. I believe it was Impossible for him to have supported him-

self there under the Circumstances he found things in. I hope they
will be able to make at last an Effectual stand where they are,
which with a repulse at New York may End this Campaign, and
make them sick of the Voagye. This success of theirs at Canada
will however give them a flush of Spirits very detrimental to our
affairs, and therefore I think you are very right in your opinion
that the Causes should be thoroughly Explored, and the like
prevented for the future.

I shall take perticular Notice of what you recommend relative
to powder, arms, stocks on Martha's Vineyard and Nantucket,
and to the Members of Congress haveing a Seat in Court, as they
all Coincide exactly with my own Sentiments, and some of which
I have laboured for without success. The discovery of the plot at
New York is a very favourable Event. I can easily Concieve deep
laid and diabolical as it was it may terminate greatly to our
Advantage. It may Accelerate the motions of the slow Bellyed
Gentry you mention, Inspire them with some Noble Sentiments,
and Excite their vigour in aiding the Execution of plans their
Timidity or wickedness have hitherto impeded.[3] I sincerely Lament the fatigues and difficulties my Friends have had so large a
Share of from these and other quarters. I hope Health, Spirits and
Strength will be given them in proportion to the difficulties they
meet with.

I know not what Intelligence General Gates has of an attack on
this Colony. It must be such as to deserve Notice or he would not
believe it himself. There seems to be no present appearance of
one. Our Coasts are all Clear and quiet since the departure of the
small fleet which hovered about for a week and then went off.
We shall Endeavour to be prepared for such an Event tho' I could
wish this Colony in a better posture both with regard to Men and
Arms. We are so drained that we have been Obliged to give an
Exorbitant Bounty and 1500 Men more are called for.[4] Surely
Congress do not Consider the Numbers of Men we already have
in service. The Continental Army, the Sea Coast, and the Sea
Service have taken half of our Men at least, and left scarcely sufficient to till the Land.

I am sorry General Ward is not yet relieved it would be certainly a Deed of Charity, both to him and the Country. He will ⟨certainly⟩ dye if Continued, and we want a Man of Spirit and Abilities to Command the Continental Troops here. Green I have always had a very good opinion of as a *Brigadier*. Mercer or his Character I know Nothing of. Whitcomb I am told will resign and perhaps it is best he should.[5] If there should be an attack here it seems necessary that all our Forces should be under one direction. If that is to be in your Commanding officer, the Appointment should be made with some delicacy. It may be hard work for some Persons in the Militia to serve under the Command of those who are not only Inferiour in age but in rank both civil and till very lately military.[6] I can give you no kind of News. We are in daily Expectation of great Events from New York, and hearing of the Operations in Canada. We have made no other progress in the matter of Goverment but the Appointment of a large Committee of the House, who have been diverted from Attending to that Business by the Calls for Men, and some other Important matters. I am much obliged to you for the new Instance of your Friendship discovered in your Letter of the 15th ultimo. As I have no private Business to Call of [f] my attention and must for the greater part of my Time be at Court, I could well enough attend to the Business you mention, and if the Appointment should be made should Endeavour to Execute the Trust with such diligence and Fidelity as should honour the Recommendations of my Friends. At the same time I doubt whether large Sums could be procured here, and Consequently the Emoluments would fall far short of the Estimation you make.

And now I am on the Subject of my own affairs permit me to trouble you with a matter which gives me great Uneasiness, as it may affect not only my Interest, but unless Understood in all its Circumstances my Character. By my Accounts Carried by Mr. Winthrop you will observe a deficiency of a Considerable Sum not accounted for. I have been tolerably easy about this matter not doubting but by Compareing my Account with the General's Account of Warrants drawn I should find some paid and mislaid without Entering but I received from Winthrop two days ago a letter which has put an End to my hopes.[7] I know not now how to account for ⟨or g⟩ this loss, but by supposeing some Body stole a Quire from him at Cambridge, for with him lyes the whole, or nearly the whole deficiency. Some there would have been without this, for no Man in paying such a very large Sum would be able to Ballance his Cash Account under my Circumstances, for you must Consider that the money was wanted long before it came, and I was always pressed Excessively in the payments. The sheets were of various denominations, and the Errors were against me. When I was first appointed the General[8] Inclined I should keep the office at Watertown. Afterwards he desired me to keep an office at Cambridge for small payments only reserving the larger ones to be paid at Watertown. This I Complied with and sent Winthrop down for that purpose and put into his hands sums of Money from time to time, of which I kept a regular account which I frequently settled with him and he always accounted for to my satisfaction, up to January when there was only a deficiency of about 16 dollars, which was not more than I might Expect. At the End of December there was no money to pay the old army. After some time I think in February it came, and then the Commissary General supplies were to be stopped, which made it necessary that they should be paid at Cambridge where his Clerks could attend with their Books. I was unhappily taken sick, came Home and was confined for 5 or 6 weeks dureing which time the Transaction of this Business devolved Intirely on Winthrop at Cambridge, the Office Constantly Crowded and he much hurried, and he can't now account for nearly 1800 collars, which is a quire. As I have never had the least occasion to question his Integrity I suppose some person dexterous in this way took the advantage and stole this money, especially as he is ready to swear that he never directly or Indirectly has Converted a shilling to his own use or disposed of a shilling in any other way but by the General's Warrants. Mr. Lothrop[9] and I are ready to do the same in the most solemn manner and we three are the only persons that ever transacted any kind of Business in the payment of monies in the office. It will be Extream hard upon me ⟨to⟩ after all the services I have done the army in and out of this office to lose this money which is nearly double to all my pay. As the matter is therefore Important to me I hope you will Excuse this long detail. I Beg you would Communicate it to my Friends the Mr. Adams's. I presume to rely on any advice and assistance you with them can give me in this matter, and am with regards to them Your Friend and Servant

Jas. Warren

Elbridge Gerry Esqr.

ALS, Frederick M. Dearborn Collection, Harvard College Library; and photographic copy, EG Papers, Library of Congress.

1. EG's letter of June 15 has not been located.
2. Eyewitness accounts of this disastrous campaign are in Commager and Morris, '*Seventy-Six*, 1:185–92. The two valuable officers were Ethan Allen (1737–89), captured, and General Richard Montgomery (1738–75), killed.
3. Samuel Eliot Morison and Henry Steele Commager (*The Growth of the American Republic*, [5th ed., 2 vols., New York, 1962], 1:205), insist, "Had it not been for the presence of Washington's force in New York City that colony would certainly have stayed loyalist: as it was, the Provincial Congress did not vote for independence until 9 July 1776, and the patriot committees had great difficulty in keeping the tories quiet by strong-arm methods."
4. In fulfillment of the resolve of June 25, Massachusetts was paying a bounty of £7 to soldiers and non-commissioned officers destined for Canada and a bounty of £3 for their counterparts going to New York. See Mass., *A&R*, 19:463.
5. Nathanael Greene (1742–86) had served throughout the siege of Boston and after the British evacuation he had commanded the army in that city. In August, 1776, he was promoted to the rank of major general in the Continental Army.
Hugh Mercer (1725–77).
6. In due time this aspect of the conflict between militia and Continental Army would provoke JW's own resignation.
7. On July 6, hence unknown to JW as he penned the present letter, Congress had approved allowances in his account for assistants, sundry articles for office use, and horse hire. (See *JCC*, 5:525.)
8. General George Washington.
9. Isaac Lothrop, friend and confidant of JW, had represented, along with JW, the town of Plymouth for years in the House of Representatives.

§

For the Massachusetts delegation in Philadelphia this was a particularly trying season. In late July, Paine was so ill that John Adams concluded, somewhat prematurely, "he never would be fit to do duty there again, without a long Intermission." Samuel Adams, John also declared, "is compleatly worn out." Of himself he wrote, "My Case is worse. My Face has grown pale, my Eyes weak and inflamed, my Nerves tremulous, and my Mind weak as Water." Repeatedly Adams urged JW and the General Court to elect some new delegates to the Congress.[1]

EG, after five months of labor in the Pennsylvania city, also needed a respite. On the eve of EG's departure from Philadelphia, John Adams wrote, "He is obliged to take a Ride for his health. God grant he may recover it, for he is a Man of immense Worth. If every Man here was a Gerry, the Liberties of America would be safe against the Gates of Earth and Hell." EG rode north on the sixteenth, his desire to get home tempered by his hope to study conditions en route and by his awareness that small-pox was raging in Massachusetts.[2]

In New York, on the nineteenth, EG was, in Joseph Trumbull's words, "better then when he left Philadelphia." From Kings Bridge, two days later, the horseman wrote his colleagues Samuel and John Adams, authorizing them to put his name upon the Declaration of Independence should that item of business arise. At the beginning of August, EG, recovered in body and spirit, met Abigail Adams for the first time. EG, she wrote her husband, "appeard a modest Man, and has a fine inteligent Eye."[3] While in the Boston-Watertown area, EG acquainted himself with the problems related to troop levies, clothing, etc. By September 2, EG had reached Philadelphia.[4]

In mid-July the Massachusetts authorities, still trying to raise 5,000 men for military service, concluded a treaty of alliance and friendship with the St. John's and Mickmac Indians. Meanwhile the spreading smallpox epidemic threatened the suspension of many activities. Terror and hope led some to seek inoculation.

His ear attuned to developments in both Boston and Philadelphia, JW divided the troubled summer between Plymouth and Boston. Upon hearing of the Declaration of Independence, he wrote John Adams, "When are we to hear of your proceedings on the first Instant what Al-liances, and Confederations have you agreed on? I want to see some French Men of War on the coast." On July 13 JW and MW journeyed to Boston to be inoculated against smallpox. In due time their sons in Plymouth received the same treatment. Abigail Adams reported JW "very cleverly spattrd" and MW somewhat given to "faintings and langour." Meanwhile JW had declined an appointment as justice of the Supreme Judicial Court of Massachusetts, much to John Adams' displeasure. "Warren has both Talents and Virtues beyond most Men in this World," John wrote Abigail, "yet his Character has never been in Proportion. Thus he always is, has been, and will be." Early in September JW was again in harness as Speaker of the House.[5]

1. *W-A Ltrs.*, 1:264, 265, 269.
2. EG to Jos. Trumbull, Philadelphia, July 8, 1776, EG Papers, Library of Congress; and *W-A Ltrs.*, 1:260.
3. Force, *AA*, 5th ser., 1:452; *LCC*, 2:20; and *Adams FC*, 2:68, 72, 78.
4. EG to John Adams, Watertown, August 3, 1776, EG Papers, Library of Congress; *Adams FC*, 2:94–95, 98; Force, *AA*, 5th ser., 1:1146–47; and *W-A Ltrs.*, 1:272.
5. *Ibid.*, 258, 259, 262, 263; Force, *AA*, 5th ser., 1:315–26, 367, 847–50; *Adams FC*, 2:65–67, 99; and Anthony, *First Lady*, 106–7.

James Warren to Elbridge Gerry

• •

Watertown, September 17th: 1776

My dear Sir.

Since my last the Intelligence from New York, a Letter from Governor Trumbull and a Requisition from Congress for more Men[1] have Interrupted our Tranquility and turned our profound meditations on Modes of Government into ways and means for raising 1/5 part of our Militia both of the Alarm and Train Band. Excepting in some of the remote Counties and seaport Towns, this is at last Effected.[2] The orders are Issued, and Executeing as fast as possible, tho I hear there are some difficulties yet to be remedied. These are to march with delay to New York, Except one Battalion to Rhode Island. We are now about riseing that the members in their several Towns may give their aid to the Officers in dispatching the Men. I beleive we shall rise this day or Tomorrow, after doing a few matters of Importance. Our Recess will be short. We have provided for the Manufactory of Cannon, and shall for that of small arms, Lead, Sulphur, and salt petre as fast as we can. We have laid an Embargo on the Exportation of all Lumber to the first November that the Enemy may not avail themselves of it to Build winter quarters.[3]

We are in good Spirits, tho sorry for the Advantages gained by our Enemies. It was Yesterday Reported that Congress had sent a Committee to treat with Lord and General Howe. I assure you this produced more sober Countenances than the loss of Long Island.[4] I want to Enlarge but I have not opportunity. I shall be Called away Immediately. I must therefore now trouble you with a little of my own private affairs.[5] Inclosed is my account of Moneys paid after the 4th May to the 15th June, and the Warrants to vouch it, and with them a Certificate ⟨that⟩ from General Ward that this was done by his desire and from the Necessity of the thing. The army were very uneasy, for want of their pay, and nobody appointed to pay them, and money in my hands. I thought it would at least salve the public. If Congress should allow me ⟨any thing⟩ my usual pay it will go only to sink the old Balance, tho' this is working as the proverb is for a dead Horse. Yet I shall be satisfied if that is done. I have made no Charge in the Account if you think that best you will please to add it. If ⟨th⟩ you think it will be of any advantage to have our affadavits, you will please to advise me. We have nothing new here. Prizes some of them very Rich are Constantly arriveing notwithstanding the vigilance and success of the Cruisers.[6] My Regards to all Friends I am Yours assuredly

J. Warren

Mr. Gerry

ALS, EG Collection of Elsie O. and Philip D. Sang, on deposit at Southern Illinois University Library, Carbondale.

1. Force, *AA*, 5th ser., 2:205–6, 266, 315–16; and *LCC*, 2:13–14. The governor is Jonathan Trumbull (1710–85) of Connecticut.

2. *W-A Ltrs.*, 1:268, 273.

3. To strengthen this action, Massachusetts, on September 2, and over the signature of JW, had recommended a similar step to New Hampshire. See Force, *AA*, 5th ser., 1:1283.

4. On September 6, the Congress named a committee of three to proceed to Staten Island to learn what authority and propositions Lord Howe might have. A conversation of three hours with Howe convinced the Americans that he possessed no unusual powers and they returned to Philadelphia on the thirteenth. Meanwhile American

patriots wondered what was afoot. See *JCC*, 5:730–31, 737–38, 765–66; *Adams FC*,
2:124; *D&A–JA*, 2:250; *LCC*, 2:91–93; and *W-A Ltrs.*, 1:274.
  5. Late in August, JW had raised this issue in conversation with Abigail Adams;
see *Adams FC*, 2:116.
  6. In late July, August, and early September, the "Hancock," "Franklin," and
"Lee" had taken four vessels, none of which carried cargo of military significance; see
Clark, *George Washington's Navy*, Appendix B, Nos. 40–43.

§

Foreign and domestic issues clamored for attention in Philadelphia
that autumn, including the terms of a proposed treaty with France, the
instructions of the agent entrusted with that diplomatic endeavor, and
a revision of the articles of war. Meanwhile the military situation in the
vicinity of Philadelphia so deteriorated that fear of British entry into the
city induced the Congress to depart that place.[1]
  On September 20, 1776, a couple of weeks after his return to Philadelphia, EG was named to a committee charged with repairing "to head
quarters, near New York, to enquire into the state of the army, and the
best means of supplying their wants." Three days of conferences and
interviews buttressed the report, which, in EG's hand, was submitted to
the Congress on October 3.[2]
  While completing his report on the state of the army, EG was appointed, on October 1, to a committee to confer with Brigadier General
Thomas Mifflin (1744–1800), who had been asked to assume the office
of quarter master general of the Continental Army. A rare exception to
EG's concentration on military affairs came, on October 17, with his
appointment, to a three-man committee "to bring in a plan for the
better regulating the treasury board."[3] Participation on the Treasury
Board became one of EG's major duties.
  The Congress, "informed that certain persons were busy in monopo-
lizing and engrossing the articles necessary for the use of the army, with
a view to enhance their price, and prevent the army from being supplied,"
named EG to another committee of three "to enquire into this matter,
and report thereon to Congress." In turn, EG's motions of November 8,
led to the establishment of yet another three-man committee, on which
he was instructed "to consider and report under what restrictions the
suttlers, who supply the army, should be laid." The new committee's
report, in the hand of EG, was submitted to the Congress the following
day.[4] In addition to his service on these committees touching military

affairs, EG's concern about that department prompted a vigorous correspondence with General Gates and Commissary General Trumbull.[5]

Shortly after Congress reconvened in Baltimore, where he found the air "so much more exhilirating," EG's activities became less exclusively military in nature. On December 24, EG was named to the five-man committee "to prepare and report a plan for obtaining foreign assistance." Congress received the desired report, in EG's hand, four days later. Meanwhile, on December 26, still another committee appointment came EG's way. Then, along with four others, EG sought means "for the better conducting the executive business of Congress, by boards composed of persons, not members of Congress."[6]

As was the case in Philadelphia and Baltimore, a variety of concerns drew official attention in Massachusetts during the autumn of 1776. In mid-September, with the frigate "Hancock" especially in mind, it was resolved that Massachusetts furnish the agent for the construction of Continental ships at Newburyport with cannon. Simultaneously every effort was exerted to raise the soldiers needed at New York. Indeed the legislature adjourned until October 9 so that its members, by going to their respective homes, might advance the rate of enlistment. "The House chose me as a Major General to lead this detachment," JW wrote John Adams, "but I thought I could not at this time support the fatigue. They excused me and chose Lincoln." In mid-October another resolve, which was intended to help Massachusetts fill its quota, attested the difficulties attending recruiting that season in the Bay area.[7]

As Speaker of the House of Representatives, JW wrestled with a variety of frustrating military problems—manpower, officers, clothing, and bills of credit. As President of the nine-man Board of War which Massachusetts had created on October 29, JW corresponded widely in pursuit of supplies.[8]

While in Plymouth with MW and the boys, JW came to consider the seventy or more Irish prisoners there such a threat to the community that he appealed to higher authority. To the Council of Massachusetts he wrote on December 8, "I dare not leave home unless they are removed or secured." Two days later that body, treating a more serious issue, certified that Hancock, Samuel and John Adams, Paine, EG, Francis Dana (1743–1811) and James Lovell would constitute the Massachusetts delegation to the Continental Congress for the calendar year 1777. Lingering in Plymouth, JW did what he could, in reference to both shipping and cargos, to advance the work of the Massachusetts Board of War, with which he repeatedly corresponded. "When you don't approve of my conduct," he wrote that body, "you will recall me."[9]

1. *JCC*, 5:768–78, 788–807, 813–17 and 6:917–1007 *passim*, 1027; and Burnett, *CC*, 210, 237.

2. *JCC*, 5:808, 842–44 and 6:904. The need for medicines and hospital administrators is pointed up in Dr. John Warren to EG, Hackensack General Hospital, November 15, 1776, EG Collection of Elsie O. and Philip D. Sang, on deposit at Southern Illinois University Library, Carbondale.

3. *JCC*, 5:838 and 6:886.

4. *Ibid.*, 906, 935, 937–39.

5. *LCC*, 2:103, 105–6, 120–21, 125–26, 127–28, 164–65, 173, 191, 203–4; and Jos. Trumbull to EG, North Castle, November 26, 1776, EG Collection of Elsie O. and Philip D. Sang, on deposit at Southern Illinois University Library, Carbondale.

6. *LCC*, 2:200; and *JCC*, 6:1039, 1041–42, 1049.

7. Mass., *A&R*, 19:565, 576–77, 583, 598–99, 604–6; *W-A Ltrs.*, 1:273–74; and Force, *AA*, 5th ser., 2:376–77, 487.

8. *Ibid.*, 3:496, 507–8, 626, 850; *W-A Ltrs.*, 1:275–86 *passim*; *LCC*, 2:189, 209; and Mass., *A&R*, 19:625–27.

9. Force, *AA*, 5th ser., 3:1065–66, 1132, 1177, 1252, 1267; *JCC*, 7:25–26; and Mass., *A&R*, 19:723.

James Warren to Elbridge Gerry

· ·

Boston, January 15th 1777

My dear Sir

When I last wrote to you, I had ⟨but⟩ no Expectation that my next must be directed to you at Baltimore. I shall not Enquire how or for what reasons you are there, but Implicitly suppose that every Motion of Body or Mind ⟨of⟩ made by Congress is prudent and right. I hope however that you are not so far removed from the Seat of War, and din of Arms, that the Timid, and the wishers for a reconciliation with Britain can forget the Late progress and wanton and cruel devastation of the British Troops. If it should rouse them and put an End to their fears and wishes, it will be happy for us. ⟨I was once in pain for Philadelphia but have now the pleasure to Congratulate you on the ⟨reverse⟩ favourable reverse of our Affairs. Every post now brings us favourable Accounts of the Success of our Arms to the Southward, the perticulars of which you no doubt have with more certainty than we have.⟩ The Troops at Rhode Island have remained till this week very quiet, and nothing of Consequence had taken place there till last Night we heard they had burnt Newport and were supposed to be going off. I hope next Spring we shall be able to open and support a Campaign with advantage. I have favourable prospects of the raising our quota of Men. Very Considerable Numbers Inlist. I beleive they will fill up our Battalions in that way, but if it is like to fail we shall levy them on the Towns. Great quantitys of Cloathing have been procured here not less I presume than a sufficiency for 8 or 10 Battalions, which is cheifly sent forward. More will yet be Collected, tho the principal Channel of our Supplies is in some measure Stopped. An Embargo now here has stopped many Privateers. The price of every thing is Extravagant, and the Extortion of Sellers unbounded. To check it we are now forming a Bill to fix the prices of provisions, Merchandize, Labour &c. Whether it be practicable to Carry such an Act into Execution or not time must discover. If it can be done it may serve us. If we attempt and fail it will certainly do more hurt than good, by Increasing the Evil, and at the same time bringing our Authority into Contempt. No new form of Goverment is yet adopted. Every Body seems to wish for it, and a Number of us are Incessantly moveing and pressing for it. What hinders I don't know Except downright Laziness. A few prizes are dropping in but not in such Numbers as heretofore. The General Apprehensions are that the Enemy Intended to make an Attack here next Spring, and when powerfully reinforced ⟨in the Spring⟩ would Enter by the way of Rhode Island. Whether this Sentiment be right or wrong it is certainly good policy to Encourage and Cherish it, that we may be the better provided. I hope we shall be ready for them, and though I should be sorry to see our Country the Seat of war, I should submit supposeing it for the good of the whole. I think they would not be able to Traverse this Country as they have York and the Jerseys. However a French War will put an End to all their Traverses here. We are frequently told that you have the Offer of French Troops. I hope that will be the last resource. Why do we not hear of French Men-of-War, when ten Sail only might answer all our purposes and all our wishes. I beleive you wonder I have never yet forwarded such a stale of facts as you mentioned. I have not been fortunate enough to get Winthrop and Lothrop together nor have I yet. Lothrop has been in a Hospital with the Small Pox. The matter is Compleated by myself and Winthrop and I Expect to have it done next week by Lothrop, when [*I*] will send it forward by first safe hand. ⟨This I suppose will go by our Friend Mr. Pliarne[1] who is a very agreable Gentleman and one in whom the Boards of War have placed great Confidence by relying on a Contract with him for the greater part of the most Important Articles we want.⟩ Please to make my regards to my Friend Mr. Adams. I will write him as soon and as often as I can. I am Sincerely Your Friend &c.

J. Warren

⟨Since writing the above I have the pleasure of yours by Mr. Rose,[2] and of one from Mr. Adams by Express.⟩[3]

ALS, Gerry II Papers, Massachusetts Historical Society; and Austin, *EG*, 1:253–56.

1. Emanuel de Pliarne, in America since 1775, had entered into contracts for arms and ammunition with the Continental Congress. Early in 1778 he drowned in the Potomac River.

2. This letter by EG has not been located.

3. The docketing reads: "ansd Feby. 18th." That letter by EG also has not been seen.

A comparison of the present text of JW's letter of January 15, 1777 with the version of it in Austin, *EG*, 1:253–56 reveals Austin's techniques in handling his father-in-law's correspondence. His editorial practices included the following: the elimination of capitalization of common nouns, the spelling out of numbers, the elimination of all material—words, sentences, etc.—that had been stricken out, the modernization and correction of spelling (e.g. clothing for cloathing, completed for compleated, chiefly for cheifly, moving for moveing, etc.), and a tendency to be reticent about or to omit material dealing with embarrassing episodes.

§

During the opening weeks of 1777, the Continental Congress was undergoing the annual metamorphosis that the emerging states and their new slates of delegates thrust upon it. The sessions continued in muddy, expensive Baltimore until February 27. A host of resolutions regarding provisions provoked the appointment, on January 17, of yet another committee, on which EG served with two others. On January 20, a report of the Board of Treasury, written in EG's hand, encouraged the advance of $100,000 which was made to New Hampshire. Two days later communications from the committee of Congress in Philadelphia and the council of safety of Pennsylvania required the attention of a committee of three, of whom EG was one.[1]

When, on February 17, "the report of the committee appointed to prepare a plan for suppressing the internal enemies of America, and preventing a communication of intelligence to our other enemies" was recommitted and the committee enlarged, EG joined the committee. Three days later the committee named to confer with Colonel William Buchanan "on the subject of a contract for supplying the army with provisions," counted EG and two others.[2]

In mid-March, EG presented to the Congress a succession of reports, the writing of which had been delegated to him. One touched claims against the United States; another treated an allowance for commissary personnel of the northern department; and a third spelled out the establishment and function of the office of secretary to the Congress.

"When we shall form our Constitution, or in what manner we shall do it I am unable to say," JW told John Adams. EG, meanwhile, was informing the Massachusetts Board of War of the nature and quantity of war supplies which Gardoqui and Sons were to procure in either Spain or France and deliver "to a port Northward of Boston."[3] Reciting bitter experiences of Massachusetts soldiers during 1776 and stressing the related reluctance of many to shoulder arms in 1777, Samuel Phillips, Jr., then lieutenant governor, asked EG, "Whether it is not of the utmost consequence to banish from the army every sutler who is trading on his own account?"[4]

MW, on March 1, drew this historical comparison: "Surely Rome had not severer tryals than America, nor was Cesar in the senate with his Flatterers, and his Legions about him, more to be Dreaded than George the 3d with his parasites in parliment, and his murdering Mercenaries in the Field." Abigail crystalized a specific problem when she reported to her absent husband, "If I would give a Guiney for a pound of flower I dont think I could purchase it. There is such a Cry for Bread in the Town of Boston as I suppose was never before Heard." Greedy profiteers provoked the lament, "I am asshamed of my Country men." At the same time Samuel A. Otis (1740–1814), of the Massachusetts Board of War, pleased with the legislative effort to cope with prices, treason and other crimes, posed this question for EG, "A Merchant and a Statesman as well as a patriot, will you forgive my asking your opinion of the Embargo?"[5]

On March 18, JW went up to Boston, immersed himself more completely in public issues, and entertained a variety of conclusions. Enlistments were speeding up, but the elements of the Continental navy at Boston gave JW pause: too many vessels were in port; some captains refused to speak to each other, much less cooperate in operations, etc. With the naval situation at Providence even worse, JW ventured to suggest to John Adams, "You must fall on some new plan for conducting your Naval Affairs at a distance from you. Perhaps to establish a Board in each district upon an honourable footing, and with extensive powers or something (I know not what) else." Turning to the issue of government in Massachusetts, he added, "one day this week is assigned to determine in what way a new one shall be formed. I fear the determination will be in favour of a Convention."[6]

1. *W-A Ltrs.*, 1:293; *LCC*, 2:231, 237; and *JCC*, 7:45, 50, 54–55.

2. *Ibid.*, 128, 134.

3. *W-A Ltrs.*, 1:288–89, 293–98, 299–301, 303–6; and EG to Massachusetts Board of War, Baltimore, February 2, 1777, EG Collection of Elsie O. and Philip D. Sang, on deposit at Southern Illinois University Library, Carbondale.

4. Austin, *EG*, 1:256–60.

5. *Adams FC*, 2:166, 172; and S. A. Otis to EG, Boston, March 17, 1777, EG Collection of Elsie O. and Philip D. Sang, on deposit at Southern Illinois University Library, Carbondale.

6. *W-A Ltrs.*, 1:303–6.

James Warren to Elbridge Gerry

·   ·

Boston, March 24th: 1777

My dear Sir

When I write to you or Either of the Mr. Adams I Consider myself in many respects as writeing to all three. I yesterday wrote a long Letter to Mr. Adams.[1] I mentioned to him every thing of Consequence that then Occurred to me. I therefore write this more to Express my Friendship and regard than for any ⟨I shall⟩ additional Intelligence I have to give. It is near a month since I had the pleasure of a Line from you.[2] As you have now returned to your *Ancient and most Convenient Seat*, a hundred miles nearer to us, I shall Expect favours of that kind at least Oftner in proportion to the distance. Yesterday arrived in Town the French Officer who came in the Ship at Portsmouth. He is said to be a Brigadeir,[3] and was to have been received with Ceremony, but his comeing on Sunday prevented. I presume he will be Considered and Entertained with all the Marks of respect and Friendship that one Brother has a right to Expect from another. We are Impatient for the Arrival of the Ships from France destined to this place. I Congratulate you on the Appearances of things in France. Tho' our account is only General, you will be perticularly Informed what we may Expect from France, a matter that has Engaged the Curiosity of every one, some from one Principle and some from another.

The principle Questions in the House are about the Army, and whether our Embargo shall be taken of [*f*], and the Privateers and Others let loose, and about mending or repealing our regulateing Bill. This Bill makes no small Noise and difficulty here, as it was designed to supply in some measure the want of publick virtue. When I think of it I can't help recollecting at the same time a decree I have ⟨seen⟩ read or heard of among the simple Natives of ⟨of⟩ some simple Country to Inspire Courage into their Inhabitants. It is however to be Lamented that their should be such a venal Spirit prevailing to the destruction of all patriotism. While I am writeing I am told that there is a Brigantine from South Carolina with an account that this Spirit is not Confined to us. We are Informed that some Men of Character among them have been playing a Curious Game for the sake of filthy Lucre, one of the Blessings derived from Civilization and its Attendant Commerce. I envy the Indians their simplicity, and the savages their Barbarism. Civilization was surely the greatest Curse

Consequent upon Original Sin. This goes by Major Ward,[4] who is a man I have a good Opinion of. I beg leave to Introduce him to you. If you find my Opinion Justified by an Acquaintance with him, and opportunity offers perhaps you may think proper to provide for him. I am Your Friend and Humble Servant

J. W.

Honourable Mr. Gerry

ALS, photographic copy, EG Papers, Library of Congress.

    1. This letter is in *W-A Ltrs.*, 1:303–6.

    2. This letter by EG has not been located.

    3. Prudhomme de Borré, who soon was commissioned a brigadier general in the Continental Army; see *JCC*, 7:256.

    4. Major Joseph Ward, formerly aide-de-camp to General Artemas Ward, became Commissary General of Musters in April, 1777. Ward also carried a letter to John Adams; see *JCC*, 7:252; and *W-A Ltrs.*, 1:306.

§

Domestic issues—manpower, supplies and hospitals for the military, finances, the formulation of the Articles of Confederation, and the expedition of its own business—crowded the agenda and debates of the Continental Congress. A portion of the report submitted to it on April 1 relative to the distribution of the tickets of the lottery of the United States was penned by EG. The following day the three-man committee appointed "to revise Dr. Shippen's plan for the regulating the hospital" included EG. On April 8 the search for the more systematic conduct of its business led Congress to name a committee "to report a plan for regulating the mode of receiving applications made to Congress." On this committee, EG also served.[1]

When, on April 17, the Congress considered and recommended, to an enlarged committee, "the report of the committee on the means of introducing better discipline in the army," EG became one of the new members of that body. In similar fashion, on April 19, EG was one of those added to the original membership of "the committee appointed to devise regulations for the commissary's department." Later that month, when the British marched into Danbury, Connecticut and destroyed the stores collected there, EG was named to the committee which consulted with the commissary general concerning the losses sustained.[2]

That spring, in the words of Robert Treat Paine, public measures in Massachusetts were "worrying on at a strange rate." The Massachusetts quota for the army remained unfilled and economic matters provoked mounting complaint.[3]

JW, who spent most of this interval in Boston attending the General Court, learned that on March 31, the Continental Congress had resolved "that the loss sustained by James Warren, Esq. whilst pay master general, in consequence of his keeping an additional office at Cambridge, at the request of the General, for the convenience of the army, as particularly set forth in the depositions of himself Isaac Lothrop, Esqr. and William Winthrop, amounting to one thousand four hundred and one and 42/90 dollars, be allowed in the adjustment of his account at the treasury office." The following day payment to JW was authorized "for the pay due to him as pay master general, from the 4 May to the 15 June, 1776, being forty-two days, at 1,200 dollars per annum, 138 6/90 dollars."[4]

For a fortnight in April, JW, unwell, withdrew to Plymouth. When he resumed his legislative labors, he longed for the close of the session. Love of Plymouth and the special attractions of spring to the landowner called JW.

1. *JCC*, 7:214, 240.
2. *Ibid.*, 274, 281, 314.
3. R. T. Paine to EG, Boston, April 12, 1777, EG Collection of Elsie O. and Philip D. Sang, on deposit at Southern Illinois University Library, Carbondale; and *Adams FC*, 2:210, 217.
4. *JCC*, 7:212, 216.

James Warren to Elbridge Gerry

. .

Boston, April 23, 1777

My dear Sir

I am almost wore out with serving as a Speaker of our House. I have been unwell and absent for some time, and returned here but Yesterday, when I found Captain Ayres designing to set out this Morning for Philadelphia. I have but little time, and there-

fore must write you a very Short letter. I received yours of the
31st March[1] with the Inclosed papers. I am much Obliged to you
for your Friendship and Attention to my Affairs. I am however
sorry to have given you so much trouble. I forgot perhaps to
mention the sum deficient. You have however I think taken it
right in the last Ballance, except by that means you have Excluded me the Advantage of 379 dollars which the Congress had allowed me for an assistant in the Office, and for horse hire, and
attendance and Expences to settle accounts in Philadelphia, and
113 dollars ⟨from⟩ for my own pay from March 31 to May 6th all
which I presume they Intended I should have. I was Accordingly
Credited for them in the account last settled which reduced the
Ballance to 27,722 dollars, and after the warrants paid by
General Ward, drafts the difference or deficiency to 1,401 dollars
Instead of 1893, but I would not wish to trouble you any further
on this head, but set down Contented with that loss.

I have long been Concerned for the ill policy towards and
⟨little⟩ false Lenity shown our Tories in this place. Your accounts
have too much foundation for them. I have long tryed to rouse
the Attention of the Court to the growing Impudence, if not
Encreasing Numbers of these people, but in vain. Indeed one
part ⟨of⟩ or Branch seem ambitious of Excelling in Charity, and
tenderness for them, but Jone Junior it seems appeared on the
Stage last Saturday and Carted of [*f*] five of them, Epes Sargeant,
William Jackson, [. . .] Cary, one Green and James Perkins. I
had rather this method should be avoided but prefer it to none.
I can't Care to see men who at the same time they are deviseing
the destruction of their Country Enjoy all the Advantages of
ease, pleasure, and profit and respect while others are sacrifiseing
every thing to save it, and are Embarrassed and plagued by the
arts of these people. A little spirit in our Assembly would prevent
the necessity of Conducting the matter in this way and nothing
else will do it. The patience of the people seems to be Exhausted.
Our regulateing Bill has Involved us in great difficulty. We are
now forming a Bill to Carry it into Execution, and if possible
restrain the Baleful Effects of that Avarice which always attends

a Spirit of Commerce. The Bearer waits and I must Conclude. He appears to me to be an active man well acquainted with Sea Affairs, has served you as a Commander of one of your Schooners. I wish you may give him further Employ (if he desires it) according to his deserts. I Sir Yours &c.

[*no signature*]

E: Gerry Esqr.

AL, Russell W. Knight—Gerry collection, Massachusetts Historical Society.

1. This letter by EG has not been located.

James Warren to Elbridge Gerry

. .

Boston, April 30th: 1777

My dear Sir

We have this day received an account of the Unfortunate, and Inglorious affair at Danburry.[1] How such an handful of Men came to be suffered to penetrate so far into the Country, to a place so secure as one ought to be where so Important a Magazine was placed, I can't tell. Perhaps the Connecticut Militia or some Body else can. We have likewise this afternoon an account of the weak State of Ticonderoga, and the apprehensions the Commanding Officer is under for that Post. These things may, and I hope will have the good Effect to rouse us. We have Just passed a Resolution to Compleat our Quota by a draft, and another to reinforce Ticonderoga with 1500 Militia from the County of Hampshire,[2] one half of the Berkshire Militia haveing already Marched at the Instance of General Gates to Albany, to quell the Tories, and Guard the posts in that quarter. I hope we shall succeed in our draft. These Circumstances will help us, tho' a draft for three Years is a little out of the common Course. We seem to be in a way to have our hands full I hope we shall by the assistance of Heaven get through. The Opening of the Campaign, and the Conduct of the Enemy strongly Indicate the Authenticity of your Intelligence. ⟨The Authent⟩ The Situation of our affairs have kept the Court together till now and will a few days longer. Our regulateing Act has produced much such Consequences as I at first Expected, Created great Uneasinesses, put some upon deviseing every species of fraud to Evade it, and others upon assumeing Impudence enough openly to violate it and Contemn our authority. We are now upon an act Conceived with severe penalties to Carry the former into Execution. We have enough to do to Combat the Avarice and selfishness of ⟨some⟩ many people and the ⟨wickedness⟩ Malicious veiws of others, who wish to throw us into Confusion. The Frenchman who arrived here lately with a Cargo of Goods was at first well satisfied with the regulated prices, and promised to Conform, but he now Insists on being free from any Controul and at Liberty to sell his goods as he pleases, and threatens to leave us if he is Obliged to Conform. As he is the first Ship and our Connections with France are Interesting we shall treat him with delicacy, but as much as we want the goods, and that others should come after him, we seem disposed to let him go rather than repeal the Act or give him a dispensation. We are fitting a fleet to clear our Coasts. They may probably sail in two or three days. We shall attend without delay to your resolution for a Certain Expedition. I hope for the honour of New England it will be Effected.

The Inclosed Letter for you I accidentally met with and took it into my hands to forward to you with as much dispatch and security as I could. I suppose it is from Bilboa. I wrote you a few days ago and then troubled you with a State of the late Settlement of my accounts, and an Error or two I suppose was made. My regards to my Other Friends, I am assuredly Yours

[*no signature*]

AL, Russell W. Knight—Gerry collection, Massachusetts Historical Society.

1. I.e. Danbury. A detailed account is in Douglas Southall Freeman, *George Washington: A Biography* (6 vols., New York, 1948–54), 4:409–11.

2. Mass., *A&R*, 19:921–23, 925. The latter resolution limited the duty at Ticonderoga to two months.

§

Indicative of the continuing friction between the military establishments, as well as the personality of JW, was his word, on May 5, to John Adams, "The Militia is so despised, and I suppose is designed with all its officers to be directed by Continental Generals, that I intend to embrace the first opportunity to quit it, that shall offer without any imputation." While this word traveled toward Philadelphia, the Congress balloted to select the board of assistants to the Marine Committee for the Eastern Department which John Adams had proposed. From the field of nine nominees, JW was one of the three named to the Navy Board at Boston.[1]

Meanwhile the town of Charlestown, seeking compensation in the amount of £163,405 for real and personal property losses experienced during the burning of the town and the subsequent occupation by the British, had presented a petition to the Continental Congress.[2]

1. *W-A Ltrs.*, 1:323–24; and *JCC*, 7:331.
2. *Ibid.*, 354, 365–66.

Elbridge Gerry *et al* to James Warren

. .

Philadelphia, May 21st 1777

Sir

Mr. Gorham and Mr. Russel, Agents of the Town of Charlesto[w]n, have presented to Congress a Petition from the Unfortunate Inhabitants of that Place, praying for a Compensation for their Losses.[1] The Petition was drawn in very decent and handsome Terms, containing a lively Description of the distresses to which the unhappy Petitioners were reduced, from a State of Ease and affluence; and the Gentlemen who presented the Petition have urged every motive which could either show the Justice and Policy of granting the Request, or which could move the humanity and Charity of those who heard it.

These Endeavors of theirs have been seconded by your Delegates in Congress, but to no other Effect than to obtain a Committee[2] to consider the Petition, whose Report altho' it expresses much Sympathy with that virtuous People in Affliction, contains a Denyal of their Request on account of the present condition of the Finances of the United States: as, the granting of Compensation even in Part, at this Time, would set a Precedent for so many and so great Demands, of a similar Nature that the public treasury would not be able to Spare so much from the necessary Calls of the War.

There was a Great deal of Delicacy shown thro the whole debate upon this Subject. Every one wished it was in the power of Congress to grant the desired Relief; most acknowledged the Justice of the Demand; but, all agreed that, at present it would be impolitic to grant it—except the delegates from the Massachusetts Bay.

Upon a Motion that a Small Part of the Losses should be made up, such was the reluctance to giving a negative that the previous Question was moved and put; so that a present determination might not prejudice the Petitioners in any Future application.

It may be doubtful whether such petetions to Congress, from particular Corporations, or Independants in any State are proper. Perhaps it would be better that each State should ascertain the amount of its own Losses, in this Kind, and represent it to Congress; that so, in the End, some Adjustment may be made between the several States.

That such an adjustment will, sooner or later, be made is not doubted by Us: because, neither Equity nor sound policy will admit that different states, contending in the same common Cause, having in View the same common Benefit, should be unequally loaded with expense, or suffer disproportionate Losses, but, as it is impossible to foresee what Course the War will take, or what State will be the greatest Sufferer, it is probable this question will be postponed untill the End of the War.

In the mean Time, our Brethren and Neighbors, virtuously struggling together with us for every Thing that is Valuable, and reduced from Prosperity to Adversity by the cruel Stroke of War, must not be left to suffer unnoticed. This would be plainly repugnant to the dictates of Humanity, to the Precepts of Christian Charity to the Rules of common Justice and the soundest policy;—a Chain of Motives which doubtless produced the Grants already made by the General Assembly of our State for the immediate Subsistence of these sufferers. But, as the unfortunate Petitioners were deprived of their necessary Tools and Materials for Business, it was remarked by the Gentleman who pleaded for them in Congress, that an advance sufficient to replace those Things would be a most essential Relief and by the far the most economical in the end. And it was suggested that such Estates of disaffected Persons as may be sequestered or confiscated, throughout the Limits of our Union, might be a Fund, to insure the Loan of Monies, for compensating patriotic Sufferers. This, however, was not formally recommended. Each State is competent to the Business, if judged proper.

Having reported this Affair as it has been conducted in Congress, we wish it to be communicated by you to the Honorable House, for any Emolument which their Wisdom may direct.

We have the honor to be with much Respect, Sir,

Your most humble Servants
John Hancock
Samuel Adams
John Adams
Elbridge Gerry
James Lovell

To the Speaker of the Honourable House
of Representatives of Massachusetts Bay

Massachusetts Archives, CXCVII: 71; Force Transcripts, Massachusetts Records, Letters, 1777, Library of Congress; and *LCC*, 2:366–68.

1. This petition, dated November 28, 1776, was read to the Continental Congress on May 14, 1777; see *JCC*, 7:354.

2. The committee, consisting of Charles Carroll of Maryland, Thomas Heyward (1746–1809) of South Carolina, and Jonathan Bayard Smith (1742–1812) of Pennsylvania, was appointed immediately; see *ibid.*

§

As the season for military campaigns gradually unfolded, so too did congressional consideration of various needs—manpower, money, supplies, and morale. The lengthy committee report touching the commissary department was principally in the hand of EG.[1]

Late in May the Committee of Treasury revised the accounts of ex-Paymaster General JW and concluded "that a warrant should issue on the loan office of the Massachusetts bay, in favour of James Warren . . . for 494 41/90 dollars."[2]

Meanwhile, in the season of the election that sent new members to half of the seats in the Massachusetts House of Representatives, a brief respite and return to Plymouth refreshed JW. On June 4 he returned to Boston, "with a full determination not to act as Speaker; but," he wrote John Adams, "I was forced to accept for a few days." Under the circumstances, his appointment to the Navy Board evoked little enthusiasm from him. "It appears to me to be a business of some magnitude, and I have taken such a lurch lately for a more private way of life that I am undetermined what I shall do. I am told here that an actual residence in Boston is required. If so I must of course excuse myself, as I should be loath to move from and loose my interest in my native Town and County."[3]

1. *JCC*, 8:375–451.
2. *Ibid.*, 388–89.
3. *W-A Ltrs.*, 1:326, 327.

James Warren to Elbridge Gerry

. .

                                                         Boston, 10th June 1777

My dear Sir.

I have many and strong Evidences of the Friendship of those at Philadelphia who profess it. I wish it was in my power to make equal returns. I am sure I feel in myself sincerity, and an Inclination to do it. I received your kind favour Incloseing a warrant on the loan office.[1] I did not design to have given you any further trouble on that head, and what I wrote you last on that subject was rather by way of Speculation or Information than from any Expectation I had of a revision of the matter.

We have Nothing very remarkable. A few prizes have lately been sent in, and we have heard of others on the Coast which have not yet arrived, perticularly one or two Transports with Hessians taken by our State Briggs. It will indeed be a disappointment if they fail, but it is so long since one of them was spoke with off Penobscot that I fear we shall not have the pleasure of seeing them at Boston. They were then well satisfied with being taken, but they may have altered their minds and taken possession of the Vessel, or she may be retaken by the Men-of-War in our Bay. No less than 5 or 6 of them are Cruising on our Coast. I suppose our frigates now out are their principal object. A Storm soon after the sailing of our Fleet seperated them. The Privateers were no doubt glad of the opportunity to proceed on their Cruises. Where the two frigates are we don't learn. I am in pain for them least they fall into the hands of the Enemy so superiour to them. We have Endeavoured to give them Intelligence but it is Uncertain whether they get it. This Fleet will greatly Interrupt our small Trade and Privateering. Three sail of them were of [*f*] the high land of Marshfield[2] last Sunday.

Were it not for the arrival of prizes I know not how we could form the Army. The last Blanket was delivered by our Board of War without knowing where to look for more when a quantity designed for Quebec, taken by one of our state Brigantines arrived which will Enable them to proceed in the supply, and the Soldiers to March.[3] This Board of War does the Continent Eminent Service, and had your Committees sent no Agents here to Embarrass them, would have done more. But we Individually shall not receive the Advantages proposed, every thing goes to the Continent. Our State Brigantines have been under their direction and have done well. They were under another direction last Summer and did little, tho' if the directors then had been governed by reason, and animated with Spirit or would have taken the Advice of Others, we might have been Able to have paid all we owe from their Captures.

In General Court you will see a great Number of New Members, and a large Representation from the Westward full charged with prejudices against Merchants and Commerce. They after trying to get the Act passed last Year for a more equal Representation repealed, and geting the Court removed from Boston, have Contented themselves a few days with acting upon the defensive in support of the regulateing Act, the repeal of which was moved for and debated for 2 days.[4] This Act has thrown us into Confusion, Created a great deal of Ill Blood, Cherished the foolish Animosity between Town and Country, hurt our Currency by Introducing Barter, and brought our Government into Contempt, and yet but 31 were for the repeal, 122 against it. We are generally agreed upon a large Tax, £200,000 is the Sum proposed. I wish to hear of the Completion of the Confederation, and of your better health. Your last was very short. I hope you will find time to write more largely soon. I am in the mean time your Assured Friend &c.[5]

[no signature]

Honourable Mr. Gerry
I hear one of the Hessian Transports is arrived at Casco Bay.[6]

AL, Gerry-Townsend Papers, Manuscript Division, The New York Public Library.

1. See *JCC*, 7:216.
2. Approximately ten air miles north of Plymouth.
3. See Mass., *A&R*, 20:19–20.
4. See *W-A Ltrs.*, 1:327.
5. This letter bears no signature.
6. Casco Bay lies east of Portland, Maine. The docketing reads: "ansd 30th."

§

The Committee of the Treasury reported to the Continental Congress, June 11, on ways and means of meeting the expenses of the current year, the floating of foreign loans receiving special attention. The following day

EG penned the report of the Board of Treasury relative to the pay of the paymaster general and his deputies.[1]

When the Council of Massachusetts insisted that Captain John Roach, commander of the "Ranger," was of doubtful character and should be subjected to an enquiry by the Navy Board of the Eastern Department, the command of the "Ranger" was assigned to Captain John Paul Jones.[2]

Despite involvement in the affairs of the new House in Massachusetts, JW also thought of European aid. "I never wish to be beholden to any other Power but that of Heaven, and to our own virtue and valour for our Liberties," he informed John Adams, "but it seems to me a war between France and England will make a diversion very favourable to us. At least it will Gratifie my resentment and curiosity. I wish to see Britain distressed and reduced to circumstances that shall make her appear ridiculous and contemptible to herself, and I have a curiosity to see the operation and the event."[3]

Unable to strike a joyful note, MW, writing to Abigail Adams, complained of "so much Avarice and Venallity, so much Annemosity and Contention, so much pride and Weakness." The next day, in a letter to John, Abigail reflected MW's strong influence upon her as she, speaking of Boston, condemned the "Avarice, venality, Animosity, contention, pride, weakness and dissapation."[4] JW, meanwhile, was in that den of iniquity.

1. *JCC*, 8:453–57, 458.
2. *Ibid.*, 464–65.
3. *W-A Ltrs.*, 1:330.
4. *Adams FC*, 2:264–65.

James Warren to Elbridge Gerry

· ·

Boston, June 15th 1777

My dear Sir

I wrote to you by last Thursday's post after which nothing Material took place till Yesterday when four Brigantines arrived here with valuable Cargoes, two of them from Bilboa, and two of them prizes, one taken by Manley, the other by the "Tyrannicide" of this State[1] all with valuable Cargoes. Manly's prize was bound to Quebec with Cordage, Duck, Iron &c., the other an outward-bound Guinea Man with a good Cargo of the Usual kind. The two from Bilboa are Ballasted with Salt and Contain besides, the Articles as below Shipped by J. W. Gardoqui[2] and Sons on your Account and Consigned to my Care by your order. As I am not Advised whether these Goods are your own property or that of the State and you have never mentioned to me any Expectations of an Event of this kind, I have been greatly at a loss what line of Conduct to take on this occasion, and after some deliberation with myself determined to open the Inclosed Letter Addressed to you, supposeing that the Advantages of Ascertaining the matter would be my Apology, if not well knowing that your Candour and Friendship would Excuse what proceeded from better motives than Curiosity. However after all I am left to form my Judgment from the Nature of the Articles and the Circumstances attending the Shipping of them, which is said to be done by the special order of Doctor Lee[3] and some People of Consequence at the Spanish Court, and these Brigantines which were sent for the purpose of Importing Salt for the Continent, and were partly unloaded to receive these Goods.

In either Case I soon took a resolution to lodge them in a place of more safety than this Town is at present Conceived to be. Infering from the above that they were designed for the Continent I applied to General Heath[4] for room for them in the Continental Stores at Watertown which are secured by a Guard, and Engaged to pay the Storage if they should be for your own private Account. He has sent an officer to prepare room for them. You may depend on the most punctual Attention to this matter and that the same Care shall be taken of them as if my own.

I shall discharge the freight, primage and all other Charges. The freight and primage are the only ones at present that I can Ascertain, which are as below, and if these Goods are not to be disposed off, may be paid to Messrs. Willing Morris and Company, and their draft on me for the same will be more agreable to

me than the Money here. As I must soon make them a remittance
for Effects in my hands, I shall be glad to receive your orders on
this or any other occasion, and to have any Intelligence you can
give me, perticularly of your welfare, and am with the Greatest
Sincerity Your obliged Friend and humble Servant

J. Warren

I just now hear of another prize of value arrived at Booth Bay[5]
taken by one of our State Vessels. Manley's prize left and McNeil
diverting themselves with the "Somerset,"[6] a 60-gun Ship and
⟨E⟩ in a fair way to get some of the Transports under his Convoy.
They both perticularly Manly sail remarkably fast and go round
him at pleasure. The Accounts from Spain are very favourable,
but I presume you know more of that matter than I can tell you.

Brigantine "Alexander John Williamson"
  8 Anchors
 24 Bales Merchandize
  5 Cables
 16 Coils Cordage   in all 28 Tons

Brigantine "Charlote William Sinclair"
  8 Anchors
 22 Bales Merchandize
  3 Cables
An Hawser
114 Coils Cordage   in all 34 Tons
                                                 62 Tons
     freight @ 90/. sterling, primage @ 10/. is £310 - sterling

Monday Morning I find there is like to be some difficulty in geting
a Store at Watertown shall send and get one there or at Muystick[7]
for myself.

Elbridge Gerry Esqr.[8]

ALS, EG Collection of Elsie O. and Philip D. Sang, on deposit at Southern Illinois
University Library, Carbondale; and photographic copy, EG Papers, Library of
Congress.

1. The brig "Tyrannicide," Captain Jonathan Haraden of Salem, took the "Sally" and its cargo of 4,000 blankets and other goods into Salem Harbor.

2. I.e. José Gardoqui.

3. Arthur Lee (1740–92), one of the four Lee brothers of Virginia and one of the earliest American agents in Europe, had been commissioned on May 1, 1777, "in behalf of the United States to transact such business at the court of Spain as shall be intrusted to him by Congress." See *JCC*, 7:318.

4. William Heath, of Massachusetts, was one of the eight Continental brigadier generals named on June 22, 1775.

5. The bay is along the coast of Maine, northeast of Portland.

6. Excerpts of Captain Hector McNeill's report are in Allen, *Naval History*, 1:203ff.

7. I.e. Mystick.

8. The docketing reads "ansd 30th."

§

In mid-June the Continental Congress elected commissaries and deputy commissaries, tried to solve problems which plagued Clothier General James Mease, and discussed, without significant achievement, ways and means of defraying the expenses of the current year.[1]

Samuel Adams, writing JW from Philadelphia, remarked, "I observe by the Boston Papers last brought to us, that you are again plac'd in the Chair of the House of Representatives, with which I am well pleased." Meanwhile, John Adams was writing JW, "You must not decline your Appointment to the Navy Board. Congress have passed no order for a constant Residence at Boston."[2]

1. *JCC*, 8:468–81.
2. *W-A Ltrs.*, 1:332.

James Warren to Elbridge Gerry

.   .

Boston, June 19th: 1777

My dear Sir

I had the pleasure the last Post of Congratulateing you on the Arrival of a quantity of valuable Goods, Shipped on your account by Messrs. Gardoqui and Sons and Consigned to my Care Consisting of Anchors, Cordage, Cables, and Bales of Merchandize. I have such Confidence that it will reach you, and haveing but little time shall not repeat the perticulars of my last. Shall now Inform you that being disappointed of Stores at Watertown, I have procured them at Mistick for the Cables and Cordage. The Anchors [*I*] shall send to Watertown or Cambridge, and the Bales go this day to Weston.[1] Some of them are damaged, and shall be properly surveyed, so that you may receive the Benefit of Insurance if any. I hear Nothing yet of the Ship "Lidia." I hope she will have the good luck to ⟨get⟩ arrive safe. In my last I mentioned to you the lodging in Willing Morris and Company the amount of the freight and primage. This I did only as I Conceived it might probably be most agreably to you, being myself very Indifferent, haveing a prospect of its being done in another way. You will therefore act your own pleasure, and be assured it will be mine. If I had time I could not give you a Single word of News. We have Entered on the matter of Government, have our Committee chose who meet this Morning. Your Friend P[aine?] is one. It is an ill wind that blows good to Nobody. If you are loosers are we not gainers?[2] Don't Envy us. My regards to all Friends. I am Yours Sincerely[3]

J. W.

Honourable E. Gerry Esqr.

ALS, Gerry II Papers, Massachusetts Historical Society.

1. Weston is due west, approximately seven miles, from Watertown.

2. Robert Treat Paine had left Philadelphia for Massachusetts on December 12, 1776 and, although reelected to the state delegation to the Continental Congress for the year 1777, had remained in Massachusetts.

3. Docketed "ansd 30th."

§

During the last ten days of June, the Congress occupied itself, without significant achievement, with military matters touching upon personnel, supplies and finances. In the words of Samuel Adams, "We are going on within Doors with Tardiness enough."[1]

From Boston, JW declared, "I wish one side or the other would open the Campaign. I long to hear of enterprizes, of battles fought and victories gained on our side." Turning to local politics, he continued his report to John Adams, "The regulateing Act has been the subject of frequent and tedious debates, and it yet remains undetermined by the House whether to repeal, inforce, or suspend it for a time." Regarding the effort in Boston to frame a constitution, he declared, "I conceive the matter of Representation will be our greatest difficulty. They have agreed on the qualification of Electors, that they should be Freemen of 21 years of age, resident for a certain time in each Town, and such as have paid publick Taxes. I could wish that a certain degree of property had been another."

"We have had a Bill before us for freeing the Negroes, which is ordered to lie, least if passed into an Act it should have a bad effect on the Union of the Colonies," JW continued. In a postscript he added, "Please to inform Mr. Gerry that the Ship expected from Bilboa is not yet arrived."[2]

EG, meanwhile, assessed the foreign situation in words that combined logic and wishful thinking: "Whilst G. Britain is daily exhausting her resources, and growing feeble, France is encreasing in strength. Spain and Portugal will be inevitably engaged in the War. The Porte and Russia are already involved in a dispute and probably will join in alliance with other powers which will make the War general." On the home front, Paymaster William Palfrey, at Camp Middle Brook, pled insistently for more cash for the military chest. "The whole Army," Palfrey reported to EG, "is two Months in Arrears, and part of them much more."[3]

1. *JCC*, 8:482–513; and *LCC*, 2:388.

2. *W-A Ltrs.*, 1:334–36.

3. EG to John Wendell, Philadelphia, June 27, 1777, and Wm. Palfrey to EG, Camp Middle Brook, June 29, 1777, EG Papers, Library of Congress.

Elbridge Gerry to James Warren

·   ·

Philadelphia, June 30th 1777

General Warren

My dear Sir

Your agreable Favours of the 10th, 15th and 19th of June with the Inclosures are at Hand, and the Goods Shipped by Messrs.

Gardoquis on board the "Charlotte," Captain St. Clair, and the "Alexander," Captain John Williamson, and consigned to you for my account are the property of the Continent; in Consequence of which I shall desire the Suret [?] Commission to take the Charge thereof, to order payment of the Freight, Insurance and other Expences by you incurred, and for your Services herein.

Messrs. Gardoqui mentioned in their Letter a parcell of Duck which they for some Time before had Shipped by Captain Hodges for my private Account, as being new appropriated to answer an order which they have received from the Honourable Mr. Lee[1] in behalf of the United States. I am much at a Loss to understand their Intention, or to know upon what principles or Misconceptions they have made the proposal. You may remember that I purchased in November last the Cargoes of Fish to import military Stores and intended that the Continent or the State of Massachusetts Bay should have the Benefit thereof and take the *Cargoes* on their own account. As the latter had been greatly drained of Arms and other Stores, and could not so easily come at Exports as the Commission employed by Congress to purchase for the Continent, I thot it necessary to offer *them* to the Board of War, and finally concluded to risque with the Board half the Cargoes on my own account. They enquired into the Quality of the Cargoes, and finding them inferior declined to be concerned, and before I was apprized thereof, I received advices that one of the Vessels which afterwards proved to have been captured by the Enemy, was a long Time out and not arrived at Bilbao. In Consequence of this I declined offering the Cargoes to the Continent or any Individual as it would be in Fact an unequal proposal, and therefore risqued the whole on my own account. Two of the Cargoes arrived, and Messrs. Gardoquis not being able to procure Fire Arms, Lead and Flints, without breaking the strictest Injunctions of the Court of Madrid, procured 16 Bales of Duck which they mentioned and Shipped them by Captain Hodges who was altogether in my Service, Specifying particularly that the Reason of thier doing this was that he could not procure for me the other Articles mentioned. The first Cost of the Fish which he received of mine was about £2200 sterling, and bad as the Quality was it must neat near 3/4 of that Sum. The whole Amount of what he has Shipped for my account, including the 16 or 17 Bales of Duck is about £700 sterling, so that he must now have about 9 or 1000£ sterling of mine in his Hands; therefore it was not from want of Interest of mine that he proposed to make the new appropriation. In addition to this, the Vessel had Sailed from Bilbao near one Month, all which Time the risque was mine, before he made the proposal, and had she been taken and car-ryed into any port of France or Spain, it must have been known and the loss would have been mine. She is also arrived and the Goods disposed off for my account without the most distant Expectation of any Embarrassment in the Affair. I have been thus particular, that you may hereafter as occasion should require, explain the Matter, as I prefer any Loss to the least Misunderstanding with the public relative to Interest; and altho I shall not neat above one-half in Bilbao of what the 3 Cargoes cost here without charging any Insurance, yet I will consent to loose the Duck including the Cost of it should it be desired by any public Authority whatever.

⟨I desired Messrs.⟩

I shall probably have occasion to obtain the Notary's Seal to some papers for recovering about £250 sterling which Messrs. Gardoqui inform me another House in Bilbao Messrs. Lynch and Company who owe me the Money refuse to pay because I sent back Bills of Exchange for the Money here which they Sent after I had ordered my Interest to be there kept and invested in prod-uce. This is something extra in the commercial World, and I shall probably trouble you for the purposes mentioned and to teach these merchants that they are in an Error.[2]

[*no signature*]

AL, copy, Gerry II Papers, Massachusetts Historical Society.

1. Commissioner Arthur Lee, then in Spain.

2. The related records, which would make this letter more understandable, are un-happily not at hand; but this document nonetheless clearly illustrates the interlocking nature of private, state, and national business in the realm of wartime imports.

§

The membership of the new five-man Committee of Commerce, vested with the powers of the old Secret Committee, included EG, who unavailingly sought release from this assignment. EG's continuing correspondence with Joseph Trumbull of the commissary department included word, in July, that Trumbull's presence was desired in connection with his petition of the previous November. Paymaster General William Palfrey, short of funds, conducting his business in a wagon in which he could not stand upright, and irritated by the lack of response to his repeated applications, was as unhappy as was Trumbull.[1]

On July 11, EG and two others were named a committee "to proceed immediately to the army under the command of General Washington . . . to make a diligent enquiry into the state of the army, particularly into the causes of the complaints in the commissary's department." This duty absented EG from Philadelphia until the end of July or the beginning of August.[2]

EG was named, on August 4, to a committee "to enquire into, and report the number of muskets and field pieces, and the quantity of soldier's cloathing imported, or manufactured, or purchased for the use of the army, the time of importation and the place, and the persons to whom delivered, together with the number of arms in the several magazines under the care of the Board of War, the number in the stores of the commissary general of military stores, and in the hands of the continental troops, and what number has been lost or condemned." Also, early in August, EG penned several reports. Confusion in the commissary department and Joseph Trumbull's resignation encouraged the resolutions by EG[3] of August 6.

Massachusetts' political activity, meanwhile, was experiencing midsummer doldrums, the General Court adjourned, and the committee charged with framing a constitution postponing its labors. JW gladly headed for Plymouth to "ramble among the herds at Eal-river." A postscript to a letter to John Adams added, "Let Mr. Gerry know the Ship "Lidia" is not yet arrived. She left Bilboa and was chased into another port by a small English privateer."[4]

The friction born of JW's affection for the state militia and its commanders—of whom he was one—and his distrust of the commanders of the Continentals erupted anew in August. Of his refusal to subordinate himself to General Benjamin Lincoln (1733-1810), JW wrote, "I don't feel afraid to fight, . . . but I have too much pride to submit to circumstances humiliateing and degradeing. I foresee the Militia are to be considered in the same light of inferiority with regard to the Continental Troops that I have been used with indignation to see them with regard to the British. I have determined no longer to submit to such circumstances, and have therefore embraced this interval of security to resign my Commission."[5]

Even as he shed his militia role, JW assumed that set forth in the newly-arrived instructions related to his appointment to the Navy Board. Anticipating that the new assignment would require his full time, he complained, before embarking upon his duty, that one clerk would not suffice the needs of the Board.[6]

1. *JCC.*, 533–34; *LCC*, 2:402, 408, 410–11; and Wm. Palfrey to EG, Camp Pumpton Plains, July 13, 1777, EG Collection of Elsie O. and Philip D. Sang, on deposit at Southern Illinois University Library, Carbondale.
2. *JCC*, 8:546.
3. *Ibid.*, 602, 610n, 613n, 620.
4. *W-A Ltrs.*, 1:340–42.
5. *Ibid.*, 348–49.
6. *Ibid.*, 350.

James Warren to Elbridge Gerry

. .

Boston, 13th August 1777

My dear Sir

I have this day received the two Inclosed Letters by Captain Andrews who with his Ship has got safe to Portsmouth. I Informed you by the last post[1] of his safe arrival at Casco Bay, and that I had by the Advice of many friends here who veiwed the risque of the Good's comeing up in the ship ⟨too⟩ as I did too great to hazard, ordered them Shipped on small Vessels for greater Security. This was presumeing upon what I thought would be Approved of by you and the Secret Committee. I therefore sollicited your and their Immediate Approbation for my Justification. I hope my Conduct on it [*which*] appears to myself prudent will be so considered and their Approbation Expressed. Pray give me orders for the disposition of these Goods as they are Extreemly wanted ⟨for⟩ both for the Navy and Army, and I am [buried?] with Continental applications for them. We have Nothing turned up since my last. I have therefore only to add that I am Sincerely Yours &c.

J. Warren

Colonel Langdon² haveing great Occasion for some Cordage for the Continental Ships at Portsmouth I have ventured to consent he should take some.

E. Gerry Esqr.

ALS, Rare Book Dept., Boston Public Library; and photographic copy, EG Papers, Library of Congress.

1. Of uncertain date, this letter by JW has not been located.
2. In October, 1777, John Langdon, patriotic naval agent, would be counted with the forces at the Battle of Saratoga.

§

In late August and early September consideration of the Articles of Confederation was sidetracked as the Congress focused on problems related to men and supplies. Discussions of reports from the Committee of Treasury and the Board of War dotted nearly every page of the journal with the need for dollars.[1]

EG's service in Philadelphia in this interval was highlighted by committee appointments and votes. He participated in every recorded vote concerning the Ticonderoga inquiry; and he favored the newly proposed method of paying the interest on the loan office certificates but he opposed the reduction of that interest from six to five per cent. When, on September 11, the Congress favored the importation of twenty thousand copies of the Bible, EG stood with the majority.[2]

1. *JCC*, 8:640–747 *passim*.
2. *Ibid.*, 669, 675, 682, 684, 725–26, 730, 734.

James Warren to Elbridge Gerry

. .

Boston, August 31, 1777

My dear Sir

I have the pleasure to Congratulate you on the Success of your Commerce with Bilboa. Yesterday arrived in this Harbour the Schooner "Neptune" Captain Lee with fifty seven Bales of Merchandize as per the Inclosed Letter and Invoice which I presumed to open not haveing any Invoice sent to me, in order the better to determine my Conduct relative to them by the knowledge of the Contents. And at the same time Arrived at Marblehead the Brigantine "Success" Captain Harris, the Letters by whom were mostly opened and Examined by a Privateer who Boarded and threatened to Carry him into Port as a prize, but after detaining him some time dismissed him. This last Arrival gave me perticular pleasure as the Cargo ⟨was⟩ is valuable and a number of Cruisers are on the Coast, and render an Approach for any Merchantman hazardous. The Schooner I shall take measures to discharge tomorrow. The Brigantine (after some deliberations on the Advantages ⟨of⟩ and Expences of landing her Cargo at Danvers or this place) I have ordered up here with Cargo the first fair wind. The Master has accordingly returned for that purpose. The Goods per Ship "Lidia" are all gone into the Country Except the Anchors which go Tomorrow, so that Nothing will then remain of the three first Cargoes. As an Opinion of Security at present prevails here and I ⟨p⟩ am in daily Expectation of orders for the disposition of these Articles, I propose to take a warehouse and Land them here at least to Lay a short time. In my last I Informed you that many of them were Immediately wanted for the Navy and Army. Mr. Cushing and the Quarter Master are Constantly Importuning me for the delivery of Cordage, Duck, and Tent Cloath, and Blankets, Shoes, Stockings, and Shirts I suppose will be in great demand.

I Could wish you would Expedite the orders, and if it be

Agreable some Cash, as the freight, primage, and other Charges amount to a Considerable Sum, and will drain me of my runing Cash. You will please also to forward me orders for the disposition of the Brigantine.

Observing a paragraph in your Letter relative to Clearing Captain Harris of any Blame for leaving his own Vessel and takeing Charge of this Brigantine to save you or the Secret Committee the trouble of an application on that head I have made one to the Board of War here. They seem apprehensive of Involveing themselves in Blame if any Misfortune should happen, have however promised me an answer this Evening. If they Comply you will find it Inclosed.

News we have very Little. The Success of our Arms at Bennington, and Fort Stanwix[1] has diffused a general Joy, and at once shews the Importance of our Militia, and the Ill policy of Considering, and treating them with the same Marks of Inferiority with regard to Continental Troops that they used to be with regard to British Troops, when perhaps their Services with each deserved the preference. But I forbear to make Comparisons. I only wish that when Congress want their services they would put them on a footing of Equality, and suffer their Officers equally with the Continental to rank according to their Commissions and the dates of them. This would make them Important, and Encourage men of rank and Character to Engage in the Militia as officers. The other will discourage them, and secretly lay the foundations of a Standing Army which your principles and mine abhor. General Gates again going to the Command of the Northern Army has revived a Spirit of Confidence which was before ⟨was⟩ in a low state, and which with the Enquiry you have ordered for the Investigation of Mysterys in that department Inspires us with flattering prospects. The Exact State of Matters Abroad is a Subject that Excites our Curiosity, while you are so profoundly secret that we can draw nothing from you. Were I at Congress it seems to me I should tell you a little more than you tell me.

The destination and design of Howe and his Mighty Fleet and

Army furnishes a fruitful Subject of Conversation and Conjecture, and is a Mystery to me.[2] Is the Man lost in a part of the Earth or Ocean where no Body lives or Travels by Land or water that we hear Nothing of him?

Our Committee on a New Constitution meets this week, the General Court Next.[3] When will your Confederation be finished? What shall we do to prevent the total ruin of our Currency by a pack of Villains that deserve to be hanged. My Compliments and regards to all Friends. I am with wishes for your Health and Happiness Your Sincere Friend &c

J. Warren

The Board of War have Informed me that they will not blame Captain Harris for the step he has taken. I am Informed by one of them that he is a very good and deserving Ship Master. As he has merited your Notice by this step, and is now out of ⟨Emp⟩ any other Employ I could wish he might not be forgot."[4]

ALS, Russell W. Knight—Gerry collection, Massachusetts Historical Society.

1. These actions, that at Fort Stanwix on August 6 and that at Bennington on August 16, are discussed in Frank Moore, *The Diary of the Revolution . . ..* (Hartford, 1876), 477–78, 479–82.

2. Howe was then moving toward and against Philadelphia.

3. The General Court resumed its labors on September 10, ending the recess which had begun on August 16; see Mass., *A&R*, 20:109–10.

4. At the bottom of this letter, in EG's hand, one reads, "1777 September 16, laid before Congress an Extract of that part of this Letter marked with the quotation ('')."

§

On September 4, EG joined Richard Henry Lee, and Nathaniel Folsom (1726–90) of New Hampshire on the three-man committee "to consider under what regulations and restrictions regimental officers shall, for the future, receive their rations." The committee immediately corresponded with General Washington, soliciting his views. Additional committee assignments came to EG on the eighth and ninth when a letter from Governor Jonathan Trumbull on the former date, and letters related to commissary problems on the latter date, required attention. Similarly, on September 10, when the proceedings of the committees from New Hampshire, Massachusetts Bay, Rhode Island, Connecticut, and New York came under consideration, EG became a member of yet another committee.[1]

In Boston, meanwhile, JW, in addition to shouldering his duties in the General Court, added those that came his way on the new Navy Board. "How shall I attend these several departments?" JW wrote John Adams. Meanwhile Abigail Adams was imploring MW to write. "I have always been sorry," she wrote her Plymouth friend, "that a certain person who once put their Hand to the pen, should be discouraged, and give up so important a service."[2]

At the Navy Board, JW was troubled about personnel and authority. For some time the Board had unsuccessfully sought a clerk at the salary assigned by Congress. As for authority, he wrote John Adams, "if our Board are not to have a power of dismissing, or at least of suspending officers, I foresee our authority will be contemptible. I will stand in no contemptible station long."[3]

1. *JCC*, 8:710, 720, 724, 731; and *LCC*, 2:483.
2. *W-A Ltrs.*, 1:358, 364.
3. *Ibid.*, 363–67.

James Warren to Elbridge Gerry

· ·

Cambridge, September 15th 1777

My dear Sir

I thank you for yours which came to hand Saturday Afternoon[1] with the Inclosed Letters &c. I am well pleased with the prospects of things. I hope the Events will be answerable. General Washington has a fine army and (if Howe don't run away) I hope will be victorious. We hear there has been Skirmishing between the two armies much in our favour. Our Affairs to the Northward wore a very good Appearance by the last Accounts. I Expect to hear of a general action very soon. Our Troops had so surrounded John Burgoin[2] Esq. that he must fight or starve. He can neither retreat or advance without our Generals are determined to give him no more Ground, but to dispute every Inch and, perhaps that he is Encamped in. God Grant us Success.[3]

You will before this have Advices of the Arrival of the Brigantine "Success." From that Cargo I have delivered to the Clothiers' Agents all the Shirts and Shirting, Blankets, Stockins, Shoes and Hatts. I was so pressed I could no longer detain them. I have repented it since as I find the Navy must be supplied with Slops or not be manned. I have just received an order from Mr. Morris[4] to deliver all the Shirting, Cloath and Blankets received by Williamson, Sinclair and Andrews so that Nothing will then be left here ⟨but⟩ of those things wanted for the Navy but a few Blankets received by the "Neptune," and a few medicines by the "Success," and I fear I shall have an order for them before the wants of the Navy are attended to. I could wish you would Interpose your good Offices in this matter and get an order for the Navy Board to receive the Duck and Cordage and anchors and also the Blankets and Medicines mentioned above, the salt on Board the "Success" and such other Articles as may arrive here which they may have occasion for. We have no sort of News here. There was none in Boston when I left it Saturday Evening. I am Just returning but must seal this before I set out, least I should not have time ⟨bef⟩ after my arrival there before the Post goes. I wish you all possible Happiness and am Sincerely Your Friend &c.

J. Warren

E. Gerry Esqr.

ALS, photographic copy, EG Papers, Library of Congress.

1. Of uncertain date, this letter by EG has not been located.

2. I.e. Burgoyne.

3. This success came five weeks later, on October 17, when General John Burgoyne surrendered at Saratoga.

4. The letters and invoices of the cargoes carried in the "Neptune" and "Success" were referred to the Committee of Commerce on September 16, 1777; see *JCC*, 8:748; and EG to [?], Philadelphia, September 17, 1777, EG Collection of Elsie O. and Philip D. Sang, on deposit at Southern Illinois University Library, Carbondale.

§

On Thursday, September 18, the Continental Congress moved out of Philadelphia. After one day in Lancaster, Pennsylvania, it crossed the Susquehanna and continued westward to York, where it resumed its work on October 1.[1] From Lancaster, EG wrote General Washington both September 24 and 25 about the best means of collecting the firearms required by the Virginia troops. In York EG, in company with John and Samuel Adams, took up residence with the family of General Daniel Roberdeau (1727–93), then a member of the Pennsylvania delegation to the Congress. Despite illness, EG plugged away in his official correspondence at the confusion attending the commissary department. To Joseph Trumbull he wrote, "The new Commissaries do not appear to be well acquainted with their Business, the army having been one whole Day without provisions."[2]

From Boston, meanwhile, JW reported that the General Court was "provideing for our Soldiers, calling in our money, laying taxes, forming a Constitution, neither of which is yet done." Regarding the constitution, JW was pessimistic; and he registered his disgust when he contemplated the extravagance, oppression, and avarice abroad in Massachusetts.[3]

1. *JCC*, 8:747–60 and 9:761–73.
2. *LCC*, 2:500–501, 506; and *Adams FC*, 2:350.
3. *W-A Ltrs.*, 1:368.

James Warren to Elbridge Gerry

• •

Boston, October 5, 1777

My dear Sir.

I shall direct this to you at Philadelphia but where it will find you I can't Conjecture as we have very Imperfect Intelligence of the operations of war in your quarter, and none at all of the situation of Congress. Wherever it meets you I hope it will find you in safety and happiness. I have the pleasure of yours of the 17th ultimo.[1] I have received several orders for the delivery of Goods which I shall punctually Comply with, tho' somewhat against the Grain as I think some of the Shoes, Blankets, stockings, Hatts, shirts, Clouths and Medicines should have been reserved for the Navy, as I foresee great difficulties if not Impossibilities in manning the Navy unless the Seamen can be well supplied with those Articles, and when these are all gone to the Army I know not where we are to look for a supply for the Navy. I wrote you on this subject 3 weeks ago,[2] and flattered myself no more orders would come till that Letter had been received by you but as it is I don't presume to dispute the orders or delay the delivery.

I can give you no Intelligence from here but of the arrival of prizes which come in pretty well both for Numbers and value. But while the Operations by Land are so very Important, that kind of success seems to have but little Effect unless on those Immediately Concerned. Every thing is absorbed in the anxious Expectation of great Events from the Armies. You will have heard before this reaches you of an Expedition to Rhode Island. The Men are all arrived and in sufficient Numbers, It is Expected they will go on in 2 or 3 days. What the Event will be time must determine. It very much depends on vigorous measures, and sound Judgment. Nothing decisive has yet taken place in the Northern department tho' we have long Expected it. They want neither for Numbers or Confidence in their Generals, or Indeed for anything else but somehow my hopes are not so sanguine as they have been. I begin to apprehend Burgoyne will find his way back to Ticonderoga and we shall never again perhaps Catch him on such dangerous Ground. As the reputation of the New England arms, as well as the Interest of the common Cause are Engaged in this matter I am perhaps more anxious and apprehensive than I should otherwise be. You will please to make my regards to all Friends, and beleive me to be sincerely Yours

J. Warren.

Elbridge Gerry Esqr.

With regard to foreign Affairs, France and Spain are so slow and Timid in their motions, that I am Inclined to think if the Enemy should be Beat ⟨to⟩ in the North and South (which God

Grant), England would get the start of them and be the first to acknowledge the Independency of America.[3]

ALS, EG Collection of Elsie O. and Philip D. Sang, on deposit at Southern Illinois University Library, Carbondale.

1. EG's letter of September 17 has not been located.
2. See JW's letter of September 15.
3. A half decade later the maintenance of British primacy in American markets was a significant influence in the changing British mind that accepted and recognized American independence.

Elbridge Gerry to James Warren

. .

York Town in Pennsylvania, 6th October 1777

My dear Sir

I am favoured with yours of September 15th, and Suppose that eer this will reach you, the orders of the Commercial Committee, for the Disposal of the several Cargoes consigned to you by Messrs. Gardoquis, will be received. The anchors and Cordage will of Course be delivered to your marine Board; and with respect to the Duck, Medicines, and Salt, I think it will be the surest way, to deliver to the Board what is immediately wanted of each, and inform Congress thereof, together with the Necessity that led to this Measure. My Reason for this proposal is that the Disposition already made of these Cargoes, ⟨that⟩ will require a Reconsideration, which Committees as well as Congress are generally averse to: whereas, there will be no Difficulty in approving your Conduct, when evidently founded on the Necessity of the Case. The Blankets, I fear, cannot be spared from the army. A timely application to the marine Board for such other Articles as may be wanted, which should be particularly enumerated, will produce the order which you desire.

Since my last, some of the Important Events that have taken place, prove that those of War are very uncertain. From Circumstances, whether favourable or unfortunate, we are apt to

expect similar Consequences; and the reverse frequently happens; from whence we may learn, in Times of prosperity, Caution,
and of adversity, perseverance and a firm Resolution not to
despond. The Loss of Philadelphia, which In the End I think
will be a salutary Event, is owing under providence to Several
Causes. The Misbehaviour of the Militia of Pennsylvania is one,
and is attributed to the Militia Act, which invests the people with
the power of appointing the regimental officers. Be the Cause
what it may, nothing could equal their Timidity; as I am
informed by some of the principal Inhabitants of the State that
twenty five Hessians put to Flight two Regiments at the Battle of
the Brandywine,[1] and that when the General ordered them to
supply the place of a Brigade, which he had ordered from Chads
Ford to reinforce General Sullivan at Jones Ford, they refused to
comply with his orders from apprehension of *Danger*, and by
these means put the Enemy in Possession of our Lines, which they
would not have attempted to attack, had they been properly
manned—another Cause, is said to have been the Circumstance
of the Country thro which the Enemy marched to the City, it
being inhabited by Tories, who gave the best of Intelligence to
the Enemy, and deceived General Washington. These are ⟨u⟩
undoubted Facts, and by the best Information that I can get,
there is not such a Collection of disaffected people on the Continent, as of the Quakers inhabiting that part of Pennsylvania. The
Disputes about the Constitution of this State, have produced such
a Division and Torpor thro out the Same as renders it at present
an inactive, lifeless unwieldy Mass. Thus much for this State;
and the Militia of Maryland and Delaware are but little [?]
better. But the principal Cause of their obtaining the City without a second Battle, which at the Time of my writing my last
Letter was hourly expected, was a heavy rain that happened on
the ⟨after⟩ Day of the Meeting of the Armies, and after their
advanced parties were engaged; this obliged them to retire, and
the Baggage of our Army was so far distant that the Tents could
not be procured; by which Means all the ammunition of the
Soldiers was destroyed, their arms hurt, and the Army so injured,

that they were under the Necessity of marching the next Day twenty Miles into the Country to avoid a Battle; which must have been fought on our ⟨their⟩ Side by Bayonets and Artillery only. But I am apprehensive, that the Vanity of the Southern States, which has produced such Instances of Invective against the eastern officers and Troops whenever they have misbehaved, stimulated them to oppose General Howe with as little Assistance as possible from the eastern States, that they might have had the Oppertunity of boasting how much the United States, owed their Liberties to the Southern, who opposed themselves to the main army of the Enemy. This I am led to beleive, from the Declarations that were made previous to the Battle of the Brandywine, and likewise from the Neglect to draw off more Troops from Peeks Kill when the Enemy landed at Elk; but since the late Occurrences, Reason seems to have taken place, the eastern officers and Troops are highly spoken of, the others ⟨very⟩ indifferently by their own People, and I hope that each will be convinced, that a party Spirit is not only unprofitable, but destructive to both. Generals Washington and Mifflin are however ever averse to such a Spirit.

We have heard from the northern Army, and I congratulate You on the Success of Colonel Brown, and the good Conduct of our Troops in the Action of the 19th September;[2] we are in daily Expectation of some decisive Action in that quarter, which may be very important.

By a Letter from General Putnam of the 29th September, he supposed that a Reinforcement of three thousand Men had arrived at New York and that more were expected; if so, we must increase our Exertions to meet the most vigorous Efforts and perhaps the last that our Enemies can make. ⟨but⟩ He received his Information from one of our field officers which he has lately exchanged, but I strongly suspect the hope that it will turn out to be a Feint, and that the Transports were sent from the Enemy's Fleet, when they arrived at the Capes of Virginia, for this purpose. ⟨this⟩ A Fleet consisting of sixty Sail was seen the 25th of August in the Latitude of the Capes, standing with the wind at SSE to the Eastward, and is probably the same that arrived at New York, but you will undoubtedly be able to ascertain the Fact, by the Time this ⟨may⟩ reaches you.

General Washington on the Morning of the 4th Instant about 1/2 past 5 surprized the Enemy's Camp at German Town; the particulars we have not yet received or a Line from the General;[3] but a Mr. McClure who is a reputable Citizen of Baltimore, and as a Volunteer was in both the Actions of Prince Town and the Brandywine, and also in this, declares that it by far exceeds the others. By his account our Army advanced in three Divisions, the left of which did not come up for Reasons unknown. The other two attacked the Enemy, drove them thro German Town to their Lines, and attacked them therein for a considerable Time, untill the General ordered them to retreat. The Carnage he says was great, and particularly on the side of the Enemy; General Nash is wounded, and General Sullivan's Brigade Majors are said to be mortally wounded. I suppose his Aid de Camps are intended.[4] The wounded were brot off, and a Field peice of the Enemy's. Our Troops behaved with great Bravery. This is confirmed by a Letter which General Mifflin, who is sick at Redding, received from an officer in his Department, and forwarded to Congress. You will soon have more authentic accounts and I hope they will be agreable from this as well as other quarters.

General Howe has issued a proclamation confirming his promises of protection and pardon to such of the Inhabitants of the middle States as remained in their Homes and returned to their Allegiance in Consequence of his proclamation when he landed at Elk, and as shall continue to merit it by their future Behaviour and excluded all other persons whatever from the Benefit thereof; this shews what the Consequences of a Conquest would be, more than Volumes could do on the Subject.

With the heartiest Wishes for your Health and Happiness I remain Sir yours very sincerely

E. Gerry

General Warren

One of the Continental Ships in the Delaware was brot against the City, and by some Means unknown to us at present, has fallen into the Hands of the Enemy, a 26 gun Ship, 10 gun Brig and 700 hogsheads Rum with about 200 of Sugar are taken by Captain Biddle in the "Randolph" at South Carolina.

Inclosed is a Copy of a Letter from General Washington containing an authentic account of the action of the 4th ⟨with names⟩. I must beg the Favour of your requesting the Honourable Assembly to send a Member to supply my place in Congress about the 1st of December, as my Health requires some Relaxation.

ALS, Russell W. Knight—Gerry collection, Massachusetts Historical Society.

1. A detailed account of the Battle of Brandywine, without mention of this specific incident, is in Douglas Southall Freeman, *George Washington: A Biography* (6 vols., New York, 1948–54), 4:485–92.

2. Colonel Brown's contribution was at the Battle of Bennington; the action of the nineteenth, at Stillwater, saw American forces under Morgan and Dearborn facing British elements commanded by Burgoyne.

3. For an account of the Battle of Germantown, see Freeman, *George Washington: A Biography*, 4:501–19.

4. General Francis Nash commanded a brigade of North Carolinians. The aides-de-camp were Majors Sherburne and White.

§

The Congress, once settled in York, gave the Articles of Confederation increasing attention. EG, in favor of the "each State shall have one vote" provision, helped to defeat three successive amendments meant to alter that ideal. On the morning of October 14, the Massachusetts delegation, unanimous in its opposition, was unsuccessful in its effort to block the idea that state payments to the central treasury be in relation to the value of improved lands. That noon EG put his "aye" vote on the side of the resolution "That no State shall be represented in Congress by less than two nor by more than seven members." The following afternoon the Massachusetts delegation, unanimously opposed to the establishment of western boundaries for those states with western land claims, voted with the majority on that issue.[1]

EG's activities in York also included service on committees and the writing of reports. On October 11, EG joined the three-man committee "to enquire of the commissary general of purchases, the measures adopted by him for obtaining the necessary supplies of provisions for the ensuing year."[2]

On October 15, EG and two others constituted a committee for recruiting the army. This committee's report, in EG's hand, gave rise to various resolutions, most of which dealt with deserters. In the course of debate concerning the rights of states to lay duties and imposts under the proposed Articles of Confederation, EG was constrained to write, "That the Revenue arising in each State from the Duties and Imposts laid therein on Exports, and Imports, shall be Considered as the Property of the said State; but the Laws of each State imposing such Duties or Imposts, shall pass the Approbation of Congress before they are carried into Execution by such State."[3]

On October 22, the committee which had conferred with the commissary general of purchases submitted, in EG's hand, a report which inspired a succession of resolutions and a new charge to the same committee. Now it was to "prepare a plan for establishing a board to superintend the departments of the commissaries and quarter master general."[4]

From Boston, JW, buttressing his previous request for authority for the Navy Board, wrote John Adams, "As the matter now stands we are little better than a Board of Agency or factorage and tho' we are ordered to do many expensive things are not supplyed with a shilling to do it with. This is as bad as makeing bricks without straw. We have wrote repeatedly to the Marine Committee and have tryed to borrow of the Loan Office. He dont like to supply without orders."[5]

For the irate man in Massachusetts one of the most fruitful days of October was the twenty-third, when a report of the Marine Committee of the Continental Congress inspired a number of resolutions and orders concerning the Navy Board for the Eastern Department. Then it was that the Navy Board was (*a*) empowered to suspend officers, (*b*) authorized to act when two of its three members were present, (*c*) authorized to increase the salary of the clerk it needed, and (*d*) ordered the release of $50,000 to the Board by the loan office of Massachusetts, and a like sum by the loan office of Rhode Island.[6]

1. *JCC*, 9:779–82, 801–4, 806–8.
2. *Ibid.*, 794.
3. *Ibid.*, 805, 813–16, 827n.

4. *Ibid.*, 829–31.
5. *Ibid.*, 761; Allen, *Naval History*, 221; and *W-A Ltrs.*, 1:371, 372–73.
6. *JCC*, 9:833, 836–37.

James Warren to Elbridge Gerry

.   .

Boston, October 23d, 1777

My dear Sir

I have only time this Morning to acknowledge the receipt of
your favour of the 6th Instant[1] Yesterday afternoon, Just as the
post arrived with a Letter from General Gates giveing an account
of the surrender of Burgoyn and his Army. We had Rumours of
this Event for some days, but not haveing them Confirmed began
to have some doubts of the Truth. When the Confirmation Came
it at once Excited an Extravagance of Joy which was manifested
by fireing of Cannon, Bonfires &c. This is indeed in many respects
a great affair, and must be humiliating to the ⟨Brit⟩ Pride of
Britain, and will give us great Reputation in Europe, but I can't
⟨but⟩ help feeling a Disappointment that Gates has suffered himself to be drawn into a Convention, so much less favourable than
it seems to me he might have had.[2] They are not to serve in
America dureing this Contest. They will releive Garrisons that
may come and serve here with as much advantage as these could
if put into winter quarters in Canada. I am sorry they are to be
quartered round us, and more so that the Officers are suffered to
be on their Parole, and mix with whom they please. Colonel
Campbell[3] and they will have now sweet Communion, but however we should make the best of it, and be Thankful. I presume
we have gained a great addition of Ordnance, Stores &c &c. and,
being releived from further Apprehensions in that quarter our
Troops may turn their arms on Hudson's River &c. I therefore
sincerely Congratulate you on this Occasion, and wish you may
soon be able to give me an account of the total defeat of Sir Wil-

liam.[4] I suppose you will be glad to hear how the Expedition against ⟨Newport⟩ Rhode Island goes on. I can tell you no more of it than if it lay where Charlestown South Carolina ⟨lays⟩ does. All Expectation from it is lost. It has not for some days been a subject of Conversation. I have Nothing further, but my regards to all Friends, and am Yours Sincerely[5]

J. W.

Elbridge Gerry Esqr.

ALS, Gerry II Papers, Massachusetts Historical Society.

1. This letter by EG has not been located.

2. Gates' demand for Burgoyne's unconditional surrender had been tempered upon hearing from Israel Putnam that Clinton's forces had penetrated the American defenses on the lower Hudson; see John Richard Alden, *The American Revolution 1775–1783* (New York, 1954), 147–48.

3. Lt. Col. Archibald Campbell, a member of parliament on duty with the 71st Regiment of Highlanders, had been captured when the brigantine "Annabella" unwittingly sailed into colonial hands in the wake of the British evacuation of Boston. General Washington's intervention ameliorated the treatment he was accorded in the common jail at Concord, to the disgust of patriots of Massachusetts. See Clark, *Washington's Navy*, 160–65; *Adams FC*, 2:161n; and *LCC*, 2:512.

4. Sir William Howe's "total defeat" never came about. During the winter of 1777–78, with Howe in Philadelphia and Washington at Valley Forge, it bore in upon the English general that his occupation of Philadelphia was not the success he had anticipated. He resigned his command in mid-1778.

5. Docketed "ansd Novr. 13."

§

"We are now upon Confederation," John Adams wrote JW on October 24, "and have nearly compleated it." EG appraised the situation quite well when he wrote, "I am in Hopes that You will receive the plan of Confederacy before the first of December."[1]

In addition to the Articles of Confederation, EG was occupied with committee assignments and the writing of reports. On October 24, in EG's hand, the committee concerned about the problems of the commissary general of purchases submitted a report which recommended the appointment of deputy commissary general of purchases for certain specified western regions. Repeatedly, on the roll-call votes of October 27 and 30 and November 7 and 12, he supported the majority position in reference to specific portions of the Articles of Confederation. Another report, penned by EG and submitted on November 3, inspired a congressional resolution on the subject of commissaries.[2]

A sequel to Lt. Col. James Wilkinson's tardy arrival in York with details of the patriot victory at Saratoga, a committee which included EG was appointed to determine the basis for "directing the future operations of General Gates." The Congress adopted the committee's recommendation that Gates make secure the patriot hold on the Hudson River. A week later, on November 13, EG joined a pair of colleagues on a new committee "appointed to enquire into the cause of the obstructions in the department of the post master general."[3]

Meanwhile, for a variety of reasons, the Congress was rapidly changing as many members exited from York. John Hancock, after more than two years in that chair, resigned the presidency of Congress, turning those reins over to Henry Laurens (1724–92) of South Carolina. Hancock's maneuvers in Boston had so antagonized the Massachusetts delegation in York that it unanimously opposed the idea of thanking him for his services as President of the Continental Congress. The Articles of Confederation required explanation and it would help for many of the delegates to talk with their constituents. Hancock departed; and John and Samuel Adams also quickly left York. The return of Hancock and the Adamses to Massachusetts presaged further factional fighting in that area. Meanwhile the Massachusetts delegation in York was reduced to two, James Lovell and EG.[4]

1. *JCC*, 9:837–900; *W-A Ltrs.*, 1:374; *Adams FC*, 2:365; and EG to [?], York, October 28, 1777, EG Collection of Elsie O. and Philip D. Sang, on deposit at Southern Illinois University Library, Carbondale.

2. *JCC*, 9:838–39, 843, 849, 850, 859n, 879, 896.

3. *Ibid.*, 859, 863, 864–65, 898.

4. *Ibid.*, 846, 852–54, 880; Burnett, *CC*, 251; and Allan Nevins, *The American States during and after the Revolution 1775–1789* (New York, 1927), 210–11.

Elbridge Gerry to James Warren

· ·

York in Pennsylvania, November 13, 1777

My dear Sir

I am favoured with yours of October 23d., and find that in the Enjoyment of the News of General Burgoyne's Surrender, you

somewhat regretted General Gates's "suffering himself to be
drawn into a Convention." I must confess that when the News
first reached this Place, I had similar Feelings, but was somewhat
reconciled upon hearing the particulars as delivered by his
Deputy Adjutant General to Congress. It seems that General
Clinton with his intended Reinforcement to Burgoyne, at the
Time of the Treaty, was within a Day's Sail of Albany, where
were the Magazines, Hospitals, and Labaratory of the northern
Army. This General Gates knew, and not being able to detach
Troops in Time to defend them hazarded the Loss of the Whole.
His Deputy Adjutant General further says, that he had but 3
Days Provisions at Saratoga, and had Albany been taken, must
have retreated without Delay or have starved his Army. But what
made the Matter still more critical, Sir Harry Clinton had con-
veyed Intelligence which the latter received the Day before the
Ratification of the Convention, informing him of Clinton's
Expectations of relieving him in a few Days, and thereupon
General Burgoyne made some cavils [?] and finally informed
Colonel Wilkinson (the Adjutant mentioned) that Hostilities
must again commence; but the latter informing as he left him
that General Gates could not be responsible for the Consequences,
as his Men considering their General deceived, were highly enraged and zealous for Action, was recalled by General Burgoyne
and desired to favour him with a little further Time to consider
of the Matter, which being granted soon ended in his agreeing to
the Convention. However was I to judge of the Matter under ⟨all⟩
Circumstances as they respect Gates alone, without recurring to
the primary Cause of our Successes, It appears to me that such a
powerful Army as he had were entitled to the Terms first demanded ⟨by General Gates⟩, "a Surrender of the other Army Prisoners
of War." But we have ever had the greatest Reason to acquiesce
in the Determinations of Providence relative to our publick as
well as private Concerns, and therefore I find myself very happy
on the Occasion.

We have this Evening finished the Confederacy,[1] and it will be
shortly sent to the several States for thier Consideration.

My Expectations from Rhode Island were never great for Reasons too obvious to mention; but I am concerned that the Honor of so many brave Men as composed the eastern Army, should suffer from ⟨the worst⟩ a Circumstance which they could not foresee or avoid. A thorough Enquiry must be made into this Matter, if We mean to correct such Misconduct, and prevent the like in future.

Our Friends the Mr. Adams left this [*place?*] two Days since, and inclosed are two Letters for Mr. J. Adams, which I must request you to deliver him. Agreable to his Desire, that I would open such Letters as should be directed to him here, I opened these, and finding the largest ⟨in what appears to me⟩ written by what appears to me a female Hand; if so, I presume it is from his Lady, and must ask her pardon for the Error into which her Friend betrayed me. The Absence of these Gentlemen occasions a Chasm in Congress, who employed the microscopic Eye of the One to penetrate the obscure Designs of intrigueing Adversaries and the deep Erudition of the other to raise Barriers against them. My Compliments to them and other Friends and beleive me to be Yours sincerely

E. Gerry

P.S. The Enemy appear to be making great preparations to attack Fort Mifflin; I hope the brave Fellows there will not fall a sacrifice to superior Numbers.[2] Quere, ought not their Attention to be diverted by occasional Visits from our Army?

ALS, Elbridge Gerry Collection of Justin G. Turner, Los Angeles.

1. See *JCC*, 9:900.
2. Fort Mifflin had repulsed the mid-October efforts of the British to open supply lines up the Delaware River to Philadelphia. Congress had rewarded the defending commanders. A month later EG's pessimism was warranted because Fort Mifflin was evacuated, under heavy bombardment, two days after he wrote this letter. See *JCC*, 9:841, 862; Allen, *Naval History*, 245; and *Adams FC*, 2:360n.

§

The delegates in York, the "valiant remnant" as Burnett terms them, were occupied with committee meetings and reports as well as the activities of the Board of War. On November 15 minor amendments, chiefly stylistic, enabled the delegates to fix the final form of the Articles of Confederation. In the course of this business, EG phrased the second half of the first paragraph of Article IV.[1]

A new committee of three, which included EG, undertook "to collect and digest the late useful discoveries for making molasses and spirits from the juice of corn stalks, and report a plan for communicating the said discoveries to the inhabitants of the several states." On Monday, November 17, the Massachusetts delegation increased to three, thanks to the arrival and seating of Francis Dana.[2]

Another communication from Commissary General of Purchases William Buchanan prompted the creation of a three-man committee on which EG served. The same committee was also instructed to confer with General Mifflin. Later that morning, the twenty-second, EG penned the resolution that allowed Deputy Paymaster General Jonathan Trumbull, Jr. $150 "for his past extraordinary services." On November 24, two more reports in EG's hand were laid before the Congress: the first treated the commissary problems raised by Buchanan; the second recommended the addition to the Board of War of "a person acquainted with the commissarial business."[3]

Meanwhile, during an interval between the submission of those two reports, EG was named to head a five-man committee which was "to devise ways and means for providing a sufficient supply of provisions for the army."[4] In this area of congressional business, EG's background and repeated committee assignments had converted the Massachusetts bachelor into a tower of strength.

1. *JCC*, 9:900–963; and Burnett, *CC*, 251.
2. *JCC*, 9:929, 934.
3. *Ibid.*, 948, 953, 962–63.
4. *Ibid.*, 962.

James Warren to Elbridge Gerry

· ·

Boston, November 24th, 1777

My dear Sir

I Received yours of the 29th October[1] and am well pleased with the Bravery of our Troops in the defence of red Bank. I hope they will Continue to repulse the Enemy till they give up the project of geting their Ships up. In short I hope to hear that Howe and his Army are reduced to at least the same situation that Burgoyne is in. Whether I Expect too much or not you can best tell, but my faith is great, and when our Northern Boys Join the Army, we here shall Expect great things ⟨Ex⟩. We are frequently flattered with great Expectations from the Accounts we have but it is Impossible to describe to you ⟨the⟩ how uncertain our Intelligence is. We used to hear as often, and with as much certainty of the operations of War in Flanders as now in Pensilvania.² We have had an account for a week as you will see in our papers of another attack on red Bank by Cornwallis,³ but cannot get the Certainty. I am glad to hear the Confederation is so near Compleat, and that you are going to have recourse to Taxation and Confiscation. The first is necessary the last is useful and shews a manly resolution. We have a large Tax this Year and to be paid in without delay,⁴ which with stoping the Circulation of all money but Continental, have already (tho the time for stoping Circulation is not by Law to Commence till the first of December) had great Effects. ⟨Merchan⟩ I see with pleasure the Merchants wanting Money, and I am told that all kind of Goods are falling ⟨some, and I hope to see more of it⟩.

Yesterday arrived here a french Merchantman from Bourdeaux with Goods, Linnen and woolen, and also one of our privateers from the same place in 9 weeks. I have tryed this morning to get you some Intelligence but can't. It is said this privateer had great Indulgence and assistance afforded him, but that there was an order for all American Vessels to depart by a certain time, but he Conceives it to be a peice of french finesse. In short the french politics appear to me mysterious, ⟨& stupid⟩. They had heard of the takeing of Ticonderoga but the People in general did not beleive it. The Court however might. These People say that it don't appear to them that the French wish for a war. They don't Conceive the Breach between England and America to be yet wide enough, and suppose we should again unite with Britain. However if we can do for ourselves so much the better and I hope with a Continuance of the Blessing of Heaven we shall. I Congratulate you on the Success in the North. I hope you will return me yours on an Equal success in the South. The ⟨Infamous⟩ Conduct of the Expedition against Rhode Island has tarnished our Glory ⟨so⟩ but that Expedition has Ended as I prophesied to you it would. We wanted nothing but a head, we had it not and ⟨di⟩ succeeded accordingly. I am obliged to write this morning in a great Hurry and can only add my regards to Friends and wishes for your Health and Happiness and am with great Sincerity Yours &c

J. W.

Elbridge Gerry Esqr.

ALS, Russell W. Knight—Gerry collection, Massachusetts Historical Society; and Austin, *EG*, 1:227–29.

1. This letter by EG has not been located.
2. Obviously the state of communications which had inspired inquiry by a committee of Congress was general and not solely related to the action that had removed the Congress from Philadelphia to York.
3. Red Bank, on the south bank of the Delaware River, lay several miles downstream from Philadelphia. There Fort Mercer was located and opposite it lay Fort Mifflin. The two positions commanded the shipping approach to Philadelphia and accordingly drew Howe's attention.
4. See Mass., *A&R*, 20:157, 175.

§

As November gave way to December a continuing flurry of committee activity and related issues, including the never-ending problems of the commissary department, occupied the men in York.[1] The unsatisfactory state of supplies prompted the naming, on November 25, of a five-man committee, of whom EG was one, "to enquire in what manner the department of the cloathier general has been executed, and report such regulations as they judge necessary to be adopted for the better execution of that office." The following day, attention fell upon a paragraph which EG had penned on the subject of the clothier general and his agents.[2]

On Thursday, November 27, EG urged Joseph Trumbull, with every logical and patriotic argument at his command, to accept appointment to the new Board of War. The following morning the Congress unanimously resolved "That a committee of three be appointed forthwith to repair to the army, and, in a private confidential consultation with General Washington, to consider of the best and most practicable means for carrying on a winter's campaign with vigour and success, an object which Congress have much at heart." EG was of the trio chosen for this mission.[3]

At the same session that the absent John Adams was elected commissioner to France to succeed Silas Deane and a series of inquiries were instituted regarding recent patriot withdrawals from Forts Mercer, Montgomery, Clinton, and Mifflin, the report of "the committee appointed to devise ways and means for providing a sufficient supply of provisions for the army," in EG's hand, inspired a number of resolutions. In that same busy session, EG voted in the negative, along with his Massachusetts colleagues, on the proposal to enter into a contract with one Alexander Gillon for supplies from Europe.[4]

The visit to General Washington's headquarters at Whitemarsh, due north of Philadelphia, required two weeks. From there, EG wrote, "Cloathing is much wanted. In some of the officers there seems to be an irresistible desire of going into winter quarters but others are averse to it as are Congress unanimously." Five days later, EG insisted, "The American army are in a better situation for an engagement in point of numbers than they have been this campaign."[5]

In the course of conferences with Washington and his general officers, the committee soon learned of an overriding reason against a winter campaign, namely the discontent which, while general throughout the army, was especially strong among the officers. Accordingly the three members of Congress, looking forward to a better disciplined army with higher morale, informed Washington that they would make recommendations to the Congress concerning officers' pay, widows' pensions, rank, and payment for back rations.[6]

1. *JCC*, 9:963–1023.
2. *Ibid.*, 966, 968–69.
3. *LCC*, 2:571–72; and *JCC*, 9:972.
4. *Ibid.*, 975, 976, 978–80.
5. EG to John Adams, Camp at Whitemarsh, December 3 and 8, 1777, EG Papers, Library of Congress.
6. *LCC*, 2:585.

Elbridge Gerry to James Warren

. .

Potsgrove,[1] December 12th, 1777

My dear Sir

I am favoured with yours of November 21st[2] on my Way from the Camp to Congress; and find that you have formed pleasing Expectations of Intelligence from this Quarter, which the Events that have hitherto taken Place will no Ways justifie. The brave officer Colonel Smith who defended Fort Mifflin informs me, that Commodore Hazlewood who commanded the Gallies and was honored with a Sword,[3] has since behaved like a Poltroon, and by not opposing his Gallies to the Indiaman that was warpt thro' a Channel, which being shoal was unguarded by the Chiveaux de Frize,[4] the Fort was attacked on every quarter, the Works beat down, Guns dismounted, and the Garrison after suffering greatly, were reduced to the Necessity of retiring. Had they been supported by the Army, who after several Days' Deliberation determined to send a Body of Men to province Island, to attack the Enemy in the Rear of their Batteries, It is generally supposed that the Garrison would have held out; but before our Troops arrived the Enemy accomplished their purpose. Red Bank or Fort Mercer, which commanded the other, was so slightly built as not to be sufficient to withstand a Cannonade of 24 Hours, and was afterwards evacuated by the advice of some General Officers sent to veiw it. Thus the Enemy have possessed themselves of a River, which might have been easily made impregnable, had this State considered it's Importance to themselves; and have been defended, had not Delays in the Councils of War prevented seasonable Releif.[5]

The Enemy soon after these Events, brot up their Shipping to the City, and are greatly benefited by the Assistance of the Seamen of 300 Transports and some Frigates now laying at the Wharves. I was at the Camp upon a Committee of Congress to confer with the General on the Expediency of a Winter Campaign, and to take such Measures thereon as should appear necessary. We were earnestly desirous of an attack on the City, that by one vigorous Exertion Mr. Howe might meet with the Fate of his brother officer General Burgoyne; and should not have hesitated to have called in Militia from Virginia to Massachusetts Bay for this Purpose; but previous to our Arrival on the 3d Instant the General had consulted his officers, and found them averse, with their present Force to an attack on the City or a Winter Campaign, and urgent to retire to Winter Quarters. However, we determined to consider what was eligible, and to have conferred with the Officers at a general Council, and endeavoured to have reconciled them to the Measures proposed, if different from their own Intentions. But General Howe rendered this unnecessary, by marching out with his whole Force in the Night of the 4th to attack General Washington. His Army consisted of about 12 or 13000, General Washington's about 20,000 Combitants, of which 4,000 only were Militia.

About 5 in the Morning of the 5th, they were within two Miles of the Right Wing of our Army and continued there untill the Evening of the 6th, when they decamped and marched to the left and in the Morning of the 7th attacking and driving in our Pickets, they made Dispositions for Battle within half a Mile of our Camp; but after remaining there untill the Evening of the 8th they marched back to the City. Several Skirmishes happened between the Enemy and Colonel Morgan's Corps[6] and the Militia, in which ⟨Colo Er⟩ General Erving ⟨of⟩ commanding the latter, from this State, was wounded and taken prisoner, Major Morris of Morgan's Corps was wounded and 40 or 50 killed and wounded on our Side. Sir James Murray Captain in the Enemy's Service was dangerously wounded, and a considerable Number of Waggons with wounded Soldiers have been sent into the City; some Inhabitants say 80, but I beleive the Account is rather exaggerated. They have lost by Captivity and Desertions ⟨about⟩ from 50 to 100 privates, ⟨&⟩ burnt several Houses and plundered without Discrimination. Yesterday Morning General Washington decamped with a Veiw of taking Post on the other Side [*of the*] Schulkyl, to cover the Country, and refresh his Men, untill by additional *Reinforcements* he might be able to approach the City; but arriving at Swedes Ford the Militia under Command of General Potter who had crossed it were attacked by the Enemy within a Mile or two of the Bridge. Whether they had Intelligence of the orders given by General Washington the Evening before, or intended to make an attempt on the Baggage Waggons, I know not, but am informed that they marched out in the Night with the ⟨Ma⟩ main Body of their Army. General Washington has not yet crossed, and should he persist in it, I have no Doubt that a general Engagement will ensue. I am sometimes induced to wish most earnestly that the two armies were ⟨under like Circumstances⟩ in the eastern States, that the Militia like a Cloud may rise and overwhelm the Enemy; but after many Instances of the most happy Events from what we supposed unfavourable Circumstances I cannot but apply to the present Contest the general principle of Mr. Pope, "Whatever is, is best."[7] Congress are exceedingly dissatisfied with the Loss of Forts Mifflin and Mercer and the Miscarriage of the Rhode Island Expedition and have ordered an Enquiry to be made into the Causes thereof.[8] This they have extended to Forts Mongommery[9] and Constitution, being determined in [*the*] future that no Fort, post or Ship of War, belonging to the United States, shall be lost by Misconduct or Cowardice, with⟨out⟩ Impunity to the ⟨Commanding⟩ delinquent officers.

The late Recommendations of Congress, relative to Taxation, Confiscation, and Regulation of Prices &c, if vigourously executed by the several States, will probably have the most happy Effects. The Measure last mentioned, is essential to the Support of the Credit of the Currency. When the necessaries of Life are exceedingly scarce, nothing will prevent Extortion, but the Interference of the Legislature; let the ⟨Medium consist of⟩ Currency be Specie, and the Quantity be much less than is requisite for a circulating Medium, ⟨&⟩ and Extortion will still be the Consequence, unless the Laws of the State prevent it. Had the Measure been general, when the New England States regulated

Prices, I have no Doubt that it would have been successful, at least, with concommitant Measures to support the Currency; but the Neglect of it in the southern States, was attended with the most enormous Exactions within their Jurisdictions, and the Report thereof reaching the eastern States made the Merchants and Traders very uneasy under their Restrictions and prompted them to send their Effects to other States for a better Market. If there are Doubts and Hesitations about the Matter, I am apprehensive that it will be defeated, and wish not to realize the Consequences; but if the several States, convinced of the Necessity, are determined to confine Avarice to its proper Bounds, I flatter myself they will succeed to their Wishes.

I have wrote to Mr. Otis on the Subject of Cloathing,[10] and desired him to communicate to you my Sentiments on the Matter. I am informed by General Washington that 3 or 4000 of as fine Troops ⟨As⟩ as any in the Service, are unfit for Duty from the Want of Cloathing, ⟨only⟩ and that sufficient Supply would enable them to take the Field immediately. The Articles therefore must be ⟨obtained⟩ taken wherever found, and at reasonable prices, since the Neglect hereof may ⟨involve⟩ weaken our Army and infer the most ruinous Consequences. I wish to have your Sentiments on the Expediency of preventing all persons whatever (excepting publick officers) from purchasing the produce or Manufactures of these States or any Commodities therein imported, ⟨without a License⟩ more than is necessary for the annual Consumption of themselves and Families, without Licence therefor, and giving Bonds not to exceed the retail prices stipulated by the States. Few Retailers are sufficient for each County, and an unbounded Licence to speculators has not a Tendency to increase Trade, but promotes Extortion. This should not be continued longer than the War, or than is necessary to execute the regulating Acts, and if any person wants to export (altho it answers few other purposes than to supply our Enemies) they may easily obtain a permit.

My Compliments to Mr. Adams', and all Friends, being Sir with much Esteem yours sincerely

E. Gerry

P.S. The politicks of France wear an extraordinary appearance, but General Howe must have received alarming Intelligence relative thereto, as he has ordered the Heights of Staten Island near the Narrows to be fortified, and the Inhabitants are obliged to work every third Day.

ALS, EG Collection of Elsie O. and Philip D. Sang, on deposit at Southern Illinois University Library, Carbondale; and excerpts, Austin, *EG*, 1:230–31.

1. In terms of nearness, route, etc., this appears to be Pottstown.
2. Apparently the reference is to JW's letter of November 24.
3. Both Lt. Col. Samuel Smith and Commodore John Hazlewood had received swords from the Congress on November 4.
4. The *chevaux-de-frise* were frames of heavy timbers sunk to the bottom of the river, from which other beams, sharpened and sheathed in iron, pointed down stream.
5. This instance of poor cooperation between militia and Continentals and between army and navy is detailed in Allen, *Naval History*, 241–46; see also John F. Reed, *Campaign to Valley Forge: July 1, 1777–December 19, 1777* (Philadelphia, 1963), 281ff.
6. Colonel Daniel Morgan (1736–1802).
7. In line 289, Epistle 1 of *Essay on Man*, Alexander Pope had written, "One truth is clear, Whatever is, is right."
8. See *JCC*, 9:975–76, 1018–20.
9. I.e., Montgomery.
10. Samuel Allyne Otis (1740–1814), MW's younger brother, had been recommended by JW; see *W-A Ltrs.*, 1:369; and Mass., *A&R*, 20:201–2.

James Warren to Elbridge Gerry

.   .

Boston, December 14th, 1777

My Dear Sir

It is now a long time since I have had the pleasure of a line from you. I suppose your Time is greatly taken up with the Multiplicity of Business, and perhaps the more so in the Absence of so many of your Colleagues.[1] In your last you Informed me that the Confederacy was Compleated. We are in daily Expectation of it, but it is not yet arrived. We propose to adjourn Tomorrow for 3 or 4 weeks, and then have a full Assembly prepared to set down and deliberately ⟨to⟩ Consider in every veiw that, and the report of our Committee on [*the*] Constitution which is at last made.[2] I could wish you could see it, and if in my power will Inclose a Copy before I seal this. We have news of no kind to give you. Burgoyne still remains at Cambridge. No Transports are yet arrived here. We are told that a Number of Transports are arrived at Newport, and that Application is made to Congress for the British Troops to Embark there. I can't suppose Congress will ever Grant a request so manifestly Impolitic, and so disagreable to the Sentiments of the people. You will be Informed before this reaches you that ⟨you⟩ the same delegates are again Chosen for this State.[3] I shall make no Observations on this Election least they should fall into the hands of the Philistines. However I presume you will be able to read them in my General Sentiments of Man and things which you know very well. We Continue to have some prizes sent in but not in such Numbers as usual. When am I to Expect to see you here? When your Colleagues will return to releive you I know not.

Our Expectation of great Event from the Southern Army have been so long in Execution that they are now dying a Natural Death. We hear Nothing, and begin to Expect Nothing. Even the rumours of victories and repulses of the Enemy, whether from their frequency or uncertainty, don't strike as they used to do. Must that small army hold Philadelphia and Employ us two Years instead of 6 weeks in destroying them?

No more Goods has arrived from Bilboa for the Continent tho the Committee of Commerce has given me reason to Expect it. I have not lately had a Line from there. The Inclosed I picked up for you. Please to give my Compliments to Mr. Lovel and Dana and believe me to be sincerely Your Friend &c.

J. Warren

E. Gerry Esqr.

If I should Inclose a Copy of the report on Constitution you will please not to give a Copy.

ALS, Elbridge Gerry Collection of Justin G. Turner, Los Angeles; and photographic copy, EG Papers, Library of Congress.

1. The absentees were John Adams, Samuel Adams, John Hancock, and Robert Treat Paine, the last-named of whom had never attended the Continental Congress during 1777.

2. Product of a twelve-man committee, among whom Robert Treat Paine, JW, James Prescott, and Thomas Cushing were prominent.

3. The seven-man delegation—John and Samuel Adams, Hancock, Paine, Dana, Lovell, and EG—had been elected on December 4; see *JCC*, 10:9–10, 26–27.

§

From Washington's headquarters, EG returned to York to lay a report before the Congress. For four reasons, it was thought advisable that the army retire to winter quarters. The next afternoon EG joined the committee concerned with matters raised by S. A. Otis, deputy clothier general for Massachusetts.

Pressures mounted in the Congress and a committee which had been established to act upon some of Washington's communications was discharged and the matters involved went to the Board of War which, for this purpose, was enlarged by three men, one of whom was EG. This new body was "fully empowered to take the necessary measures for supplying the army with provisions and other necessaries."[1]

EG's New Year's day report of the Committee on the Clothing Department to the Congress provoked no immediate action. Four days later the committee which had studied the propositions derived from the recent meeting with General Washington at Whitemarsh submitted, in the hand of EG, a report which received inconclusive consideration. On January 14, EG joined a three-man committee charged with the revision of the commissariat system.[2]

Weary, worn, longing to return to Massachusetts and overwhelmed by unfinished business, EG's spirit was not lifted by the January mail which included the fearful words of Henry Knox concerning military intrigue and the reiterated complaints of Joseph Trumbull.

A certain desperation beset the Massachusetts delegation. On January 13, James Lovell wrote, "Now only 3 are here, 3 are essential in Congress. This, at the worst season of the year, to 3 shabby constitutions is irksome; more especially as each is on 2 standing committees, and . . . are seldom forgot upon perplexing transient calls. Mr. Dana goes to Camp. Poor Geary will get a double portion of Treasury-toil by this."[3]

1. *JCC*, 9:1029–31, 1065.

2. *Ibid.*, 10:10–12, 18–22, 49, 51.

3. Austin, *EG*, 1:238–41; Burnett, *CC*, 279–85; Jos. Trumbull to EG, Windham, January 12, 1778, EG Collection of Elsie O. and Philip D. Sang, on deposit at Southern Illinois University Library, Carbondale; *JCC*, 10:26–27; and *LCC*, 3:31–33.

Elbridge Gerry to James Warren[1]

· ·

[*Philadelphia, January 14, 1778*]
Mr. Dana has been ordered by congress on a committee to camp.[2] He will probably be absent a month. I am alone of our delegation, and the state will lose its vote. It will be very injurious to the interests of the government to be in this situation, as will often be the case while the presence of three delegates is required to give a vote.[3] I am worn down with fatigue, and have been waiting with some impatience to return to Massachusetts; but I have wished to see certain measures accomplished before I left congress; when those were finished, others presented themselves equally important and I waited for them, and so on; but this mode of travelling will never get me home. I must therefore determine at all events to leave this place in the spring.[4]

Excerpt, Austin, *EG*, 1:174.

1. The second sentence of JW's letter of April 5, 1778 (*q.v.*) establishes the fact that he was the recipient of the letter from which Austin took this excerpt.
2. *JCC*, 10:40–41.
3. This regulation was established by Massachusetts; see *ibid.*, 27.
4. This springtime departure never materialized; EG remained active in the Congress throughout 1778.

James Warren to Elbridge Gerry

· ·

Boston, January 22d, 1778
My dear Sir
I Received with great pleasure your favour of the 12th December last, and freely own that I deserve the Censure of my Friend for not acknowledgeing it before. Between the Navy Office, and

the House (where I cannot prevail to be Excused from serving as Speaker) I am so perplexed with business as to find it difficult these short and Cold days to attend to any thing but the duties of my two Stations and Indeed I have consoled myself with an Expectation that you would the more readily forgive a Neglect of this kind while your friends the Mr. Adams[*es*] are here, and I suppose give you the best and earliest Accounts of whatever takes place. We have sent Mr. Cushing, Mr. Paine, and Colonel Porter[1] a Committee to New Haven. What will be the determination of that Convention I know not.[2] The Avarice and Extortion prevalent throughout all the States, and the Consequences of them are what I beleive neither you nor I had any Idea of when we Entered into this Contest. It must Mortify and provoke every Honest Man whose ⟨fortune⟩ virtue or good fortune has kept him free from these pollutions to see the best Cause and the fairest prospects Embarrassed and Clouded by such infamous practises. The folly of this ⟨People⟩ Conduct is equal to the wickedness of it, and Contempt keeps pace with Indignation. The most Guilty will acknowledge this, and such is the Situation of things that those who are willing to reform know not how to begin, and Indeed that is the grand question how ⟨these⟩ to find a remedy for the Evils. It is a question that has Employed and puzzled my Mind very much. A strong Enthusiastic Faith has supported me in many stages of this Contest. I firmly beleive we shall get through, and this faith operates like a Mathematical demonstration. I own I see no rational prospect but from the slow but I hope certain operation of Taxes and reduceing the quantity of Money. ⟨You⟩ I at first had no Opinion of regulateing Acts and Experience has abundantly Justified my Sentiments. You can hardly Conceive the Injury they did us. They depreciated the Currency by Introduceing Barter. They weakened our Goverment by attempting what appeared in its Nature Impracticable. They appeared as our *ne plus* and at once the Apprehensions and dread of a Controul subsided and gave a Loose to the most Unbounded Sallies of Avarice and Extortion. I have no doubt that Measures ought to be taken to supply any perticular Exigencies of the public, but to Extend it so far as the Cases you mention and ask my Sentiments about, appears to me a matter of great delicacy. It is true that our Trade supplys the Enemy in some measure but then it is as true that in this part of the Continent we can't subsist without it, and if we should add to the present Embarrassments I fear the Consequence. You can hardly Conceive the Expence of supporting Navigation, and the difficulty of getting Seamen. Nothing but the prospect of Considerable profitts can Induce any one to be Concerned. The matter is indeed so Extensive and Complicated in its nature that I find it a matter of no small difficulty to form an Opinion that I would venture to pronounce upon.

We have not yet gone upon the Consideration of the Articles of Confederation. They however, meet a general Approbation, and we only wait for the Instruction of the Members, and I have no doubt will be approved of in the Course of a few days. We have for some time past been Considering the report of the Committee on the Constitution, and here we have but a poor prospect. A great part of the Convention appear to have wild sentiments of Goverment, and such as are better Calculated to answer the present Licentious disposition than the happiness of posterity. We go on slowly and I could wish I could say surely.

We are doing every thing in our power to releive the distresses of the Army, and have it in Contemplation to send the Army a strong reinforcement of Militia to do the Business at once, (will it be done if we do?) and are takeing measures to fill our quota. I am not able to say we shall fall on any that will Effect it. I sometimes wish we had at first so regulated the Militia of the Continent as to afford a Constant supply to an army. The Advantage of discipline in a standing Army is a very pretty subject to Contemplate in Theory, ⟨but⟩ while Experience has taught us, that the Militia without it ⟨can't⟩ have done almost every thing. I own I felt a pleasure in seeing your Spirited resolutions with regard to those who have supplied the Cloathiers' Agents, tho' I don't find it true that any of them have witheld the Goods till paid for. Yet I think they deserve the severest Reprehension for demanding such an Extravagant price for what they came so easily by, and which the war afforded them an opportunity of possessing, and was to be Employed in the security of their newly acquired Immense fortunes. We have no foreign News. The politics of ⟨France⟩ the European powers especially France are to me extraordinary. It seems to me they will refine so Exquisitely as to loose advantages they will never again have.[3] The Ship "Boston" will Sail in the Course of 10 or 14 days. With her will go [. . .].[4] You will join in wishing her a good passage. This Ship has lain so long in port, and been so Expensive, that it is a Capital point with me to get her out of Sight. I shan't be easy till it is done. I am somewhat unhappy in my new Station. All Ideas of Oeconomy are lost in the Extravagance of the Times, and we are kept so short of money that not only the public service, but our own reputations must suffer. The people at large will Consider us as a set of Blunderers that do not Understand our Business. Time won't admit me to Enter into detail. I can only say I fear from these Circumstances your Expectations won't be answered. You will please to make my Compliments to Mr. Lovel and Dana. I shall write the former soon. When your Brothers will join you I can't say. The General[5] talks of ⟨it⟩ doing it soon. In the mean time he is a very active and popular Member in the House. I am with wishes for your prosperity Your sincere Friend &c.[6]

[*no signature*]

Honourable E. Gerry Esqr.

AL, Gerry-Townsend Papers, Manuscript Division, The New York Public Library.

    1. Elisha Porter, colonel of the Fourth Regiment of the militia of Hampshire County, represented Hadley in the Massachusetts House of Representatives at this time. Immediately prior to this appointment he was busy establishing the regulations to govern the embarkation of Burgoyne's troops. See Mass., *A&R*, 20:5, 54 and 234.
    2. One of three regional price-fixing conventions, the New Haven body, presided over by Thomas Cushing, met January 15–20 and established a scale of remuneration to be allowed by agents of the Commissary Department for supplies seized by the army. Cushing forwarded the proceedings of the convention to the Congress; see *ibid.*, 234; Nevins, *The American States*, 618; and *JCC*, 10:172.
    3. Unknown to JW, the diplomacy which produced two treaties with France on February 6, 1778 was much advanced at this time.
    4. JW's reluctance to trust the mails forbade his writing the name John Adams in this blank space. See *D&A–JA*, 4:6–7.

5. I.e. John Hancock.
6. This letter is docketed "ansd April 29th."

§

Robert Treat Paine, at the New Haven convention, wrote disheartingly to EG, "I don't know whether we should have agreed upon a regulation were it not that we considered the requisition of Congress as being peremptory."[1]

After letters from Dr. William Shippen, Jr., director general of the hospital, and Dr. William Brown were read before the Congress, a five-man committee, which included EG, conferred with the two doctors. On February 6 the committee's report inspired various resolutions aimed at better regulation of the hospitals. Meanwhile the Board of War's concern about contracting for brass cannon prompted the naming of a four-man committee headed by EG.[2]

Reporting the mounting business and the shortage of delegates at York, EG informed Samuel Adams, "few can stand it as well as our Friend Mr. Lovell; he writes Morning Noon and Night, sickens once a Fortnight, and devotes a Day to Sleep, after which, like the Sun from behind a Cloud, he makes his Appearance with his usual Splendor."[3]

As Congress faced past failures and eyed future prospects, a variety of new assignments fell to EG. In the latter half of February he served on four committees related to the British prisoners at Boston—on which subject he wrote a report—and correspondence between Generals Washington and Howe. Between mid-February and mid-March EG served on committees inspired by letters from Governors Caswell (North Carolina), Johnson (Maryland), and Livingston (New Jersey). Four other committees on which EG served prior to April 1 concerned certain papers before the Committee of Commerce, a letter from the Board of War, a written representation from the Council and Assembly of Pennsylvania and the consideration of Colonel Jeremiah Wadsworth for the post of commissary general of purchases.[4]

During the same period, EG was embarrassed on twelve occasions when Massachusetts' failure to maintain three delegates in York kept his vote from being counted. The last week of March he wrote Jeremiah Powell, President of the Massachusetts Council, "The State of Massachusetts since January last, has been unrepresented in Congress. It may hereafter be found necessary to have at least four Members present."

Unburdening another complaint Lovell wrote on March 10, "It was mortifying to hear the Delegates from several states this day assert that they were instructed respecting the Confederation, while the two Cyphers from Massachusetts could produce nothing." Coincidence found Massachusetts, where JW was still Speaker, ratifying the Confederation that same day, news of which would not reach York for ten days.[5]

In Massachusetts, meanwhile, JW was occupied with political and naval matters. To her absent husband, MW expressed her fears and hopes. She feared conspiracies at Cambridge, traitors at Boston, the Conway cabal against Washington, and the taxes and regulations emanating from the General Court. Hopefully she countered, "I strike out three fourths of this gloomy tale as only the vague rumours of the day and reverse the scene and view America finally triumphant though innumerable difficulties may rise up in her way."[6]

1. R. T. Paine to EG, New Haven, January 26, 1778, EG Collection of Elsie O. and Philip D. Sang, on deposit at Southern Illinois University Library, Carbondale.

2. *JCC*, 10:93–94, 118, 128–31.

3. *LCC*, 3:76.

4. *JCC*, 10:172–73, 179, 185, 196, 207, 222, 238, 239, 293.

5. *Ibid.*, 104–267 *passim*; *LCC*, 3:121, 137n, 139, 145–46; Mass., *A&R*, 20:324–25; and Massachusetts House of Representatives, Resolve, March 11, 1778, EG Papers, Library of Congress.

6. *W-A Ltrs.*, 2:7.

James Warren to Elbridge Gerry

.   .

Boston, April 5th, 1778

My Dear Sir

It is now a long time since I had the pleasure of a Line from you. The Last I received ⟨fr⟩ was of the 14th January, since which many Interesting Events may have taken place, and put it in your power to have gratified me with an account of. I have indeed not wrote to you so often of late, as my Esteem, and regard for your Friendship required but this has not been voluntary. I have been

Extreemly pressed with Business, and somewhat out of Health which may Extenuate ⟨if⟩ my fault if not Excuse me.

You have been doubtless advised of the departure of our Good Friend Mr. Adams.[1] I hope before this he is safe arrived in France,[2] ready to do that Service to his Country which his great Abilities and Zeal Eminently qualify him for.

We have no kind of foreign Intelligence worthy your Notice. No Arrivals from France for a long time, and one only from Spain which brings Nothing Material. This Vessel is from Bilboa, and brings sixty-seven Bales of Goods: four of them Containing Ravens Duck, two Stocking and the remainder Blankets. I am not able to ascertain the Quantities. Your Letters were sent forward while I was out of Town, and doubtless Contain the Invoice which Messrs. Gardoqui and Sons write me were Shipped by order of the Honorable Arthur Lee Esqr. on account of Congress. I have received them, and paid the freight and primage and other Incidental Charges, and they not appearing to be the Goods you mentioned in your last I shall deliver them according to former orders and render the Accounts as usual to the Commercial Committee. The Goods you mention may be soon Expected in some Vessels to ⟨be⟩ sail in a few days after this. When they arrive[*I*] shall take perticular Care of them, as I shall at all times take peculiar pleasure in rendering you Service with regard to our domestic affairs. We have still our difficulties and Embarrassments oweing principally to the State our Currency is reduced to by the rapacity and folly of the People which continue as Boundless as ever. The Calling in [*of*] our Money and the Operation of Taxes, has ⟨mo⟩ brought money into great demand and Excluded every Idea of Barter, and had in some degree its Effect on the mercantile part. But the Extortion of the Farmers has enriched them to that degree, that they don't seem to feel the Lessening [*of*] the quantity of money and the Taxes on them. The Nature of the Commodities they are possessed of, the little demand there is for foreign Imports among them give them every advantage, which they Improve without remorse as Interest suggests, and a foolish as well as wicked and growing animosity

between Town and Country inclines them to, so that I think the
Sea ports must be Beggared. You would be amazed at the
Extravagant price of the necessaries of Life here. The great
Question is for a Remedy. The Convention of New Haven reported a Regulateing Bill. This report was debated a long while in
Committee of both Houses together in our Room, and at last
accepted by a small Majority. When the report came to us, it was
again debated and Carried by a still smaller Majority. A Committee was appointed to bring in a Bill when the Small Pox
obliged us to put an End to the Session. The Court was prorouged
for a fortnight, and are now met at Roxbury.[3] I have not yet been
with them. What further will be done I can't say. The People
abroad as well as the Court are so divided, I have no prospect of
any advantage from that quarter. We have Taxed for the whole
Sum required by Congress, [*and*] are takeing measures to suppy
our Quota of the Army in full, and to satisfy our Soldiery. These
are the most material things. We have Compleated and sent
abroad the Constitution.[4] I will Endeavour to Inclose you one.
I Expected before this Mr. Hancock would have been on his way
to Congress he is still here and attending very diligently the
General Court. I don't hear Mr. Pain talk of going. Whether
Doctor Holten the new Delegate, Intends to accept I don't know.
He is now under Inoculation. Mr. Adams proposes to go the first
of May.[5] I shall be glad to see you when you can leave Congress.
My Compliments wait on your Brothers, Mr. Lovel and Mr.
Dana. I shall write to Mr. Lovel if I can by this opportunity.
Captain Burke[6] will hand you this. You know him better than I
do. I Suppose he will make Application for an Appointment. I
know Nothing against him he is said to be a Seaman and a man
of Spirit and Capacity. I am with Great Esteem Your Friend and
Servant

J. Warren

Upon recollecting that the Constitution is published in the Papers
I shan't Inclose a Pamphlet

    Honourable Elbridge Gerry Esqr.[7]

ALS, EG Collection of Elsie O. and Philip D. Sang, on deposit at Southern Illinois University Library, Carbondale; and photographic copy, EG Papers, Library of Congress.

1. The frigate "Boston," which Adams had boarded on February 13, had sailed from Nantasket Roads the next day; see *D&A–JA*, 4:6–7.

2. John Adams had first set foot ashore on French soil on April 1, at Bordeaux; see *ibid.*, 2:293.

3. Mass., *A&R*, 20:340. Roxbury lay inland, several miles southwest of Boston.

4. Finished and approved in committee on February 28, 1778, this constitution, submitted to the vote of the freemen, was rejected by a four-and-one-half to one margin; see Nevins, *The American States*, 176–77, and Oscar and Mary Handlin (eds.), *The Popular Sources of Political Authority: Documents on the Massachusetts Constitution of 1780* (Cambridge, 1966), 188, 202–323.

5. In 1778, Samuel Adams first attended Congress on May 21, John Hancock on June 19, and Robert Treat Paine never did attend. Dr. Samuel Holten (1738–1816), elected on February 10 to replace John Adams, first attended Congress on June 20; see *LCC*, 3:liv.

6. Probably Captain William Burke, late commander of the armed schooner "Warren," who soon memorialized Congress; see *JCC*, 10:412.

7. Docketed, "ansd 29th." That letter has not been located.

§

In early spring, EG was ill, but the nature and duration of his distress are unknown. On April 18, Lovell wrote Samuel Adams of "Brother G being very ill." Some indication of the seriousness of that ailment is apparent in EG's inability to join Lovell and Dana in Congress the previous day when, once more, a twosome from Massachusetts was synonymous with no vote for the Bay State. Although other votes of record, beginning with April 21, found EG once more regularly on hand, his failure to be named to any new committee in the seven weeks between the end of March and mid-May, and his writing but a single report, suggest that he was barely able to keep going for many weeks. Nonetheless, in the continuing hassle between Drs. Rush and Shippen, the latter sought EG's friendly interposition.[1]

In Massachusetts, meanwhile, JW was less informed than usual about Congress for several reasons: friend John Adams was abroad, friend Samuel Adams was close at hand, and additionally, JW was himself very busy and less pessimistic at a time when EG, ill and overworked, was widening the intervals between his letters.

1. *LCC*, 3:173; *JCC*, 10:293–94 and 11:415–507 *passim*; and W. Shippen to EG, Hospital Headquarters Manheim, April 12, 1778, EG Collection of Elsie O. and Philip D. Sang, on deposit at Southern Illinois University Library, Carbondale.

James Warren to Elbridge Gerry

.   .

Boston, May 7th, 1778

My Dear Sir

I have often had it in Contemplation to write to you of late. I have much to say, and some things that you may wish to hear. But my Friend I am so Crowded and Embarrassed at this Time that I can add but little more ⟨but⟩ than my Congratulations on the present Situation of public Affairs. I think we have now the Game in our own hands. Let us play it well. Congress have both Abilities, and Zeal to do it and I have faith to beleive it will be well done. I now Inclose you a Letter from Messrs. Gardoqui and Sons which I presume will give you an account of Goods Shipped by him on several Vessels to my Care which shall be taken good care of, and disposed off agreable to former Orders. The Goods received per Schooner "Nancey" are already disposed of. I have since received Bills of Loading Shipped on Board four other Vessels, two of which are arrived. I fear the others may be taken but they may yet be well. This will bring me in advance for a Considerable Sum. You will oblige me, by Engageing Money to be sent me. I could wish to have my old account settled, and a proper reward allowed me for the Care and trouble of receiving, Transporting, storeing and delivering the Goods for which I left a Blank. I have furnished all the Vouchers, and nothing that I know of is wanted. Our Good Friend Mr. Adams I hope will soon be with you. I hope you will be ready to meet the British Commissioners if they are stupid enough to send them out which I doubt stupid as they are. You must suffer me to Conclude haveing wrote this in a Crowd, and am with every Wish for your Happiness Your Sincere Friend

J. Warren

You can hardly Conceive how the Naval Service, and the Clothiers departments suffer for want of a Supply of Money. I wish your attention to this matter.

E: Gerry Esqr.[1]

ALS, George M. Conarroe Collection, American Authors Series, The Historical Society of Pennsylvania.

1. The docketing reads, "ansd May 25," but EG's reply (*q.v.*) is dated May 26.

§

From Boston, on May 8, JW could write, "We are now enjoying the first fruits of our New Connections, several of the fleet from France are arrived, with large quantities of Cloathing, etc." The next day JW attended an elegant entertainment which the Massachusetts Council had arranged for the visiting Frenchmen. The strengthening Franco-American ties also bred a counter-sentiment in Boston. "The Tories," JW declared, "are very Industrious in Instilling prejudices into the minds of the people against our Connections with France. The danger of Popery is held up to them, and every other Art that Wickedness and weakness can devise is practised, but I hope with little Effect." The towns of Massachusetts generally were either electing or preparing to elect their representatives to the next General Court.[1]

1. *W-A Ltrs.*, 2:8–10.

James Warren to Elbridge Gerry

·   ·

Boston, May 13th, 1778

My dear Sir

I very seldom of late have the pleasure of your favours. I very frequently Conjecture the reasons, but never among my Conjectures Contemplate the want of Friendship. I beleive your hands are full, and if mine were not so, you would oftner be troubled with my letters. We seem here to be in the full Bloom of Prosperity, Intelligence of the most Interesting and agreable kind daily arriveing which you have at Congress in perfection, Commerce Extending her Wings, Ships daily arriveing and this

Harbour makeing a brilliant appearance which we like the Patriarchs of old who were permitted to look at the promised Land, are suffered to behold without Enjoying the fruits being Employed in serving the public for no other reward than the satisfaction of a Good Conscience. Breakfast, Dinner, and Supper we see however with more pleasure perhaps than some others ⟨the⟩ who have goods to dispose of the great Abundance of Continental Supplies. Immense quantities of Cloathing &c have lately arrived here from France and Spain. I hope never again to be Tormented with agoniseing Compaints of the Nakedness of our Soldiery. They come here Nevertheless some of them in a Strange way without any direction to any perticular person or Body of Men. Would it not be best to appoint some Person for that purpose? This Navy Board tho' out of their Line, have been obliged to receive the Cargo of the Ship "Queen of France," and must receive the Articles on Board the Dean frigate which has Just arrived. I wish you would Speak to the Commercial Committee on this Subject and desire their orders for the disposition &c. I flatter myself with the pleasing Expectation of seeing you before a great while and am Sincerely Your Friend and Humble Servant

J. Warren

Honourable Elbridge Gerry Esqr.[1]

ALS, Gerry II Papers, Massachusetts Historical Society.

   1. Although docketed "ansd Novr.6," EG's reply to this letter bears the date November 8.

§

A welcome addition to the company in York, Samuel Adams took his seat in Congress on May 21, and at once supported the monetary needs of the Navy Board in Boston, adding, in his first letter to JW from York, "I will not fail to do what in me lies to forward that Service, as our Navy has always lain near my Heart." Beginning with May 27, the date of his appointment to the Marine Committee, Adams had ample opportunity to demonstrate his concern about the navy.[1]

In Massachusetts, meanwhile, election day was approaching for JW but he was principally occupied with the affairs of the Navy Board, some of which pertained to the Plymouth-owned sloop "America," about which he could add, "Some of my Friends are Concerned in that Vessel."[2]

Yet another Massachusetts man was concerned with shipping that season for EG, on the first special committee to which he had been named since late March, was considering a problem posed for the Board of War by Gardoqui and Sons of Bilbao.[3]

1. *W-A Ltrs.*, 2:12; and *JCC*, 11:517,537.
2. *W-A Ltrs.*, 2:11.
3. *JCC*, 11:507.

Elbridge Gerry to James Warren

. .

York Town, May 26th, 1778

My dear Sir

In answer to your agreable Favour of the 7th Instant I have communicated to the commercial Committee the Invoices of the four Cargoes shipped by the House of Messrs. Gardoquis. Since they dispatched the "Nancy," And suppose you will receive their Directions for disposing of the Captains Dupee's and Knight's Cargoes, or so much of them as belongs to the States, I am apprehensive that the other two have miscarried, and should this be the Case, their amount of the Invoices will be but a moderate premium for all the Goods shipped by that House on account of the Continent. I have communicated to the commercial Committee your Demand for Money, and desired them to determine the allowance which You are to receive for your Services and to settle your former accounts.[1] 50,000 Dollars are ordered to be sent You for the use of the naval Department and 650,000 to Messrs. Otis and Andrews to discharge the Debts which they have contracted for the publick.[2] Our Friend Mr. Adams arrived here last Week and is pleased with the appearances of Things; Our Army is well officered, Generals Washington, Lee and Steuben with the main army, Gates, McDougal and Starks at the north River, Arnold and Lincoln in Reserve;[3] no Complaints from the Want of provision, Cloathing, Medicine, Arms, Ammunition or Pay, ⟨and⟩ the officers Minds made easy with Respect to the latter, and a Style of Discipline introduced by Baron Steuben who is appointed Inspector General with the Rank of Major General, to which the Army have hitherto been Strangers.[4] ⟨for⟩ This great officer has his Inspectors and Sub Inspectors with every Corps of the Army; and an Emulation prevails amongst the officers ⟨for⟩ to merit his Approbation by qualifying themselves for the places which they hold. In speaking of the officers pay I meant to allude to the half pay Establishment lately made for the officers who shall continue in the Services to the End of the War, which provides that they shall be entitled to their half pay for the Space of Seven Years, and has had a happy Effect by making the Commissions of the officers valuable, introducing Subordination ⟨of War⟩, preventing Resignations which of late have been so frequent as to prove very alarming, and promising the most happy Consequences. The Measure was exceedingly disagreable to Congress, as You will suppose when I inform You that it was debated near three Weeks, before it was adopted,[5] and the Necessity of it on account of the State of the Currency was so apparent at length as to make the House unanimous in the Measure. ⟨the⟩ The Soldiers are also provided for, each being entitled to 80 Dollars who shall continue in the Service to the End of the War. If Congress should be then of opinion that there is Danger of introducing ⟨the f⟩ or fixing a plan of burthening the publick with pensionors and placemen, they may redeem the half-pay and put an End to the precedent; for I presume few officers would refuse an offer to discount the Interest if they could be furnished at any Time with the remaining Sum arising on the half pay Establishment. ⟨T⟩ Two Things remain to be accomplished, filling the Batalions, and fixing the

Value of the Currency, the first is the Business of the several States the last of Congress who are determined forthwith to attend to it. To accomplish this and Confederate are the only Considerations that detain me here ⟨at⟩ so late in the Spring and induce me to consent to ride Home in the warm Month of June. I most heartily congratulate You on the late Events in Europe; what a marvellous Change in the System of the political World; the Goverment of England, advocates for Despotism, and endeavouring to enslave their ⟨most⟩ once most loyal ⟨Subjects⟩ Subjects of ⟨the⟩ their King; the Government of France advocates for Liberty, ⟨and⟩ espousing the Cause of Lutherans and Calvanists, and risking a War to establish their Independance; the King of England branded by every Whig in the Nation as a Tyrant; the King of France by every Whig in America, applauded as the great protector of the Rights of Mankind, the King of Britain establishing Popery,[6] the King of France endeavouring to free his people from ⟨the⟩ this Ecclesiastical Tyranny, Britain at War, and France in Alliance with America. The Express is waiting which deprives me of the pleasure of touching on other Matters; I can only add my Compliments to your agreable Lady and Family, and remain with much Esteem your Friend and humble Servant

E. Gerry

ALS, EG Collection of Elsie O. and Philip D. Sang, on deposit at Southern Illinois University Library, Carbondale.

1. A warrant was issued on August 4, 1778 in the amount of 1759 15/90 dollars "in favour of the Committee of Commerce, to enable them to pay James Warren, Esq. of Boston, his account of freight and charges on sundry merchandise belonging to the United States." See *JCC*, 11:746.

2. The former sum was ordered on May 23, the latter on May 25; see *ibid.*, 529, 531.

3. Baron Frederick William Steuben (1730–94), Alexander McDougall (1732–86), John Stark (1728–1822), and Benedict Arnold (1740–1801). For brief modern military appraisals of Washington, Lee, Gates, Arnold, and Lincoln, see George Athan Billias (ed.), *George Washington's Generals* (New York, 1964).

4. Baron Steuben's appointment dated from May 5. Alden insists that Steuben's services "have commonly been overpraised" (*The American Revolution*, 202n). If so, EG contributed his small bit.

5. Adoption occurred on May 15; see *JCC*, 11:502–3.

6. Possibly a reference to the Quebec Act of 1774, which had protected Roman Catholicism in Canada.

§

When John Hancock and Samuel Holten arrived the third week in June, the Massachusetts delegation in Congress swelled from four to six. EG labored with the problems of the Commerce Committee but he experienced no additional committee assignments in this period. When the conduct of late Quarter Master General Mifflin invited court martial proceedings, EG was the only member of the Massachusetts delegation who defended Mifflin.[1]

For JW, a political defeat made this a peculiarly trying time. On May 31, he wrote, "The Papers will Inform you that I am no longer a Member of the General Court. My Town left me out, and the House did not take Notice enough of me to Elect me a Member of the Board." Accounting for the defeat, which he ascribed to the influence of Hancock's faction, he wrote at length to John Adams, "If you Enquire how all this came to pass I must tell you it is oweing to various Causes. The people feel themselves uneasy and don't know the reason, they have therefore shifted their Members more generally than ever. I scorned to make or suffer any Influence in my favour. The Tories and the Influence from Boston, and some other places had their full play, which are the reasons I am not in the House. The greater part of the C[ourt] from Envy, and other reasons never loved me and the Complextion of the House, Consisting of Members (the most Influential of them) whose politicks are very different from mine, and who are of the moderate Class which you know I never belonged to, may account for my not being Elected. But above all the partiality of my Friends which has rendered me Obnoxious to a Certain great Man, and his numerous party by holding me up to view in Competition with him, the Policy therefore has been to get me out of sight and prevent my being an Obstacle to his Glory and Ambition."[2]

Chagrined at the outcome of the election, MW raged against the ingratitude and baseness of her husband's constituents. From York, Sam Adams commiserated with JW, saying, "Believe me, you cannot long be unnoticed by your Country." When the new Court moved from Boston to Watertown in the face of the well-nigh annual threat of smallpox, JW, proud, crushed and embarrassed, remained in the former place, devoting his energies to the business of the Navy Board. As he did so, he recommended a greater delegation of authority to the Board by the Marine Committee.³

1. *JCC*, 11:591, 621, 629.
2. *W-A Ltrs.*, 2:13, 20.
3. *Ibid.*, 17, 23, 26.

James Warren to Elbridge Gerry

. .

Boston, July 7, 1778

My Dear Sir

I have not wrote to you for sometime, not because I feel any Abatement of Friendship or respect, but because I Expected to have seen you here before now¹ and *viva voce* to have told you more than I could in many Letters. Mr. Taylor arrived here this Morning and Informs me he left you well, and thought you would Tarry a little longer. I hope you will get away before you are sick. I am now too much in haste to recollect or write many things I have thought of. I must refer you to our Friend Mr. Adams for some of them.² Capt. Manley will deliver you this. He had been much disappointed. He had reason to Expect the new frigate at Salisbury. The Marine Committee have appointed a French Gentleman to Command her.³ I fear this will occasion Confusion, it certainly must Increase our Business to man her. A Stranger is always under disadvantage where popularity and the People's Confidence are necessary, and it is perhaps not more so in any Instance than in Maning your Ships. Besides is it right to put younger Officers over the Heads of older ones whose Characters are good?⁴ But I can't Enlarge.

We have no kind of News but what comes from the Southward. Our Coast is pretty clear of Men-of-War, and several prizes have lately arrived. I wish you every happiness, and am Sincerely Your Friend &c

J. Warren

The Court Martial has honourably acquitted Manley and sentenced McNeil to be dismissed and rendered Incapable of serving in the Navy again.[5] They exercised great patience. I believe their decision was grounded on Justice and Impartiality, and marked with Tenderness and delicacy. You may rely on that whatever you may hear.

Elbridge Gerry Esqr.[6]

ALS, EG Collection of Elsie O. and Philip D. Sang, on deposit at Southern Illinois University Library, Carbondale; and photographic copy, EG Papers, Library of Congress.

1. EG's plans, which never materialized, called for his departure for Massachusetts as soon as Hancock arrived to augment the delegation to Congress; see *W-A Ltrs.*, 2:13.

2. JW had written to Samuel Adams on May 31 and June 26 and 28; see *ibid.*, 13–14, 24–29.

3. The frigate was the "Alliance," and her commander was Pierre Landais; see *JCC*, 11:555, 625.

4. Samuel Adams, anticipating this problem, appealed to JW for his assistance; later JW informed Adams of specific American captains who, neglected, were resentful; see *W-A Ltrs.*, 2:22–23, 30–31.

5. Captain John Manley was tried in June for the loss of his ship, the frigate "Hancock"; and Captain Hector McNeill was tried for not properly supporting the "Hancock"; see Allen, *Naval History*, 1:313.

6. Docketed "ansd Novr 8."

§

On July 9, EG was among the representatives of nine states who signed the Articles of Confederation. Above and beyond his ranging duties on the Commerce Committee, EG drew a number of special committee assignments in this period. The dual appointment of John Holker as agent to the royal marine of France in the ports of the United States and as consul at Philadelphia posed precedent-making problems. EG was one of five to whom the issues involving Holker were referred on July 23. A week later, EG was named to the committee concerned with the Board of Treasury's recommendation of a new board.[1]

In Massachusetts, meanwhile, JW occupied himself with the business of the Navy Board. At the end of July, Samuel Adams reported favorable action on JW's requests for additional funds for the Board, adding, "The Marine Committee have agreed that the Navy Board shall appoint Commanders for Vessels of War under Twenty Guns." When Captains Manley and McNeill appeared in Philadelphia, hoping to reestablish their tarnished reputations and win assignments, Samuel Adams and other members of the Marine Committee were inundated by letters from interested parties. "To yours," Samuel Adams wrote JW, "I shall pay a particular Regard, because I am well satisfied you never suffer Prejudices to divert your Attention from the great Object—the publick Good."[2]

1. *LCC*, 3:323n, and *JCC*, 11:713, 731.
2. *LCC*, 3:339–40, 352.

James Warren to Elbridge Gerry

· ·

Boston, August 4th, 1778

My dear Sir

As the principal Operations of War are again in our quarter, you may now Expect some Intelligence from your Friends here, and while you are Engaged in Treaty with an Embassador of a Grat Monarch and acting the part of a Sovereign of a great State, Condescend to read with some pleasure a Line from a Person as obscure as I am. You have every Capital Intelligence so direct from the persons Intrusted with the Execution of the principal parts of the great Drama that it will be to Little purpose for me to tell you of the arrival of the French Squadron before Rhode Island &c. I shall therefore Content myself with Congratulateing you on this Event which seems better Calculated to do Execution than laying before New York, and to Inform you that their arrival has diffused a General Joy here. There seems to be a Spirit prevailing to afford every aid to the Expedition against Rhode Island. The Council of this State have ordered

out the Men General Sullivan has requested, and I am told they
turn out with alacrity in general. Besides several Companies of
Volunteirs are offering themselves ⟨so⟩ one of which of 84 very
respectable men from Salem are now in this Town on their
way to Providence, so that I think we have at present every
reason to Expect Success, unless an English Fleet of superiour
Force should arrive and spoil the Sport. The Troops from this
State are to be Commanded by two Brigadeirs. No Major General is ordered to that command. I am told General Hancock
talks of going, and says he is *determined* but if his Health
would not permit his Tarrying at Philadelphia, at such a Time
as this, perhaps it may be a good reason for altering his mind
with regard to this matter—more especially as he will not
Command there any more than he did preside with you.[1] We
have no foreign Intelligence, no late arrivals from Europe nor
any prizes in. I presume the "Warren" has before this Joined the
French Squadron. The Brigantine "Resistance" will sail in a day
or two, and the "Raleigh" perhaps in 10 or 14 days. To Effect
even this we have been forced to make great Exertions. I find I
must soon leave this Business, and then when you return Home
if you will take the pains to make a Visit to Plymouth, you shall
be received with great Cordiality by a Simple and I assure you
a very honest Farmer, who never in all his Employments got a
Single Shilling from the public dishonestly. The Business of this
Board is Extensive, Complicated, and as we are supplied Embarrassing and besides is too Expensive for me. My Single Board,
Horsekeeping, and Barber has Cost me a dollar a day more than
my pay since I have been in the office. What then is to become of
our Families? It has always been my Fortune to break the Ice
for other people. I flatter myself we have done a good deal and
got things in a tolerable way. I suppose others will succeed us
with good Salaries, and find a beaten Track to walk in. Whoever
serves you in such an office should be paid for it. It is Mortifying
to serve always for Nothing a Silly and ungrateful Generation of
people wallowing with unmeaning dissipation in ill gotten
abundance, and with all the fopperies and fooleries of high head

dresses and large Cocked hatts &c. while their own Families are to be reduced by the Terms of their Service to Poverty. I will not detain you any longer, at this Time but only to assure you that I am with great Sincerity Your Friend &c

J. Warren

I have not paid my Compliments to Mr. Hudson who is here with Genl. Hancock. He lodges at his House. I should have seen him if he had lodged any where else, but for many reasons I did not Incline to go there. None of my Friends mention this Gentleman to me. No doubt they have a reason for it. I forgot to mention to you an Extraordinary Step of the Board of War, in Impowering our Council to appoint some Body to receive, take Care off, and forward the Cloathing while Otis and Andrews were on the Spot, and Capably doing it much better than any Body here and who by their Exertions have certainly deserved the public thanks rather than the [. . .] of any public Board. The Council have appointed Mr. Samuel ⟨Thatcher⟩ Fletcher, a Contrast Indeed but he is related to great Men. If you don't know him you may apply to Mr. Adams for his Character, History and Connections, from all which you will be able to form a Judgment of the situation of your Goods Imported here [. . .] a very great value, and perhaps won't won[der] if I tell you this ⟨in⟩ in every part is a matter of much Speculation.

ALS, Russell W. Knight—Gerry collection, Massachusetts Historical Society.

1. A later assessment of this politician in uniform refers to him as "King Hancock, that insufferable piece of bravery." See Moore, *The Diary of the Revolution*, 619.

§

Late in August, EG became a member of the committee to which General Robert Howe's letter of June 23 was referred. The last week of August EG joined Robert Morris and three others on the committee "appointed to consider of the state of the money and finances of the United States, and report thereon from time to time." To EG and two others, on September 15, were referred those parts of a report concerning the treasury that related "to a confederal fund, and to the mode of is-

suing and accounting for loan office certificates." Successive letters from
Major General William Heath posed problems for committees on which
EG served as chairman. A petition from Paymaster Hezekiah Stoakes
of Virginia, and letters from Deputy Commissary General of Purchases
for the Eastern District, Peter Colt, and from General Washington also
represented committee labor that involved EG. Similarly EG served on
committees concerned with the amended report of the committee on
finance and the British manifesto and proclamation which aimed at
promoting sedition.[1]

His health restored, EG apparently forgot his announced intention of
returning to Massachusetts in 1778. The monotony of the congressional
labor was occasionally relieved, however, by evening walks with Samuel
Holten, visits with members of other delegations, dinner at the home of
Robert Morris, and other such social pleasantries.[2]

Informed of the simple forms attending the reception of the French
minister, JW told Samuel Adams, "I think Congress have pitched on a
person to settle Ceremonials who will not be in favour of what I hate,
pompous parade, etc."[3]

As months passed, and he remained separated from his family, JW
hinted his resignation from the Navy Board. Alerted to JW's thinking,
Samuel Adams countered, "I intreat you not to resign your Seat at the
Navy Board." While Adams' letter was still en route to Boston, JW sub-
mitted his threatened resignation, explaining his action to Samuel
Adams. Congress, however, did not accept his proferred resignation, and
action by the Marine Committee removed JW's urge to press the matter.
The first week of November Samuel Adams informed JW that additional
funds were being forwarded to the Navy Board at Boston and that
"Congress has increased your Salaries to three thousand Dollars per
Annum."[4]

To prod EG, whose letter-writing was stymied by work, ill health, and
the prospect of seeing his friends in Massachusetts, JW had requested
Samuel Adams, "desire Mr. Gerry to let me know under his own hand
why he has done writing to me."[5]

---

1. *JCC*, 11:816, 843 and 12:915, 936, 949, 970, 983, 988, 1007–8, 1013.
2. *LCC*, 3:374, 380, 407, 481.
3. *W-A Ltrs.*, 2:41.
4. *Ibid.*, 52, 59, 60–63; and *LCC*, 3:477.
5. *W-A Ltrs.*, 2:50.

James Warren to Elbridge Gerry

. .

Boston, November 1, 1778[1]

My Dear Sir,

I have looked for you a long time, and tho' I shall be glad to see you when you come, I am not sorry that you are still at Congress. Every Step taken by that Body that I see is marked with dignity, and every Measure with true policy, and I presume without flattery you have your Share in them. But why do you not write to me as usual? I have not had a single line for many weeks. Are you too much Engaged in matters of more Importance or would you willingly get rid of the Correspondence? My Friendship remains the same, my Curiosity as great as ever. I want to know what you are about, what new alliances are forming, how the Confederation stands, what is doing to save your Currency from absolute Insignificancy and what other great things you have in Contemplation, for next to Heaven, I look to the Wisdom and virtue of Congress, and indeed to them only to save a wicked and foolish People degenerating fast into every Species of Luxury, Extravagance and folly unfeeling to the distresses of the public, and the Misery of Individuals, and loosing fast even the semblance of virtue and public Spirit. How the present Manners of the Southern States are I can't say, but if you don't return home prepared for Unbounded Licentiousness in dress, Equipage and Liveing you may in some respects make as small a figure as I do, besides you may be surprised at the present System of politics here. Inattention has supplanted that vigour that has Conducted us thus far in this great Contest, and the Moderation preached up by Tories in the days of Hutchinson and Bernard[2] has succeeded that true Policy, and determined resolution necessary to support such a Cause as ours is. The last Session however of the General Assembly produced one Act marked with the Spirit of our Times, but that was rather a Compromise for the failing of a Confiscation Bill than the result of the old Spirit. No Motion was made that I know of during that Session for a Constitution of Government. The Bill for Confiscation passed the House but in such a way that I think the Council was right in rejecting it, and I supposed the most Cunning and perhaps some of the most Influential ⟨ones⟩ Members Calculated it on purpose. The Currency here is depreciated beyond all description. At the same time the Spirit of Avarice keeps full pace with it, thus while Avarice and Extravagance are Contrasted in the same Breasts, while dissipation, Moderation, Carelessness, and self Interest are prevailing over public and private virtue what are we to Expect if the Enemy leave us, the most favourable supposition is that the Voayge is not half through. However I don't despond we have Hitherto been saved by Miracles, and I beleive shall be still.

I wish I could tell you some News, but we have none. The French Squadron are ready for the Sea and I think would have sailed this day had the wind been fair. Their destination is a subject of Conjecture only here. You may know it better than any of us. This Movement affords an ample subject for discussion among the Politicians on Change. Time must determine by their going to France, the West Indies, Hallifax, or Newport which Judge Best. We have but few prizes in lately a Number of British Cruisers have been on our Coasts, and taken many Vessels.

Captain Johnson a Captain in our Navy will hand you this. I wish some provision could be made for the good officers out of actual Service, and proper Encouragement given to all to rise ⟨ag⟩ agreable to their Merits. You will please to make my regards to Mr. Adams and Mr. Lovel, and any other of your Friends and accept a large Share Your self from Your Assured Friend and Humble Servant

J. Warren

I have made my resignation to Congress of the place I hold at the Navy Board, and Expect soon to be at Liberty to retire, and in Solitude admire the Wisdom or despise the folly of those that Steer the great Machine, both in the upper and lower departments.

Honourable E. Gerry Esqr.

ALS, Miscellaneous Manuscripts, Gen. James Warren, The New-York Historical Society.

1. Courtesy of The New-York Historical Society, New York City.
2. Sir Francis Bernard (1712–79) served as Governor of Massachusetts between 1760 and 1769.

Elbridge Gerry to James Warren

. .

Philadelphia, November 8th, 1778

My dear Sir

I am a little apprehensive that some of my Friends will consider Silence to their Letters, which an indifferent State of Health and much Fatigue has for some Time rendered inevitable, as an abatement of Friendship, but conscious of the sincerest Esteem for my Friend General Warren and having long experienced his Candour, I flatter myself he will consider such omissions, as they really are, the Effects of Necessity. I shall trouble you with little in Answer to your several Favours of the 13th May, 7th July, 4th August, and 3d September last,[1] as their early Dates renders it unnecessary. The Marine Committee, I presume, have taken the proper Steps to do Justice to Captain Manly;[2] the bravery of this Officer seems not to be questioned, but many appear to Want Confidence in his Abilities and Experience, and on that Ground oppose his being high in office: I presume not to judge of their Motives and Designs on this Occasion, or without further Information, of his Character as an officer. I am much concerned to find, that you intend to quit the Business of the Navy Board, as it will be soon an important and respectable Department. Under the present State of affairs it is impossible to do Justice to the Commissioners, but Congress have increased their Salary to 3000 Dollars per Year.[3] Perhaps you consider the Levity of the

Times as an Argument for quitting the Service, if so, I will readily acknowledge that the Vices of some and Follies of others are very displeasing; but in a Revolution like the present, neccessarily producing an entire Change of the Governments and Constitutions of thirteen States, the Suspension of Law and Justice, the Want of necessary Arrangements for preventing Frauds, and the most favorable oppertunities for Speculators and Engrossers, it must reasonably be expected that the Morals of the people will be greatly injured, and for a while, present a gloomy prospect. But I trust, there is yet Wisdom and Virtue enough in America to recover her Citizens from their Errors, and lead a brave and and deserving People into paths conducive to their Happiness. True it is, the Work is arduous, and it is equally true, that it is necessary; for should We exceed in Power and Wealth every Empire on Earth, and neglect the Morals of the people, is it not evident, that our Independance, instead of Freedom would produce a Slavery, far exceeding that of every other Nation. If the best and ablest Friends of America, who under providence have opposed the corrupt Arts, not less than the powerful Arms of Great Britain, will unite in checking the Career of Vanity, Vice, and Folly, the Leaders of this feeble Train will vanish at the Appearance of Opposition, and leave the Way clear to the promotion of the opposite Virtues; but if on the other Hand, those on whom we have principally relied, should suffer themselves to be disgusted at the natural appearance of *Bubbles* on the mighty Ocean of our affairs, and withdraw from the Service, I fear that our Liberties, like such shortlived *phaenomenons* will burst, and leave not behind, a Trace of their former existence. I know that you have had much Fatigue and Tryal, and met with many Things that are very disagreable. I assure you that We have had a full Share of these in Congress; I most ardently wish to return to my native Country, and cooperate with my Friends in their salutary Measures. Pray confer with our Friend Mr. Dana⁴ on these affairs, as I am persuaded he can inform you of many ⟨T⟩ Things which will assist you in pursuing the necessary Measures.

Adeiu my Dear Sir after receiving my warmest Wishes for the

Health and Happiness of your Lady, self, and Family and beleive
me to be your sincere Friend and humble Servant

E. Gerry

General Warren

ALS, Mercy Warren Papers, Massachusetts Historical Society; *LCC,* 3:482–84; and
excerpt, *W-A Ltrs.,* 2:64–65.

1. JW's letters of August 4 and September 3, 1778 have not been located.
2. The Marine Committee's handling of Captain Manley's case—as well as Samuel
Adams' part therein—consumed much time and provoked considerable ill will; see
JCC, 11:724, 749; *LCC,* 3:270n, 352, 397, 409, 419; and *W-A Ltrs.,* 2:31, 42, 43, 47.
3. This salary had been established October 31; see *JCC,* 12:1085.
4. Shortly after obtaining a leave of absence, on August 7, Francis Dana had
returned to Massachusetts.

§

On December 19, as the dwindling Continental Army faced another
winter of hardship, some of which was born of financial distress, EG
joined a committee which was instructed "to confer with the Commander in Chief and the principal officers of the staff, on ways and means
for retrenching the expences of the army."[1]

As 1778 gave way to 1779 the Massachusetts delegation in Philadelphia counted Samuel Adams, James Lovell, Samuel Holten, and
EG. In addition to that quartet, Massachusetts had named Hancock,
Dana and Timothy Edwards to its seven-man delegation for 1779.[2] None
of that trio, however, ever attended Congress that year but successive
replacements for Edwards did result in George Partridge's (1740–1828)
participation, beginning in late summer, by which time Adams had
departed the Congress. The primary burden of providing Massachusetts
with continuous representation in Congress consequently fell upon
Lovell, Holten, and EG, the last of whom would be spending his second
full year there without return to Massachusetts.[3]

EG's committee work in 1779, in addition to the continuing heavy
duty that was his in reference to the Commerce Committee, was in three
areas: foreign affairs and domestic matters related to both the military
and finance. On January 20, EG was named, as the Massachusetts
representative, to the thirteen-man committee "to take into consideration
the foreign affairs of these United States, and also the conduct of the late
and present commissioners of these states in Europe." In mid-March

Henry Laurens moved that a replacement be named for EG because the latter's "necessary attention to the affairs of the treasury would not admit of his attending the Committee on Foreign Affairs" but EG fended off this effort to remove him from that body.[4]

In Massachusetts, meanwhile, JW had withdrawn his resignation from the Navy Board and his continued identification with it filled his days with labor and lament. Quickly, as the Navy Board served the needs of both the French and American squadrons, JW repeated his plea for more funds. In the Christmas season of 1778 he spent a brief period with MW and their children in Plymouth. Ordinarily his life in Boston was a lonely one, brightened by MW's occasional visits. With three of their children old enough to be away from home, it was not very difficult for her to make arrangements for the other two when she planned such trips to Boston. The "Assemblies, Gameing, and the fashionable Amusements" of wartime Boston impressed JW as the height of folly and wickedness. Lifting his eyes above his Navy Board papers to survey the swinging of the political pendulum on the local scene, JW was pained to note the continuing popularity of Hancock and his faction.[5]

In mid-February, 1779, amid small receipt from Congress and large demands by ships, JW told Samuel Adams—and indirectly the Marine Committee, "you must haul up your Ships or supply us Immediately with a much larger Sum." On occasion, as when Richard Henry Lee wrote, "If all men like General Warren possessed wisdom, integrity, and discernment," his gloom surely disappeared for a time. JW mingled caution with determination as, when thinking of peace negotiations, he said, "The doctrine that almost any peace is preferable to a Continuance of the war is a dangerous one, because it pleases the Feelings and Taste of the Many who have abandoned every valuable Consideration to a rage for Ease, Luxurious Living and Expensive diversions."[6]

1. *JCC*, 12:1235.

2. Mass., *A&R*, 20:535–36. Timothy Edwards, of Stockbridge, served on the Massachusetts Council in the period 1777–79.

3. *JCC*, 13:17; and *LCC*, 4:liii–liv.

4. *JCC*, 13:93, 322.

5. *W-A Ltrs.*, 2:77–78, 81–82, 87.

6. *Ibid.*, 88, 94, 97.

James Warren to Elbridge Gerry

.   .

Boston, March 18th, 1779[1]

My dear Sir

Are you so Engaged with the Great Matters of the public as to be Unable to write to an old Friend, or have you other reasons for neglecting it? I can only suppose the first, because my own Mind suggests to me no reasons that could originate on my part. I know you are much Engaged, and have many difficulties to struggle with, but it is a great while since I have had a single Line from you. You may write to others whose Correspondence may afford you more pleasure, but I am sure no one will receive your Letters with more pleasure. I wish it was in my power to give you any Interesting Intelligence but we have Nothing here but what you must have in greater perfection at Philadelphia.

The Internal Circumstances of this State are in some respects similar to those of others. We suffer in Common with them all the disadvantages of the depreciation of our Currency, and in addition to that we have a real Scarcity of provisions, Bread especially of which in some places there is actually a famine.[2] However People submit to it with more patience than could be Expected. Few are shaken in the great Principle by their wants and difficulties, Joined with the Insidious Arts of the Tories, which are very Industriously Employed on this occasion. What is the Policy of suffering them among us?

Have you as we hear great and Important Secrets? When are we to know them? Will they stop the depreciation of our Currency and make it better? I fear more from that than any thing else. You can hardly Conceive what State things are in here. On that account meat 61 [. . .], meal 23 dollars bushel, flour 40 dollars [. . .]. Labour and every thing in the same proportion. I am sick paying Bills that would surprise you and yet I dare say you think we spend more Money on the Navy than you should

Expect. I must Conclude, and am with Great Esteem Your Friend and Humble Servant[3]

J. Warren

Honourable Elbridge Gerry Esqr.

ALS, Miscellaneous Manuscripts, Gen. James Warren, The New-York Historical Society.

1. Courtesy of The New-York Historical Society, New York City.
2. When Massachusetts, in need of bread, applied to Congress for relief, the delegation from that state sped congressional consideration of the matter; see *JCC*, 13:257; and *LCC*, 4:128, 156–57, 179–80.
3. Docketed "ansd Jun 14th 1779." That letter by EG has not been located.

§

EG's attention to foreign affairs was intense in late summer and autumn when a variety of special assignments related him to trifling and significant issues: congratulating the French minister on the king's birthday, preparing instructions and a commission for the American designated to negotiate a treaty of alliance and friendship and commerce with Spain, preparing instructions for the person empowered to negotiate a loan with Holland, and establishing a table of salaries for ministers plenipotentiary and their secretaries.[1]

In regard to military matters, EG served during the summer as chairman on committees that recommended decisive efforts by the states to fill their respective battalions and considered the question of further allowances for army officers. In fiscal affairs, EG drew many special committee assignments related to the financing of the war and the creation of a better system of handling fiscal matters. He was chairman of a committee "to confer with a committee of the general assembly of Pennsylvania, on the subject of the emissions of continental money ordered to be taken out of circulation."[2] His motion inspired a committee, on which he served, "to devise and report without delay further ways and means of supplying the treasury, and prepare an address to the several states." EG also was Massachusetts' representative on the thirteen-man committee "to consider and report the sums to be paid into the continental treasury by the respective states." Numerous nominations by EG to fill offices of the treasury led to another committee on which he served, that "to report a plan for an executive board to superintend officers of these United States."[3]

On the floor of Congress, EG insisted upon the American right in the North Atlantic fisheries; and there he agitated, unsuccessfully, for an address to the Irish people which might provoke their revolt against the British. On these and other issues, EG expressed himself; on scores of occasions he cast votes which, in the aggregate, aimed at a free America.[4]

JW, who, under certain conditions "had rather the War should Continue the remaining part of my Life," was deeply religious. On Sunday, June 6, for example, he wrote Mercy from Boston, "I have read one Excellent Sermon this day and heard two others." That same season the smell of politics was heavy in JW's nostrils. When his name was suggested as a congressional replacement for Timothy Edwards, he squashed the move. Explaining the matter to John Adams, he wrote, "Your Friend and Servant who is now a Member of the House might have been chose but prevented it, and promoted another."[5] Obviously the man who felt ill at ease because of the distance between Boston and Plymouth was not about to exchange Boston for Philadelphia. Reelection to the Massachusetts General Court for the 1779–80 term permitted him to live and operate at the level he preferred, the state level.

In June the representative from Plymouth successfully petitioned in behalf of the citizens of that community for the right to take herring in a certain brook running through the town of Sandwich. Loyal to the Navy Board, JW retained his post, did his work, and voiced his complaints. "I am still drudging at the Navy Board for a morsel of Bread," he wrote John Adams, "while others, and among them fellows who would have cleaned my shoes five years ago, have amassed fortunes, and are riding in chariots." For JW, life in Boston was "a world turned topsy turvy, beyond the description of Hogarths humorous pencil or Churchils Satyr."[6]

1. *JCC*, 13:488 and 14:988 and 15:1083–85, 1118, 1186.
2. *Ibid.*, 13:262 and 14:740, 952, 978–79.
3. *Ibid.*, 15:1019–20, 1148–49, 1241–42. The report of the committee of July 23, for which EG was chairman, is in the EG Collection of Elsie O. and Philip D. Sang, on deposit at Southern Illinois University Library, Carbondale.
4. *JCC*, 14:749, 967; and *LCC*, 4:275, 366.
5. *W-A Ltrs.*, 2:97, 101, 102, 106.
6. Mass., *A&R*, 21:45; and *W-A Ltrs.*, 2:105.

James Warren to Elbridge Gerry

. .

Boston, November 9th, 1779

My Dear Sir,

I have now given you a long respite from the Trouble of my Letters,[1] partly because I had nothing very Important to write, and partly out of Compassion to you, as I hear from all Quarters that you are so deeply engaged in Business, as to have no Time to Spare upon small Matters. However I find by your Letter to Mr. Adams that you have not forgot there is such a Man as I am and that he may be Confided in.[2]

We have no foreign News to be depended on. A new Constitution of Goverment now forming by the Convention at Cambridge, a Plan of which as reported by the Committee you have from our Friend Adams by this Post.[3] The Meeting of the General Court this day, but principally the Confusions occasioned by the depreciation and the regulations and other Plans to obviate or remove them Engross the attention and Conversation. The People seem Convinced of the Necessity of a new Form of Goverment, and I think are well disposed to receive one, but the Business goes on slowly, and the Convention talk of adjourning. I fear the Consequences if they do. Mr. Adams and Mr. Dana will sail in 3 or 4 days.[4] I wish them safe in France. Two Ships one of 50, and the other of 44 [*guns?*] have been Cruising sometime here for them. A Storm must first Clear our Coast and then they may go safe. We have four Continental Ships ready for the Sea, ordered to Lay for Count D'Estaing's or General Washington's orders. I wish they were gone. It is a public Misfortune to have them detained long after they are ready. We could if we had powers direct them to profitable Cruises, but we are only Servants, and allowed to use but little discretion.

I am Sir with Great Esteem Your assured Friend and Humble Servant

J. Warren

My regards to Mr. Lovel shall write him by next Post, not haveing Time at present.

Honourable E. Gerry Esqr.[5]

ALS, EG Collection of Elsie O. and Philip D. Sang, on deposit at Southern Illinois University Library, Carbondale; and photographic copy, EG Papers, Library of Congress.

1. On March 30, 1779, JW wrote EG a letter which has not been located. JW's handling of the cargoes consigned by Gardoqui and Sons on the schooners "Scorpion" and "Hawke" prompted a motion by EG which referred JW's services to the Commercial Committee for reimbursement; see motion, [n.d.], EG Collection of Elsie O. and Philip D. Sang, on deposit at Southern Illinois University Library, Carbondale.

2. John Adams had returned in August from his first trip to Europe; see *D&A–JA*, 2:400n; and *LCC*, 4:458, wherein EG's words, "I wish that our Friend General Warren may peruse this Letter," served to inspire JW's comment.

3. The first two sessions of the Convention called to frame a new constitution for Massachusetts met in Cambridge between September 1 and November 11, with John Adams a major participant in its labors. In its third session the convention completed the constitution of 1780. See Nevins, *The American States*, 179–80; and *D&A–JA*, 2:401n.

4. On September 27, John Adams had been named minister plenipotentiary to negotiate a treaty of peace and commerce with Great Britain; two days later Francis Dana was designated his secretary. Adams and his party boarded the French frigate "Le Sensible" at Boston on November 13. See *JCC*, 15:1113, 1128; and *D&A–JA*, 2:191.

5. Docketed "ansd Novr. 23d." That letter by EG has not been located.

§

In addition to the mountain of work he shared with others on the Commercial Committee, EG drew in November and December a variety of special committee duties related to domestic affairs, financial and military.[1]

On November 15, EG joined the three-man committee "to report a proper allowance for the officers of the Treasury, Board of War, Marine and Commercial Committees, and Secretary of Congress from the last adjustment of their accounts." A bigger responsibility, couched in fewer words, fell to EG as chairman of the committee appointed "to devise ways and means for supplying the public treasury." More directly related to the military were EG's role in writing the report inspired by the letter of November 18 from General Washington, his consideration of Major General Greene's letter of December 12, and his conferences with the Board of War on the subject of plans for procuring supplies for the army.[2]

On the floor of Congress, EG demonstrated, often unsuccessfully, the high regard in which he held certain individuals. When nominations for three commissioners on the Board of Admiralty were in order, EG nominated JW, but the proud son of Plymouth did not win that post.[3]

EG was also capable of casting an eye toward the indefinite future. Under circumstances that remain unclear, he put himself on record as one concerned about the ultimate history of the Revolution. John Adams recalled EG's unsuccessful labor when he wrote, many years later, "Had your Motion in Congress been adopted, and a Man of Sense and Letters appointed in each State to collect Memorials of the Rise Progress and Termination of the Revolution: We should now Possess a Monument of more estimable Value than all the Histories and Orations that have been written."[4]

JW, at end of year, wallowed in disappointment born of his failure to be named to the Board of Admiralty. James Lovell informed him that his case had been damaged by anonymous letters which spoke of handsome commissions garnered by the Navy Board member. Terming the charges "groundless and ridiculous," JW declared that the Navy Board of which he was a member could bear the severest scrutiny. Once more the militant man from Plymouth declared his willingness to resign his post.[5]

On December 22, the General Court instructed EG to urge in Philadelphia "the expediency of limiting the prices of articles of produce and merchandize."[6]

The new year demanded EG's continuing attention to domestic financial and military affairs. A number of resolutions, on January 10, relative to a systematic reduction of the army encouraged EG to recommend that the matter be referred to a committee, which body, in turn, he thought should repair to Washington's headquarters for consultation. The idea of the committee was approved, and EG became its chairman; but Congress disapproved the idea of its going to headquarters. Less than ten days later, however, a related matter did produce a committee which was expected to go to Washington's camp. This three-man committee, with EG its chairman, was instructed, "in conjunction with the Commander in Chief to arrange and regulate the Departments of the Quarter Master, Hospital, Commissary General of Military stores and Issuing Commissary."[7]

Besides taking a hard look at the military establishment, EG, in January, 1780, served on a committee charged with "apportioning to the

States their quotas of the bills of credit emitted by Congress." Similarly, when estimates of quotas of supplies were referred to a thirteen-man committee, EG served as the representative of Massachusetts.[8]

1. *JCC*, 15:1252–1427 and 16:1–89.

2. *Ibid.*, 15:1261, 1285–86, 1312, 1324, 1358–59, 1389, 1421.

3. *Ibid.*, 1263, 1271, 1318, 1333; and Charles P. Whittemore, *A General of the Revolution: John Sullivan of New Hampshire* (New York, 1961), 150–51.

4. *W-A Ltrs.*, 2:380; and *LCC*, 4:527–28.

5. *W-A Ltrs.*, 2:121–22.

6. Mass., *A&R*, 21:307–8.

7. *JCC*, 16:36–38, 73.

8. *Ibid.*, 41, 68.

Elbridge Gerry to James Warren

.   .

Philadelphia, January 25, 1780

My dear Sir

It is a long Time since we have heard from our Friends eastward, and We impute it to the Severity of the Winter, but yesterday I received by the Post your agreable Favour of the 27th December,[1] the Desire of which was increased by the Detention.

I should have been glad to have seen your Remarks on the anonymous Letter, but Mr. Lovell informs me he has not yet received them.[2]

The Policy of America will succeed or fail in my Opinion, in proportion to her Exertions for establishing a Navy. I well remember that you was the first to promote it, and altho it was disapproved by some in Point of Time, the Benefit derived from the Measure has clearly manifested the Wisdom of it. The State of our Finances will check it's present Growth, but I doubt not that it will soon flourish, and that Time will suggest Improvements in the Arrangements and Regulations of the Boards that are appointed to cherish and conduct it. I am very sensible that the

Officers of these Departments have been poorly rewarded, and was lately of a Committee who reported that their present Salaries should have a Retrospect to November 1778, but the Subject is not yet considered by Congress.[3] I think however that you have their fullest Confidence.

Congress have not yet determined whether to remove eastward or southward; both are talked of, but your Remarks respecting the Navy, are conclusive in my Mind, in Favour of the former.

The great objects of Attention in Congress are Oeconomy and Resources. Necessity dictates their Measures, and I hope will produce salutary Effects. The Departments of the Muster and Barrack Masters are abolished and the Business of the former annexed to the office of Inspectors.[4] Generals Schuyler and Mifflin and Colonel Pickering are appointed a Committee[5] with full Powers to inform themselves by Inspection or otherwise of the State of the Staff Departments, to call on any of the officers thereof for Information, to discharge all persons therein that are supernumerary or delinquent, to break up unnecessary issuing Posts and establish others where requisite, to stop all Issues of Rations not indispensibly necessary for the Service, and in Conjunction with General Washington to reduce the Number of Horses and Waggons in the Service and Expence of Transportation, and to adopt a general Reformation of the Departments. The States are to be also called on for their respective quotas of Supplies[6] and authorized to stop all purchases by continental officers, when ⟨said⟩ Measures are adopted for complying with the Requisitions of Congress; and to induce the States to purchase cheap, they are to be credited equal prices for Articles of the same Kind and quality, and in proportion for other Articles.

I inclose you the Newspapers containing three sensible Letters by a Gentleman in Maryland on "Appreciation,"[7] and can give you nothing new, excepting certain Information from the Court of France that by their Interposition the British Court have failed in their Applications for Recruits ⟨from⟩ to the several Powers of Germany.

The Massachusetts Delegates are sitting in Congress by Virtue only of a Certificate of their Appointment from the Deputy Secretary. They have never aspired to be *commissioned*,[8] but wish not to loose their Rank as warrant officers.

I observe your Apprehensions relative to a new Quarter Master General but have no Reason to suppose them well grounded, altho the Matter has been suggested in Congress.

I remain Sir with every Sentiment of respect your Friend and humble Servant

                                                            E. Gerry

General Warren

ALS, Mercy Warren Papers, Massachusetts Historical Society; *W-A Ltrs.*, 2:123–25; and *LCC*, 5:14–16.

    1. This letter has not been located.

    2. EG wrote this letter of January 25 just hours before James Lovell received the undated letter in which JW unburdened himself regarding this matter; see *W-A Ltrs.*, 2:121–22; and *LCC*, 5:19.

    3. *JCC*, 15:1261.

    4. These actions of January 12 and 20 are detailed in *ibid.*, 16:47, 76.

    5. Of this trio, Philip Schuyler (1733–1804), a New York delegate then absent from Congress, refused to serve; Quartermaster General Thomas Mifflin had been nominated by EG; and Timothy Pickering (1745–1829) was destined to become Quartermaster General in August (*ibid.*, 77, 79 and 17:698).

    6. *Ibid.*, 16:68.

    7. Presumably from the pen of a man named Usher; see *LCC*, 5:14.

    8. The certificate was dated November 18, 1779, while the commission and instructions bore the date December 2, 1779. The latter document, read into the journal of the Continental Congress on February 7, 1780, must have suffered delay in Massachusetts; see *JCC*, 16:2, 130.

§

During the wintry weeks of early 1780, the purchasing power of American money and the resources and prospects of the military establishment under Washington merited and received attention from Congress, EG participating in both areas of concern. When the Chevalier La Luzerne, who had replaced Gérard as the French diplomatic representative in Philadelphia the previous autumn, admonished Congress to plan and push with vigor the campaign which would result in British acknowledgment of American independence, he posed questions which prompted the naming of a committee. EG was one of seven charged with receiving La Luzerne's communications and reporting them to Congress. EG's letter of January 12 to Washington, wherein he attacked the complacency exhibited by some regarding the manpower needs of the army, suggested that he was vitally concerned about the issue raised by the French diplomat.[1]

In like fashion EG's identification with fiscal matters, persistent because of his duties on the Commerce Committee, deepened in response to a motion of February 14. It was then moved that "it be recommended to the legislatures of the several States to revise their laws making the continental bills of credit a tender in payment of debts and contracts, and frame them so as to prevent injustice to creditors or debtors." The committee to which the matter was referred counted EG one of its three members.[2]

On February 17–18, a piece of routine business provoked the procedural snarl—and as EG saw it, violation of privilege and principle, which abruptly terminated EG's attendance at Congress. The report of the committee for estimating supplies was under discussion when EG moved modification of the prices set for both flour and beef and requested that the yeas and nays be required. Enraged when it was determined that he was out of order with that request, he immediately absented himself from Congress. Writing to Samuel Huntington, President of Congress, EG insisted that the decision violated the rules and practices of Congress and deprived him of a privilege which belonged to him. Determined to battle for principle, EG hoped that Congress would recognize his position by reversing its ruling. Receiving no immediate response from the President of Congress, and learning also that his letter had not been considered on the floor of that body, EG wrote Huntington a second time, saying, "I conceive that the privilege contended for, is an essential one, and that without it, a Member cannot discharge his Trust."[3]

EG's refusal to attend Congress broke a record of continuous association which had marked him the most regular representative of Massachusetts in recent years. His reluctance to withdraw is evident in his continued presence in Philadelphia. EG expected Congress to admit that it had erred, thus paving the way for his triumphant return. Congress, meanwhile, expected the aggrieved Gerry to take his place and be heard. Because EG insisted upon clarification of the issue before his return—indeed as the price of his return, both sides assumed adamant positions which admitted of no retreat. When friends and colleagues failed to effect a solution, EG wrote Huntington on April 3. That day, when his letter was read in Congress, George Partridge unsuccessfully sought to win a hearing for EG the following day. However, on April 15 it was resolved that Congress consider on the seventeenth the substance of all three of EG's letters to President Huntington. EG refused to meet the Congress on its terms and the issue once more subsided, even though EG remained in Philadelphia. While staying abreast of many developments, he was drawn into one. On May 18 EG felt constrained to pen a lengthy letter to Huntington on the subject of Benedict Arnold's accounts.[4]

As the months dragged on, EG refrained from bringing the matter of his estrangement from Congress to the official attention of authorities in Massachusetts. Instead, when the Massachusetts delegation corresponded with Jeremiah Powell, President of the Massachusetts Council, EG was a party to the action. In truth, however, after Partridge's departure for home early in April, EG's stubborn abstinence left Massachusetts with but two effective men in the Congress, Holten and Lovell. That EG continued to keep abreast of official activity in Philadelphia is evident in letters written on both domestic and foreign affairs in early May.[5]

On June 3, the rupture between EG and the Congress widened as that delegate set out for Massachusetts. Despite the weariness, pique, pursuit of principles and unpredictability that was "just Gerry," the man from Massachusetts did not withdraw from congressional concerns. In Morristown, on June 11, the congressional committee at army headquarters urged him, as he journeyed homeward, "to give such information to the Executive powers of the Eastern States, respecting the distressed situation of the Army, as you, from your own observations, and our communications, are enabled to afford." That same day cooperative EG, discussing "the present reduced State of the Army and the Want of every Species of Supplies," penned his proposed remedies for the situation in a letter to Robert Morris. On June 23, a resolve of the General Court of Massachusetts approved the conduct of EG and Samuel Adams in requesting Brigadier Fellows to hold his brigade under marching orders to proceed to North River, New York upon application by General Robert Howe. In late July and early August, EG reported orally and in writing to the Massachusetts Council regarding military matters.[6]

In the Bay State EG spent most of his time in the Marblehead-Boston area. Yet even as he reimmersed himself in state and local matters, he kept up with developments in Philadelphia. Not until the mid-September gathering of the General Assembly did EG make a public statement of his reasons for withdrawing from Congress.[7]

In this lengthy period that witnessed EG's departure from Philadelphia and reentry into Massachusetts politics, JW also was a party to changing circumstances. Increased quantities of consumer goods direct from England led him to assert, "my own Judgment is we can do very well without it, and that all Intercourse with that accursed and barbarous Nation should be intirely broke of, and that we should use ourselves to the Manufactures and Merchandize of other Nations, to prevent as much as possible the hankering after those of Britain."[8]

1. *JCC*, 16:89; and Burnett, *CC*, 442–43.
2. *JCC*, 16:165.
3. EG to [Samuel Huntington], Philadelphia, February 22, 1780, copy, EG Collection of Elsie O. and Philip D. Sang, on deposit at Southern Illinois University Library, Carbondale; and *LCC*, 5:41–43, 45–46.
4. EG to [Samuel Huntington], Philadelphia, April 3, 1780, copy, EG Collection of Elsie O. and Philip D. Sang, on deposit at Southern Illinois University Library, Carbondale; *JCC*, 16:324–25, 368; and *LCC*, 5:102–5, 115, 151–54.
5. *Ibid.*, 126, 136.
6. *Ibid.*, 205–8; Mass., *A&R*, 21:577; and Austin, *EG*, 1:348–53.
7. J. Lovell to EG, [n.p.], July 24, 1780, EG Collection of Elsie O. and Philip D. Sang, on deposit at Southern Illinois University Library, Carbondale; and *LCC*, 5:326–27, 361–62, 370–71, 382–86, 451–53.
8. *W-A Ltrs.*, 2:136–37.

James Warren to Elbridge Gerry

• •

Boston, August 24th, 1780

My Dear Sir

I received yours of the 15th Instant[1] and have attended to your request with regard to the package Shipped on Board the "Alliance" but as yet without any success. Every thing is in such Confusion on Board that Ship, that no Body seems to know any thing about one thing or another. Quarrels and altercations among themselves seems to have taken all their Attention. I am seeking for a Trunk Mr. Adams writes me he had Shipped without being able to find it. I shall pursue a further Enquiry and find both if possible.

I thank you for the kind Letter you Inclosed for my Son,[2] and shall forward it to him at Newfoundland where he has had the Misfortune to be Carried as a Prisoner, but where he is very politely Used, and I dare say will be permitted to receive Letters without any Inspection.

I thank you also for your Attention to my Hobby Horse,[3] and the prospect you afford me of Considering you a Brother Farmer as well as a Political Brother. I wish to see you at Boston. Do you not Intend to see Doctor Lee?[4] I had a long private Conversation with him this day. I wish you had been present, I am sure it would have given you pleasure, and I think it would give ⟨you⟩ him pleasure to see ⟨him⟩ you. It is my private opinion you should not loose the opportunity of seeing him. I should be pleased with the Honour of Introduceing you to him. I think your Politics and Souls are so Congenial that they would soon Unite in the Service of your Country. How does your Electioneiring succeed? I think you will be disappointed and if you are, other good folks will also but we must submit to fate and to folly. I am Yours sincerely

J. Warren

Honourable E. Gerry Esqr.

ALS, Russell W. Knight—Gerry collection, Massachusetts Historical Society.
1. This letter by EG has not been located.
2. Winslow Warren.
3. This allusion, despite the persistence evident in MW's use of it in her letter of February 6, 1791 (*q.v.*), remains obscure. Possibly it refers to JW's love of farming.
4. Arthur Lee (1740–92) had served earlier as commissioner to France and Spain. In 1781 he entered the Continental Congress.

§

In Massachusetts a joint committee of the state legislature concluded that EG had been denied his rights in Philadelphia. At the same time a resolve granted him payment of £23,203.4s.2d. for services and expenses between January 1776 and July 1780. The legislature also included EG on its slate of delegates to Congress for the year 1781, despite his request that he not be so designated. While unsuccessful in his efforts to keep Hancock from the governorship, EG was himself popular enough to be named simultaneously a senator from Essex County and a representative from the town of Marblehead. The former post he declined; the latter he accepted.[1]

On November 23, EG was named by Speaker Caleb Davis to the Massachusetts House committee "to devise Ways and Means to supply the Treasury to pay this Commonwealth's Quota of the Army and other Exigencies of Government & to sit immediately and constantly untill the Business is perfected."[2]

At the Navy Board, JW kept informed about privateering activities, the threats posed by British naval power, and the insignificance of the Continental navy. His own unsettled accounts induced him to declare, "if Congress will not do us Justice, I will Instantly quit, or rather I must."[3]

JW's second son, commercial-minded Winslow, upset the Warrens when his mid-summer voyage to Europe aboard "The Pallas" caused him, in company with Henry Laurens, to fall into enemy hands. Although he adhered to the rugged political outlook of his parents, Winslow, uninterested in Harvard or the sea and distinctly interested in acquiring money and enjoying society, was unlike either his parents or his brothers.

JW, meanwhile, kept thinking of returning to the farm he loved. Increasingly ill at ease amid changing manners and principles, he found the social whirl of Boston so distasteful. Like her husband, MW glimpsed and condemned the class-consciousness and conspicuous consumption of the wartime patriot *nouveau riche*. In closing weeks of the legislative session JW presented the memorial which, approved, permitted Plymouth to choose a new collector.[4]

Sharing EG's distaste for Hancock and company, JW witnessed the September election with disgust and disappointment. He failed to continue as spokesman for Plymouth in the House, declined the post of lieutenant governor, and was unsuccessful in his efforts to have Samuel Adams named secretary of the Commonwealth. To Samuel Adams, he cautiously phrased his disgust, "I have feelings on this Occasion which I shall not Attempt to describe in a Letter."[5] Informed of affairs in Philadelphia by Samuel Adams and aware of some Continental prospects via correspondence with John Adams, JW and EG, reunited in Massachusetts, had little reason to write one another.

1. J. Avery to EG, [Boston], September 30, 1780 and EG to the Massachusetts legislature, Boston, September 30, 1780 and Report of the Committee, [Boston], October 4, 1780 and EG to President of Senate and Speaker of the House, Boston, October 31, 1780, EG Collection of Elsie O. and Philip D. Sang, on deposit at Southern Illinois University Library, Carbondale; and Mass., *A&R*, 21:633, 660.

2. C. Davis to EG, Boston, November 23, 1780, EG Collection of Elsie O. and Philip D. Sang, on deposit at Southern Illinois University Library, Carbondale.

3. *W-A Ltrs.*, 2:141, 153.

4. Anthony, *First Lady*, 112–14, 127–29; and Mass., *A&R*, 21:632.

5. *W-A Ltrs.*, 2:138–39, 145.

James Warren to Elbridge Gerry

. .

Plymouth, December 3d, 1780

My dear Sir

I have arrived Home in safety but I have not left all my public Cares behind.[1] I think this on all Accounts a Critical period, that requires great Attention. I did not Expect to see dissipation of Manners, and Inattention to public Principles United as the Characteristic of America so early as the Year 1780, but I do now see it or dream that I do. If the late Example of our Cheif Magistrates and the Taste for fashionable and Expensive diversions do not prove the first, and one of the Resolutions of the Hartford Convention[2] does not prove the last, I may yet dream only and am alarmed without reason. But Dream sometimes give as much pain as reality.

A Riseing Republic in its dawn vesting the Military with Civil powers is a Solecism in Politics, and at least forebodes a short Life, and the Absurdity is heightened by doing it in an Instance where their own ⟨Inst⟩ Interest is concerned. It is more than probable to me that if they are Impowered to Collect the Levies from deficient States for their own pay and subsistence, they will soon find a way to Impose New ones to satiate that Uneasiness so apparent among them, and which they give us frequent Instances of. I always supposed that half pay for Life was all that was wished for, but a late Letter shows we were mistaken. The Resolution I refer to must be opposed *totis viribus* or we may be undone. I have wrote largely to Mr. Lovel on this subject. I wished to have some private Conversation with you on many subjects, but the hurry was too great. I hope to see you next week, and am Your Sincere Friend &c.

J. Warren

Honourable E. Gerry Esqr.[3]

ALS, Frederick M. Dearborn Collection, Harvard College Library; and photographic copy, EG Papers, Library of Congress.

1. JW is but remarking his move from Boston to Plymouth.
2. Declining purchasing power had induced a convention of five states (New York and New England) in Hartford, Connecticut on October 20, 1779. This gathering, publicizing its proceedings, directed wider attention to the issue of regulating prices by legislation but successive efforts to hold meetings in Philadelphia proved abortive in the early months of 1780. Congress, afforded copies of the Hartford proceedings, had followed this effort with interest. See Burnett, *CC*, 423–25; Nevins, *The American States*, 619; and *JCC*, 15:1254, 1289.
3. This letter was addressed to EG at Boston.

§

EG, temporarily withdrawn from the national scene and immersed in trade, privateering and Massachusetts politics, kept abreast of developments in Philadelphia, chiefly through his correspondence with James Lovell.

In this otherwise bleak period, a move from Plymouth to Milton presented the Warrens with a refreshing prospect. In January, 1781, JW purchased Milton Hill, formerly the property of Governor Thomas Hutchinson. There, some fourteen miles from Boston and not far from the Adamses at Braintree, JW hoped to give farming more attention than he had accorded it in recent years. In addition, Milton meant less isolation for Mercy and a closer physical identification with the bustle of the Boston area.[1]

1. Anthony, *First Lady*, 132–33.

Mercy Warren to Elbridge Gerry

. .

Plimouth, January 22, 1781

Sir

With my thanks I return a Manuscript handed me by Mr. Warren, and as you seem fond of the Musical strain, I have sometimes had thoughts of attuning the Harp and giving my opinions in Metre—both of the poetical Ladies—of the fair Chloe's gentle passive song, and of Collia's patriotic Numbers, urging the Hoarse [?] Clarion of War, in spite of Beauty, Fortune, and Love. But the Manners—the Exigences—the Taste—and the Times Require Heroics.

I could wish to Awaken the sleeping Muses, and call back the wandering Dieties. But Alas! Clio is Deaf, perhaps irrecoverably stuned till the Noise of War shall cease. The Harmony of Calliope suffers by the jaring of patriots. Melpomene is frighted by the Cry of the Miscerery, and the Fire of lost Urania quenched by the tears which flow for the loss of public and private Virtue.

In short I beleive the sacred Vine sickened by the unpromising aspect of the Decayed Village of Plimouth (though once the early Asylum from the Hand of Tyrany) and grown Weary of their old Friends. Sensible they had heretofore endeavored to cultivate an unthrifty soil, have bid an everlasting Adieu. And as their Ladyships have taken Wing probably in pursuit of some more Happy Clime. I hope they will not Rest till they Alight in the Head of some Votive Genius whose productions will do Honour to the admired Train—as well as to the Cold Regions of the North.

But if they should ever again condescend to make a Temporary Visit to one almost secluded from society (which Brightens the Idea, or gives a polish to Expression) you may depend upon it though more trivial matter may be Neglected, an Exertion shall be made (perhaps by way of Atonement for your sires and the iniquities of your Friend W[arren]) to offer a Libation to the Image set up in Dura.

A celebrated female writer has observed that "poetry is the most convenient Vehicle for Flattery,"[1] and as I think before the Vernal Equinox every class of your own sex will leave Exhausted all the powers of prosaic competition, in the sweet Incense of Adulation offered to the Work of their own Hands—another garb must be assumed, and when the "Herald crys aloud" for a New Emission, it will be Necessary the Dulcimer, the Harp, and the Lute be put to Musick, that the [. . .] of the seasons may be more highly perfumed least they flatten in the Nostrils of the Golden Calf.

Then "if ye be ready to fall down and Worship it is well." If not the Fiery Furnace of slander will be heated seven Times hotter than before, and it may be Necessary for some kind Guardian angel to Interpose and Deliver Daniel and the Righteous three from the Fury of the Devouring flame.[2]

But there are certain seasons, in the History of Man, when the Human Mind is Warped to Error and no Investigations of Reason can trace the hidden cause. Genius, Virtue, and patriotism frequently Nod over the Vices of the Times, Whether the Reigning Folly be Avarice, Dissipation, or Idolitry, and when their Nap is out May some Masterly Hand with a Delicacy peculiarly his own point the Ridicule when, (and only when,) it ought to Fall. Improve the Taste, correct the Morals and Learn the satyrist not to tread over a Line that will make itself Ridiculous.

Mean time I hope ⟨not⟩ the sermons of the Great—the smiles of the *Little* and the Buz of popular censure or applause will ever be Disregarded by the few, the very few, whose Fortitude is unshaken, and whose Virtue Remains uncorrupt at a period when Honour, property, and principle are afloat.[3]

I am sir, with Respect and Esteem, Your Friend and very Humble Servant

M. Warren

ALS, Russell W. Knight—Gerry collection, Massachusetts Historical Society.

1. The author and work have not been identified.
2. The quotations and parallels are derived from the Book of Daniel, chapter 3.

3. It would be difficult, in any other one short letter, to exceed this as a demonstration of MW's wide reading and ornate writing.

§

One of James Lovell's enigmatic letters, stolen from the mails and published by Rivington's *Gazette*, briefly threatened EG's friendship with Washington. In February, 1781, Massachusetts tendered EG the sum of £871.16s. additional payment of his expenses and salary while serving as a delegate to Congress for the period January, 1776—July, 1780.[1]

In this period EG's political outlook was determined largely by two circumstances: his opposition to Hancock and the willingness or unwillingness of the state to back him in his continuing battle with Congress over the question of privilege which had precipitated his absence from that body. Although repeatedly named a member of the Massachusetts delegation, EG refused to return to Philadelphia until Massachusetts endorsed his stand of 1780. When notified, on May 30, 1782, that he had been chosen a senator for Essex County, EG wrote from Marblehead, "being unable at present to discharge the Trust, I am under the necessity of declining the appointment."[2] Four months later, on September 23, his fighting spirit led him to write the Massachusetts Assembly, "If one publick Grievance is unnoticed, is it not usually productive of another, and do not the Evils multiply, untill the Constitution, like a fortress besieged, is rendered defencless by numerous Breaches?" Less than a month later the government of Massachusetts, "approving his right of privilege as a member of Congress, and directing the delegates in Congress from this Commonwealth, to enquire into the complaints," so backed aggrieved EG as to clear the way for his return to Congress.[3]

Meanwhile, with regard to matters at large, a growing optimism crept into EG's letters to John Adams and John Jay. To the latter he wrote, as hostilities were drawing to a close, "We have not only resources for continuing the War, but also the Power of drawing them forth in quantities equal to the most pressing Necessities."[4]

For JW, meanwhile, the last stages of the Anglo-American conflict brought sorrow and change. To second son 22-year-old Winslow, detained and under surveillance of British authorities in London, went the letters in which MW expressed the concern of all the family. Even when his freedom of movement was restored, Winslow remained in Europe, to the disappointment of his parents. They, in this same period, faced another sorrow when the crippling wound that cost 24-year-old James a leg returned him home after five years of naval service. Coupled with the termination of his work with the Navy Board and his failure to be re-elected to the Massachusetts House, JW had his reasons for entertaining a full measure of pessimism.

But to John Adams, in Europe, JW, the revitalized farmer, wrote, "I shall certainly take pleasure in roving with you among the Partridges, Squirrels, etc. . . . do ascertain what Marle is that we may know whether we have it here or not." Close upon Boston and aware of the political pulse of Massachusetts and posted on European developments by the letters of Adams, JW rounded out his political intelligence from a flow of correspondence from Philadelphia, chiefly from the pen of Arthur Lee. Accordingly it was but partial truth when he wrote John Adams, "I am quite a private Man, a distant Spectator."[5]

1. *LCC*, 5:532–33 and 6:5–6, 27, 30, 37–38, 174–75; J. Lovell to EG, [n.p.], February 1 and May 8, 1781, EG Collection of Elsie O. and Philip D. Sang, on deposit at Southern Illinois University Library, Carbondale; J. Lovell to EG, [n.p.], April 10, 1781, EG Papers, Library of Congress; Austin, *EG*, 1:340–44; and Mass., *A&R 1780–81*, 253.

2. *LCC*, 6:300–301; and S. Adams to EG, [Boston], May 30, 1782 and EG to S. Adams, Marblehead, June 1, 1782, EG Papers, Library of Congress.

3. EG to Massachusetts Assembly, Marblehead, September 23, 1782, EG Collection of Elsie O. and Philip D. Sang, on deposit at Southern Illinois University Library, Carbondale; and Mass., *A&R 1782–83*, 340.

4. EG to John Jay, Marblehead, September 20, 1781, EG Collection of Elsie O. and Philip D. Sang, on deposit at Southern Illinois University Library, Carbondale; and EG to J. Adams, Marblehead, January 10, 1781, EG Papers, Library of Congress.

5. *W-A Ltrs.*, 2:166–74, 178–79; and *LCC*, 6:389–90.

James Warren to Elbridge Gerry

·   ·

Milton, October 20th, 1782

My Dear Sir

I think I may now fairly Consider you as a Member of Congress without any possibility of retreating if the General Court has out maneuvered you. They Certainly have given you a Compleat

Victory over the Governor.[1] They have taken up the very Individual Resolve that he made, or did not make any Objections to. The very Resolve however that his ⟨his⟩ Cunning or something as Contemptible prevented passing into an Act last Session, and they have passed it very Unanimously and sent it to him in such Season that he can't avail himself of any Evasions. He must now either pass it, or make his Objections like a Governor, at least in the Form prescribed by the Constitution. If he passes it, every Stroke of his pen will be a pointed Mortification. I say Nothing of Inconsistency, whatever is common and familiar makes little Impression even where Sensibility is delicate. If he does not Sign it The Two Houses will make it an Act without him, and that Certainly must be more agreable to you, than if his fiat of approbation ⟨con⟩ Constituted a part of it. I have no News to give you. I Look for the "Argo" every day. It would give me great pleasure to see her. We recollect with great pleasure every Stage of our agreable Visit at Marblehead. You will please to make our Compliments to the very agreable Circle. I am Your Friend and Humble Servant

J. Warren

Honourable Elbridge Gerry Esqr.[2]

ALS, EG Papers 1772–1882 (gift of Samuel Eliot Morison), Massachusetts Historical Society.

1. John Hancock.
2. This letter is addressed to EG at Marblehead; it is docketed "ansd 23, 1782."

§

For a moment, at least, in mid-autumn 1782 it appeared that EG and JW would return to the political arena as colleagues in the Massachusetts delegation to Congress. Immediately after the stand taken by that state in support of EG's conduct and withdrawal from Philadelphia in 1780 cleared the way for acceptance of the congressional seat which awaited the Marblehead man, JW was chosen to represent Massachusetts in that body, for the year beginning November 1, 1782.[1]

JW and MW were unreservedly reluctant regarding the political prospect before the man from Plymouth. Mercy, writing about JW's election, told John Adams, "So little prospect of success is there to the struggles of the uncorrupted few, that I do not find myself quite willing your much esteemed Friend, Mr. Warren, who has but just retired from the public Walks (sickened by the servility and weakness of Man and wearied with the remiting Vigalence of Near twenty years in the Field of Politics) should again return to the *Embarased scene.* Yet Convinced of the Necessity of sending our *best men* to Congress, and knowing you deem it a point of the utmost importance, I dare not urge my Arguments against his repairing to Philadelphia to you." A week later, JW wrote the same overseas friend, "The Legislature [of Massachusetts] is in the Usual Stile, sometimes making wise Laws and sometimes not; however, constantly making New, or repealing old ones. The present Members of Congress elected are, Gerry, Osgood, S. Higginson, Gorham, Holton and J.W. I believe the last must stay at Home and cultivate his Farm."[2]

1. *LCC*, 7: lxviii–lxix; and Mass., *A&R 1782–83*, 323.
2. *W-A Ltrs.*, 2:180–81, 183. Samuel Osgood (1748–1813) served in the Continental Congress for the period 1780–84, and Stephen Higginson (1743–1828) served during 1782–83. Nathaniel Gorham (1738–96) spent 1782–83 and 1785–87 in Congress, serving as its president during some of the latter interval.

James Warren to Elbridge Gerry

· ·

Milton, December 2d, 1782

My Dear Sir

Upon my return from Plymouth I found your Letter of the 13th November[1] and Intended before now fully to have Complyed with your request but tho' I have seen Mr. Capan the Snow on the Ground, at one time, his Absence from Home at others, and some other Circumstances have prevented my seeing the Farm, and being able to form any opinion of that, or the reasonableness of his demands for it. But I am determined to see both him and the Farm in the Course of this week when I will do myself the pleasure to write you again. Mr. Marquand has delivered me your very polite favour dated Ipswich March 19th 1782,[2] which

I suppose was really wrote on the 19th of November and that the mistake in the date may be easily accounted for by supposeing ⟨you⟩ that some very agreable Circle of Ladies, or what is still a more adequate Cause that some very agreable Lady[3] in that quarter had Inspired you with all the fervor and Spirit of the Vernal Equinox. But however that may be, I am fully sensible you had not lost the feelings and partiality of Friendship. I think I Cannot go to Congress, but if I could, it certainly should be an Indespensible Condition that my Friend Mr. Gerry should not only be my Companion, but my Colleague in a public Capacity. I have many reasons for makeing that such a Condition, but they must be given *viva voce*. While I hesitate the Lady you refer me to says Nothing, and the little patriotic Circle being not quite so well Instructed in the Maxims of prudence Chatter away, but divided in Sentiment decide Nothing but all agree that Mr. Gerry should go. ⟨wi⟩

I have long Contemplated with pleasure the safe Arrival of the "Argo" with a good Voayge to my Friend. I leave you then to Conceive my Feelings on hearing of the Misfortune that had befallen her. I won't say it affected me like a loss of my own, but it has given me more pain than if it had fallen any where else.

I beg you to Enquire of Mrs. Bourn whether she has wrote to Mr. Winslow, and in what manner and desire her to give you a Copy of the Bond, and the Endorsments, and her permission to put it in suit in her Name, as I think I have a Chance of recovering 60 or 70 pounds without any kind of Injury to her demands on me.[4] You will please to accept Mrs. Warren's and my Compliments to yourself and the agreable Circle at Marblehead. I am Yours Sincerely

J. Warren

E. Gerry Esqr.[5]

ALS, Gerry II Papers, Massachusetts Historical Society.

1. This letter has not been located.
2. This letter likewise has not been located.
3. Despite the strong hints that romance had entangled the 38-year-old bachelor, EG did not take the marital plunge at this time.

4. This somewhat enigmatic passage probably refers to the unsuccessful importing business that contributed to Winslow Warren's mounting indebtedness at this time.

5. This letter, addressed to EG at Marblehead, is docketed "ansd 20th Decr." The letter of that date also has not been located.

§

Proud and adamant, EG sat out the winter of 1782–83 politically, awaiting the reaction of Congress to the Massachusetts resolution in support of his right of privilege. Learning that the resolution had been transmitted to Congress, EG wrote Stephen Higginson of the Massachusetts delegation, "whenever they may have considered the Matter, I wish to be informed of their proceedings."[1]

JW, meanwhile, was being importuned from abroad, by John Adams. Out of Philadelphia came the additional urging of Arthur Lee, "The mode of settling the Quotas of the States, and of establishing funds for the payment of our debts are questions now before Congress. I wish we had your assistance in discussing them."[2]

1. EG to S. Higginson, Boston, February 28, 1783, EG Collection of Elsie O. and Philip D. Sang, on deposit at Southern Illinois University Library, Carbondale.

2. *W-A Ltrs.*, 2:189, 190.

James Warren to Elbridge Gerry

· ·

Milton, February 25th: 1783[1]

My Dear Sir

I have taken another ⟨rid⟩ ride this day, and in the Course of it met with Mr. Capon and find by him that he sold his Farm to the Man he was in Treaty with when I saw him at your desire. I have also Learned that the Brush Hill Farm formerly owned by Mr. Smith and which I hear is both a good ⟨one⟩ and a pleasant one is on sale. I never saw it, and therefore cannot give you an opinion of it, but Mr. Robbins our Representative now in Town has the Conduct of the Business. If you please you may Enquire of him the Terms &c and if you will come here when you please,

I will wait on you and see it. I want you for a Neighbour but my own Interest shall not Betray me into a Judgment of it that shall be disadvantageous to your Interest.

Let not the Government delay the operations we talked of, and if my Opinion of Men and things can be supposed necessary bring some or all of them here, and let us Enjoy one Evening at Milton. Mr. Parsons has often promised and may come if he pleases. I write in a hurry and must Conclude. I am Your Friend

J. Warren

E. Gerry Esqr.

ALS, HM 22596, The Huntington Library, San Marino.
   1. The Huntington Library, San Marino, California. Reproduced by permission.

James Warren to Elbridge Gerry

· ·

Milton March 2d 1783

My Dear Sir,

I received your message by my Son.[1] I do not think I shall be able to be with you Tomorrow Evening without takeing the Hazard of a long Confinement, which I have now a prospect of Escapeing. Nor do I think it necessary, as I dare say I shall readily Embrace the plan you will agree on. I am sorry that you came to no determination at your last meeting. You know my Sentiments and may act for me, by Proxey. The only Object is to fix upon those men who are the most likely to Obtain the suffrages. Upon that subject you know my Sentiments. We are all certain that a deviation from the present Line cannot be for the worse. You will let me hear from you soon. I am Your Friend &c

J. Warren

E. Gerry Esqr.

ALS, Russell W. Knight—Gerry collection, Massachusetts Historical Society.

1. Apparently the bearer of the message was 17-year-old George, the youngest of the five sons of the Warrens.

§

Late in May, when delegate Osgood returned to Massachusetts and reported that as yet Congress had taken no action on the resolution concerning EG, the latter, on tenterhooks, wrote delegate Holten that he was in "a State that is by no Means agreable."[1]

In the spring of 1783 fun-loving Winslow Warren, having amassed debts rather than a fortune in commerce in Marseilles, returned to the United States, desirous of a consular post. Loyal to the father of the young man whom he had never seen, EG urged Samuel Holten, in Philadelphia, to support the application of young Warren.[2]

1. EG to S. Holten, Boston, May 19, 1783, EG Collection of Elsie O. and Philip D. Sang, on deposit at Southern Illinois University Library, Carbondale.
2. *Ibid.*

Mercy Warren to Elbridge Gerry

. .

Milton, May 19th, 1783

Sir

You desired me to Recollect and Mention the places named by a young Gentleman[1] where he should like to reside. He says he has no perticular place fixed, should like England, France, Barcelona, Maliga, Allacant,[2] or Lisbon. Would not your application to Mr. Morris[3] be Influential in his favour?

I have such an oppinion of your Friendship to Mr. Warren and Family that I think an appoligy unnecessary Either for this Interruption or the Maternal Attentions you may at other times have observed.

Mr. Warren having many letters to write has left this to me. I have informed my son that you are his Friend which perhaps you will confirm (if leasure permits) by a line from your own Hand. I am Sir with Great Sincerity and Esteem Your Friend &c.[4]

M. Warren

ALS, Frank M. Etting Collection, American Authors Series, The Historical Society of Pennsylvania.

1. Winslow Warren.
2. I.e. Málaga and Alicante.
3. Robert Morris was then serving as Superintendent of Finance.
4. This letter was addressed to EG at Boston.

§

In late spring EG's desire to return to Congress was common knowledge. Early in June, the Massachusetts delegation (Holten, Gorham and Higginson) finally complied with the order of the General Court and remonstrated against the conduct of Congress which had led to EG's withdrawal from that body in 1780. Charles Thomson, Secretary of Congress, endorsed the protest and filed it with EG's letters of 1780. This trifling act apparently removed the final obstacle to EG's return to Congress.[1]

Another sorrow, this one tempered with mercy, touched the Warren family on May 23. Then it was that "The Patriot," James Otis, MW's insane brother who, decades earlier, had sparked the rebellion now crowned with success, was struck dead by a bolt of lightning.[2]

1. W. Ellery to EG, Newport, May 24, 1783 and Massachusetts Delegates to the Continental Congress, [Philadelphia], June 6, 1783, EG Collection of Elsie O. and Philip D. Sang, on deposit at Southern Illinois University Library, Carbondale; and *LCC*, 7:181.
2. Anthony, *First Lady*, 144.

Mercy Warren to Elbridge Gerry

.   .

Tremont, June 6th, 1783

Dear Sir

It is an undoubted truth that there are seasons in human affairs, when genius, virtue, and patriotism, nod over the vices of the times, perhaps this drowsy disposition was never more remarkable than at the present period. I am at a loss whither the reigning folly is avarice, dissipation, or idolatry; but when the nap is out, I hope we shall see the reanimation of patriotism take place of the apathy which has for some time hung on the lids of this people, and that some masterly hand will arise and correct the morals, improve the taste, and learn the *satyrist* to discriminate, that the pen of genius may not make itself ridiculous, as it has done in some late instances, by mistaking its cue. Every country has its Caesars and its Catalines, its Brutii and Octavii, and the spirit of idolatry is more easily cultivated among mankind, than rational modes of homage and respect both in religion and politics. The artful hipocrite of specious manners frequently creates an influence that counteracts the efforts of undisguized probity; thus we often see the supple multitude, lick the hand that is unable to protect, and adore the footsteps of the man, who to secure his popularity, would tread down their dear bought privileges. We have set Great Britain at defiance, we have weathered the shocks of war—we have hazarded all, and waded through rivers of blood to establish the independence of America, and maintain the freedom of the human mind. But alas! if we have any national character, what a heterogeneous mixture—we have a republican form of government with the principles of monarchy, the freedom of democracy, with the servility of despotism, the extravagance of nobility, with the poverty of peasantry.

I could tell you some very surprizing truths relative to your state, but letters are dangerous vehicles of intelligence. While Caesar meditated triumphs over the citizens, and trampled on the liberties of Rome, he scattered largesses among the people. How did he succeed? The Romans indeed were not then capable of enjoying that freedom that Brutus would have purchased not only with the blood of the tyrant, but with the generous current that flowed from his own breast. Is not America tainted with many of the vices that stained that ancient republic? It is easy to give a long list of the absurd follies that have crept in among us;—but where are the virtues that will make a balance sufficient to support a free commonwealth?

Caesar had talents,—he had valour, intrepidity, activity, and magnanimity as well as ambition,—he had the capacity and inclination for the dispatch of business—thus qualified, it was easy to deceive by intrigue, while he captivated by generosity. But modern times exhibit more wonderful phenomenons;—we have seen a man without abilities idolized by the multitude,[1] and fame on the wing to crown the head of imbecillity;—we have seen a people trifling with the priviledge of *election*, and throwing away the glorious opportunity of establishing liberty and independence on the everlasting basis of virtue, we have heard them trumpet the praises of their idol of straw, and sing of sacrifices he never had the courage to make. You very well know, Sir, he was first brought into political existence, and supported, on the shoulders of men of less fortune, but infinitely more merit than himself. We have seen this state *baby* of the Massachusetts repeatedly chosen the first magistrate of this Commonwealth;—we see him triumph in the zenith of popularity, though so debilitated, as literally to be borne about on the shoulders of his sycophants.[2] Much artifice has been necessary for this general deception, but nothing has had a more powerful effect, than squandering gratuities among the weak and the worthless. Meantime your philosophical friend and myself are retired from the crowd, to the calm and delightful shade of *Tremont*, where with little interruption but such as we choose, we can smile at the ambitious canvassing for *place*, and the courtier practising dissimulation;—or contemplate the inconsistency of human nature, the frivolity of mankind, the sudden revolutions of states, which seldom better their condition by their struggles; the rise of kingdoms, the fall of empires, and the convulsed state of human affairs from the death of *Abel*, to the slaughter of many of the heroes of America. But no situation either in the public or private walks of life, will render us unmindful of those few virtuous and patriotic characters, without whose exertions, neither the union, nor the independence of the American States, would ever have had an existence;— nor is it any degree of flattery to say that Mr. Gerry stands high on the list, in the opinion of his assured friend

M. Warren

To the Honorable Elbridge Gerry Esquire

LC, Mercy Warren Letterbook, 469–70, Massachusetts Historical Society.

1. The reference is to John Hancock.
2. Without interruption Hancock had occupied the governor's chair since 1780 and with the exception of one brief interval he would continue in it until 1793. Although only in his mid-forties at this time, Hancock, severely and repeatedly afflicted with gout, had the appearance of an elderly man; see Herbert S. Allan, *John Hancock; Patriot in Purple* (New York, 1948), 308.

§

Informing EG of the step taken in his behalf in Philadelphia, Samuel Holten wrote, "I hope, I shall soon have the pleasure of paying you my personal respects in Philadelphia." EG's reply promised himself "the Pleasure, by the middle of July, of an agreeable Interview with my Friends at Philadelphia." When he informed the General Court that he intended to take up his post in Philadelphia, the Commonwealth readied his credentials.[1]

JW, in this season, was adept with excuses that eased himself from the firing line of political action. Commenting on EG's departure for service in Congress, he remarked to John Adams, "if you ask why I dont go, I will tell you because I have been Sick the whole Spring, and dare not Venture to go at this Season."[2] Handy for the moment, this excuse could not dim the fact that, given his prior service and present outlook, JW was not interested in serving in the Congress.

1. S. Holten to EG, Philadelphia, June 7, 1783, and EG to S. Holten, Marblehead, June 16, 1783, EG Collection of Elsie O. and Philip D. Sang, on deposit at Southern Illinois University Library, Carbondale; *JCC*, 24:510; and Mass., *A&R 1782–83*, 692.
2. *W-A Ltrs.*, 2:219, 220.

James Warren to Elbridge Gerry

. .

Milton, August 5th, 1783

My Dear Sir

You have really in the true Modern Stile taken a French Leave of us. After Expecting you every day for some time, I see it announced in the public papers that Mr. Gerry is gone on to Congress. I wish him a good Journey. If we had known the Time, we should have Joined the Party, and done ourselves the pleasure of dining with him at Lynn, and the Honour of being marked among the number of his perticular Friends. But why has he gone without the Visit he promised, or a single Line to tell us why he did not make it; if we were Enemies in force and well posted, I should think this Maneuvre an Instance of Great Generalship. In such a Case I might have harrassed your rear with my light Horse. As it is I shall pursue you with (what is worse) trifleing Letters, and perhaps you will find more Inconvenience from my Friendship than Enmity but it is an Inconvenience you must submit to for I cannot find it in my Heart to be your Enemy nor shall unless I find you Betraying or forsakeing the great Principles of the American revolution which I beleive there is no danger off.

Foreign News we have none, and you have not been gone long enough to Expect any Alteration in our domestic Affairs. This Letter therefore you are to Consider only as a substitute to takeing you by the hand, and bidding you Good By and for the same reason I make this substitute for that purpose. I Inclose a Memorial[1] which I had not an Oppertunity of putting into your hands. You will use it as you think proper. Please to make my Compliments to Doctor Lee, General Lincoln, and your Brother Delegates.[2] I will presume that I shall very often hear from you and am assuredly Your Friend &c &c

J. Warren

Honourable Elbridge Gerry Esqr.

ALS, Gerry II Papers, Massachusetts Historical Society.

1. The contents of this memorial are unknown. Inasmuch as JW had unsettled accounts, his son Winslow was seeking a consular post, and his son James was a wounded veteran, the memorial might have turned upon any of several matters close to the Warrens.

2. Arthur Lee, one of Virginia's delegates in Congress, was a frequent correspondent of JW's; and General Benjamin Lincoln, of Massachusetts, from whom JW had received a lengthy letter under date of April 5, 1783, was then serving as Secretary of War. The Massachusetts delegation then in Philadelphia counted Nathaniel Gorham, Stephen Higginson and Samuel Holten.

§

"Mr. Elbridge Gerry, a delegate for the State of Massachusetts," the opening entry in the journal of Congress for Thursday, August 14, 1783, in Princeton, New Jersey read, "attended, and took his seat."[1] During the forty-two months since his withdrawal from Congress in February, 1780, much had occurred; but only recently, in June, had Congress moved from the Pennsylvania city to Princeton.

Basically, the war, then prosecuted, had been won; the peace, then sought, had been obtained; and the structure of the national government of the United States, then struggling toward fruition, had been instituted under the Confederation. Accustomed to facing a wide variety of problems in the former period, EG was ready to grabble with those plaguing the infant state.

Meanwhile, based in Milton but with eyes and ears on state, national and international developments, JW continued to dedicate his energies, along with those of Mercy, to winning support from influential friends for the application which Winslow had made on July 2 for the post of consul.[2]

1. *JCC*, 24:508.
2. *Ibid.*, 428n; and *W-A Ltrs.*, 2:220–21.

James Warren to Elbridge Gerry

· ·

                                                    Milton, August 17th, 1783
My Dear Sir.

My Last to you was wrote at a Time when I Expected my Son[1] every day. I therefore did not mention him, supposeing ⟨you⟩

he would not have an opportunity of seeing you, nor shall I trouble you any further at this time than to desire your Care of the Inclosed Letter, and to desire you to return it in Case you have no opportunity to deliver it before he sets out for Home. You will easily suppose my silence with regard to him and his Affairs proceeds from that Opinion of your Friendship which makes me beleive it of that kind which requires no solicitations. I presume he will be happy to see you and proud to make himself worthy of your Friendship. I hope he will succeed in both. I wish to know from you what prospects he has.

I suppose by this time you are Engaged in the great Field of Politics, that you have before you, and in full view, all the Movements of the Great Machine, whether they proceed from those Sources that Characterize the Great and Good Statesman, or the cunning and designing Politician and your Reverence and Contempt may alternately rise and fall as the different Objects pass in succession before you. From my Humble Station I veiw the great Operations at a distance. If it be my duty to view them with respect, Contempt and Indignation will sometimes Intrude, and how can I help it while Consciousness of our past Labours remains and Recollection frequently brings to view not only our Conduct, but the motives that Governed it. The fault is in the Contrast I am not to Blame. But enough of this, I would tell you News if I had any, but there is a Dead Calm. Inactivity has succeeded the Bustle and Turmoll of War. Peace and Plenty give it Countenance. We must wait for Time, or some Occurrence to rouse ⟨some⟩ a Genius that shall make a figure in Tranquility. Perhaps such an one may arise soon, and Blaze like a New Constellation. We may then hope to see ⟨public⟩ a Mode devised for Establishing public Credit without sacrificeing or hazarding our dear earned rights. I am with Great Esteem Your Sincere Friend &c. &c.[2]

J. Warren

Honourable E: Gerry Esqr.

ALS, EG Collection of Elsie O. and Philip D. Sang, on deposit at Southern Illinois

University Library, Carbondale; and photographic copy, EG Papers, Library of Congress.

1. Winslow Warren, who had gone to the seat of Congress to press his application for a consular post.
2. Docketed "ansd Sept. 3d." That letter by EG has not been located.

§

EG immediately served on committees burdened with pressing issues: the public credit, the army, and relations with the Indians, among them. With mounting attention assigned the choice of a permanent residence for the Congress, he became a leader among those actively seeking a solution which would promote unity. EG moved "That buildings for the use of Congress be created on the banks of the Delaware, near Trenton, or of Potomac, near George-Town." At the close of debate he became one of the members of the five-man committee which was to visit the vicinity of the falls of Delaware and report back to Congress. Sensing that general assent to any single site would be extremely unlikely, he moved "for the alternate residence of Congress in two places," the second location to be on the Potomac. Furthermore, until two permanent sites were selected and built upon, he urged that Congress alternate between Trenton and Annapolis.[1]

In foreign affairs these same weeks found EG concerned with maritime issues, interpretations of the peace treaty, the issuance of an exequatur to the consul general of France, and the study of the diplomatic dispatches received from American representatives abroad. Unsuccessfully he insisted that only American citizens be appointed to the posts of consul and vice consul. In this area, then so interesting to the Warrens, he also studied the need for an agent or consul at Madeira.[2]

Arthur Lee, one of the friends enlisted in the effort to win a consular appointment for Winslow, wrote JW, "No day is fixed for entering upon the business of Consuls." To John Adams, in midautumn, JW wrote, "at Work among my Potatoes, instead of being in Congress. I am quite contented with a private life, and my Ambition is quite satisfied by excelling in the perfection of my Composts, the Culture of my Lands, and in the Quality and Abundance of my Crops; but I own I sometimes wish to be at the Wheel to serve my Country." Regarding the rise of an oligarchy in the powers and position of certain department heads, JW insisted, "if this Oligarchal System is not Annihilated, I think our Liberties must be."[3]

1. *JCC*, 24:512n and 25:571–73, 577–84, 590n, 654–59, 693, 697–99, 708.
2. *Ibid.*, 24:518, 518n and 25:536–38, 554, 587, 617, 621–22, 628, 637, 778–79; and Austin, *EG*, 1:381–84, 398–400.
3. *W-A Ltrs.*, 2:226, 229, 230.

James Warren to Elbridge Gerry

· ·

Milton, November 16th, 1783

My Dear Sir

I thank you for your favours of 25th September and 22d October[1] and heartily Congratulate you on the late determinations of Congress. They are the Tryumph of Patriotism and Independence, and restore in my Mind a great degree of that Confidence I used to have in the Virtue and good Sense of that Body.

It has been difficult to say whether the Insolence of a few (whose characters I was never taught to revere) or the Tameness and submission of Congress were the most astonishing. I have for sometime supposed that if a stop was not put to the Career of the aristocratic System before their Success was Carried much further, Members of Congress must of Course be Considered with less respect than the Clerks in their Offices. Every Body else who was not Calculated to unite in their plans has been Insulted and ill used, and it must have come to their Turn soon. The little Attention that has been paid to this matter has surprised me. While an Accumulation of Power totally Inconsistent with the Principles on which we Ground ourselves has made the most rapid Strides that ever were seen in a Country under like Circumstances, almost every Body has been so hush and silent as to make me at times almost doubt my own Senses and Understanding, and to make me suspect that neither Villany nor Insolence existed where I was at other Times sure I saw both. You have begun well but you have much more to do yet. You must Change the whole System. The People see the Cloven foot and have no Confidence in those or rather in him who is Invested with such Indefinite powers.

The Impost as proposed by Congress should never be adopted because it is Impolitic and wrong in every view of it, and will never take place in some other States, tho' it has been Carried through our Assembly after a great deal of Art and Management by a Majority of three only in the House. I shall rejoice if this does not take place, but I shall wish to see other Measures more safe and more Effectual for paying not only the Interest but the principal of the National Debt adopted. But such seems to be the prevailing want of Confidence that I doubt whether any will succeed while the Management is in his hands. The Oligarchy feel themselves so strong as to take of [f] the Mask without fear, or at least not to take much pains to disguise their Plans, or to show a decent regard to the public honour and Interest. The late sale of the Frigates is an Instance in point. The selling[of] them at all is a disgrace to the Nation, and the Manner in which it is done is an Insult that amounts to a defiance. They were first fitted up at a great Expense to the Continent, and then sold to the Person that ⟨y⟩ had the direction for less than the fixing had Cost, by which means his Agents first got their Commissions, and he a good Bargain. If this is a barefaced prostration of National honour and Interest, it has been done Boldly in open day Light, and without any Appearance of Fear or Shame. A permanent Fund for payment of the Interest of the Debt, or little more than the Interest, in such hands would be a pretty Affair, and afford a Curious Sceen but I leave this matter to wish you a good Journey, and an agreable Session at Annapolis.[2]

I have lately received a Number of Letters from our Friend Mr. Adams. They were of an old date none later than April, but Contain many things that I wish I could Communicate to you in the Spirit and feelings with which they were wrote.[3] He has been ill used. He has been thwarted and Embarrassed in all his Measures, but I think he will not bear much more of it. Mr. Jay is a good Man,[4] and is certainly right with regard to the Appointment to Britain. Mr. Adams is the most suitable Man, and it is his right.[5] The Appointment of any one else would at least imply a Censure upon him, and I am sure he would feel it to the quick, If he is Jockeyed, he had rather any Body should be the Jockeys than Vergennes[6] and Franklin. I am Astonished at the Instructions that have been given by Congress to their Ministers. If they wished to humble them, they should have done it in some way that would not have hazarded the safety, and Interest of the Country. Have not our foreign Affairs in General been strangely Conducted?

But I will not Scold any more in this Letter, not because I don't feel disposed for it this Cold Morning but because I fear you will be more tired of it than I am. I am obliged to you for your Attention to myself and Son.[7] His wish is to go to Lisbon, but Beggars must not Choose. He refers the Conduct of the whole matter to your Judgment and would be Glad to ⟨be⟩ have one of the first Appointments rather than wait and take his Chance for another if it should be more eligible, as he has nothing to do here and wishes to be engaged in Business.

It is said and beleived here that the definitive Treaty was signed the begining of September.[8] Mrs. Warren desires her Compliments to Mr. Gerry. I am with Great Esteem Your Friend and Humble Servant

                                                              J. Warren

I have taken the Liberty to Inclose two Letters for Mr. Ellary and Mr. Howel[9] requesting their Influence in favour of my Son, and referring them to you for any Information with regard to him. Will you be kind enough to deliver them, and answer their Questions? I am a Troublesome Acquaintance. Tell me how I shall make returns for the services you do me. If Friendship and Esteem will compensate I am not in Debt if not I am greatly.

Honourable E. Gerry Esqr.[10]

ALS, EG Collection of Elsie O. and Philip D. Sang, on deposit at Southern Illinois University Library, Carbondale; and photographic copy, EG Papers, Library of Congress.

1. Neither of these letters by EG has been located.

2. On November 4, Congress adjourned its session in Princeton pursuant to a resolution calling for it to resume its labors in Annapolis on November 26; see *JCC*, 25:807.

3. Those of March and April, 1783, apparently the ones to which JW refers, are in *W-A Ltrs.*, 2:190–99, 205–15.

4. John Jay (1745–1826) of New York, then a member of the American peace delegation but previously on diplomatic duty in Spain.

5. Eventually, in 1785, John Adams did become the first U.S. Minister at the Court of St. James.

6. The Count de Vergennes, the French Foreign Minister, promoted a policy of the continuing dependence of the United States upon France.

7. Winslow Warren.

8. Referring to this event, participant John Adams wrote, "The third of September will be more remarkable for the signature of the definitive treaties than for the battle of Naseby or Worcester, or the death of Oliver Cromwell;" see Austin, *EG*, 1:381.

9. William Ellery (1727–1820) and David Howell (1747–1824) were members of the Rhode Island delegation to Congress.

10. This letter is docketed "ansd Decr. 19th." EG's reply has not been located.

§

Fortified with credentials certifying that he had been reelected to Congress for the term November 1783—November 1784, EG was ready for work in Annapolis before the needed quorum could be mustered. Late in 1783, prior to becoming involved in issues regarding possible enroachments on the eastern boundary and refugees from Canada, EG had written John Adams, "Our domestic affairs are much deranged."[1]

When, on December 18, more than three weeks later than planned, Congress resumed work with seven states represented, the Massachusetts delegation consisted of EG, Samuel Osgood and George Partridge.[2]

1. EG to J. Adams, Philadelphia, November 23, 1783, EG Papers, Library of Congress.

2. *JCC*, 25:810, 815.

James Warren to Elbridge Gerry

. .

Milton, December 17th 1783

My dear Sir,

When I received yours of the 22d October[1] my feelings so strongly Inclined me that I wrote to you on the subject of public matters with so little reserve as Indicated a full Confidence in the Coveyance by the Post, and indeed I had not a suspicion of the mails being Intercepted in our present state of Peace. It did not occur to me, as bad an Opinion as I had of them, that the Aristocratic party could take such measures to answer their political purposes. I hope my Letter has reached you in safety, but I am uneasy about it especially since I received yours of the 26th November.[2] However if they get it, they will find nothing but the honest Effusions of Truth, and Patriotism, which if rightly Improved may do them more good than the discovery can Injure me. I have not yet received from Mr. Thaxter the Pamphlet and News Paper you mention. Shall Comply with your request and send them to Mr. Higgison as soon as I have read them. I have always been suspicious of the Institution, and wished to know the real design. I could hardly be satisfied that it originated only from vanity, and had no other Object but the Importance and distinction their Merits, or Imaginations had suggested were peculiarly due to their Class. I shall talk with General Lincoln and some others on the subject.

We have Nothing new here, tho' we have been threatned with a very Extraordinary Event, the Resignation of our Governor.[3] He declared before very large and respectable Companies, among which were at one time the Supreem Court, and at another the Governors of the College that the Last thing he Intended to do as Governor was to Nominate a Person to fill the Supreem Bench, and that he would absolutely resign on the 26th of November. That Time is past without a resignation, and there are those who do not despise him secretly, nor ridicule him openly. However singular his good Luck is. If you ask what determined him to make such a declaration, I can only say that opinions are various. Some say it arose from disappointment and Chagrin that his Speech was not Echoed Back in the usual stile of fulsome address, and the late publications of some of his small Fools Justify this Opinion, while others say that it happened at a Certain time, that an Idea of the dignity of General Washington in retireing to private Life happened to float across his Pericranium, and to make such an Impression as Induced him to think he should be a great Man too, if he followed the Example. But alas, his Fortitude did not support his resolution, and enable him to do this wise and prudent thing. But it is a matter of very trifling Consequence and so I dismiss it.

I suppose you are now set down to Business at Annapolis. Small matters must give place to great Objects. My own Business excites no Impatience, but as your Young Friend[4] wishes to be gone, and be Engaged in Business and waits for nothing else, I feel some for him at the same time I know there is no hurrying such matters and have full Confidence you will accomplish it as soon as possible. Will you write me soon if you ever received the Letter I mentioned above. It Inclosed two letters to Mr. Howel and Ellery. My Son also wrote to you not long before. Mr. Dana arrived here a little unexpectedly.[5] I have not yet seen him. I wish to. Mr. Adams refers me to him for many Curious Anecdotes, not of Voayges and Travels only but of Negotiations &c. I suppose he will be with you soon. Will you make my regards to Doctor Lee, Major Osgood, and Mr. Partridge, and Beleive me to be Your Friend &c &c

J. W.

Honourable E. Gerry Esqr.

ALS, Russell W. Knight—Gerry collection, Massachusetts Historical Society.

1. This letter by EG has not been located.
2. This letter by EG likewise has not been located.
3. John Hancock.
4. Winslow Warren.
5. Francis Dana had served as the U.S. Minister to Russia 1780–83.

§

A simple, yet formal, set of arrangements for the public audience of General Washington, who had indicated his desire to resign his commission, was penned by EG as the report of the committee in charge of the occasion. Foreign affairs, especially the problem of instructions for the diplomatic representatives of the United States, also absorbed EG's time and attention. Immediately after Christmas, the committee charged with studying the Delaware River valley sites to be considered as a permanent seat of Congress submitted a report which EG had penned.[1]

As 1784 opened, the under-manned Congress found EG, one of the oldest and most experienced persons present, studying numerous foreign and domestic issues. In the realm of foreign affairs, his service on committees, his authorship of reports, his motions and his votes all demonstrated his concern about the appointments, instructions, salaries, and reports of our ministers abroad, as well as the formulation of commercial treaties and the structure and operation of the office of the secretary of foreign affairs.[2]

1. *JCC*, 25:818, 820–28, 841, 841n.
2. *Ibid.*, 26:4, 5, 104–356 *passim*; Austin, *EG*, 1:400–402; EG to J. Adams, Philadelphia, November 23, 1783, EG Papers, Library of Congress; and Tristram Dalton to EG, Newburyport, December 1, 1783, EG Collection of Elsie O. and Philip D. Sang, on deposit at Southern Illinois University Library, Carbondale.

James Warren to Elbridge Gerry

. .

Milton, February 25th, 1784.

My Dear Sir,

My Conscience by severely reproaching my Indolence has at last roused me to Action, and dictated to me in a Strong light my Negligence. It tells me that I have not wrote to you for many weeks. I see the fault and the folly of this Indolent Neglect and Friendship and Wisdom unite in my repentance and Amendment. The Consequence is this Letter which, if it gives you no pleasure, may Engage your Candor and forgiveness.

My last was principally on the subject of an Intended resignation or at least a pretended one,[1] but for your Comfort and Consolation I have the pleasure to Inform you, that we hear no more of it. We may still be happy in the possession of a Chief Magistrate, whose Merits are of such an Extraordinary kind that no Conduct on his own can sully them with ridicule or Contempt.

The General Court has set for some Weeks without my being able to Inform you what they have done of a public and Im-

portant Nature. Except the Choice of Mr. Dana in the room of
Judge S[ulliva]n as a delegate to Congress.[2] Good Providence
takes care of us and this is an Instance of it. A more fortunate
Event than the resignation could not have taken place and a
more Judicious Choice could not have been made to fill the
Vacancy. Mr. Dana dined with me lately and will soon be with
you unless prevented by an Adjournment of Congress.[3] When
he stands upon your floor as an Independent Member, his
Abilities and rectitude may give honest Men pleasure while they
detect the Malice and Corruption and Excite the Shame of the
servile, if there should be any such among you. I receive your
Letter of 19th December[4] and am pleased to find you had such
Expectations of a free and Independent Congress. I have done
your several Messages. they thank you for your attention. My
Son[5] goes for Europe in a few weeks and proposes to set down in
Lisbon, and will be happy to be honoured with the Commands
of Congress. An Adjournment of Congress, if the Committee
behave well, will certainly add to their dignity and consequently
be a public Advantage. I presume your final determination with
regard to Consuls must have been formed and probably your
Elections made before now.[6] I wish to know why the Commercial
Treaty with Britain is suspended. If the delay is occasioned by
want of Instructions from Congress how has that happened? Is
it not a Misfortune that it should be delayed till disputes and
prejudices have time to operate, and rancle? are not Treaties to
be made with Denmark, Portugal, the two Empires, with
Morocco, Algiers, Tunis and Tripoli? And if made with them,
and perhaps with Sardinia and Naples, is it to be left with a
Single Commissioner, as that with Sweden was, while the others
are in Europe and might be Engaged in the Business much to our
Advantage without any Additional Expense? For my own part
I freely own I shall be sorry to see the Extensive Management of
these great matters in the hands of a Single Man which if not
grown feeble by age may have become suspicious from worse
excesses.[7] Penobscot is Evacuated. After desireing our Government to send a Commission to receive the delivery of the place

and waiting in vain for some Months they went of *san Cérémonie* after Burning the Barricades and some of the Houses. I think they did right, for why should they leave them standing if we cared Nothing about them? We have had what we call a tight Winter and been continually tortured with Cold. I hope you have Enjoyed the sweet Temperature of a Southern Climate. My Compliments to my Friends Major Osgood and Mr. Partridge and also to Doctor Lee. I will write him soon. In the meantime am not Inattentive to his Business without being able to get it Effected. there seems to be some fatality or strange Inattention in the Conduct of it. Mrs. Warren desires her Compliments to you. I am with great Sincerity Your Friend and Humbl Servt

J. Warren.

I had forgot to tell you that by some Inadvertency in Mr. Thaxter I have never recd the strictures you mention.[8] I have however seen one and have the pleasure to tell you they have a good Effect here. People are Justly Alarmed at the Cunning deep laid plan. It is a subject of general Conversation and Execration without a Single Exception, where neither Interest or Expectation are Engaged. I think it must be given up or reduced to a Simple Benificent Standard.

Copy, EG Papers, Massachusetts Historical Society; and Massachusetts Historical Society *Proceedings*, 59 (1925–26), 85–87.

1. See JW's letter of December 17, 1783.
2. When James Sullivan resigned, the General Court unanimously selected Francis Dana to replace him; see *W-A Ltrs.*, 2:236.
3. Adjournment did not come until June 3rd; Dana took his seat in Congress on May 24.
4. This letter by EG has not been located.
5. Winslow Warren did go to Lisbon but his departure did not take place until June.
6. Far from fact, this is wishful thinking on JW's part.
7. The reference is to Benjamin Franklin.
8. The strictures probably were in regard to the Society of the Cincinnati.

§

EG continued to face foreign and domestic questions in Annapolis. He unsuccessfully agitated for congressional access to the papers of the office of foreign affairs; and he successfully moved for higher salaries for our ministers abroad and he it was who nominated John Jay to fill the vacant post of secretary for foreign affairs.

On the domestic front, Indian affairs, the grand committee charged with revision of the treasury department, frontier posts, the inadequate number of delegates attending Congress, the site of the federal town, and western lands competed for EG's attention. In addition, he supported Timothy Pickering for the post of Secretary of War and favored the abolition of the Society of the Cincinnati.[1]

"You want to know how I like Annapolis," he wrote Samuel Holten in mid-spring, "It is of all Places the best for transacting publick Business."[2] During the summer adjournment, Dana represented Massachusetts on the Committee of the States and EG departed Annapolis for Massachusetts.

In that state, JW, surveying the state, national, and international scenes as well as his acreage at Milton, entertained doubts and fears, even though much of his pessimism of late war years had diminished. Of the General Court of Massachusetts he wrote, in late February, "I hear of nothing very important being done." Since Abigail Adams' departure to join her husband in France, twice as many Adamses supplied the Warrens with foreign intelligence. Meanwhile another calamity was settling upon the Warren household. Twenty-two-year-old Charles had returned home from Harvard with tuberculosis.[3]

1. *JCC*, 26:104–8, 122–55 *passim*, 172, 180n, 201, 212, 221–25, 245, 269–71, 317–19, 324–31, 339–40, 353–56 and 27:365, 376, 444–45, 477; T. Pickering to EG, Philadelphia, February 20, 1784, EG Collection of Elsie O. and Philip D. Sang, on deposit at Southern Illinois University Library, Carbondale; and *LCC*, 7:455–56, 522.
2. *Ibid.*, 498.
3. *W-A Ltrs.*, 2:236–37, 240, 242–47; and Anthony, *First Lady*, 140.

James Warren to Elbridge Gerry

· ·

                                    Milton, November 23d, 1784

My dear Sir.

I this day received your favour of Yesterday,[1] Informing me of your Intention to set out for Congress on Thursday morning without makeing us a Visit ⟨to⟩ at Milton. We all sincerely regret the last Circumstance but must Join with the Good and the Sensible in rejoicing on occasion of the first. I am fully Convinced of the Absolute necessity of your presence there. I hope to hear from you often, and that every thing will succeed to your wishes.

I presume so much on your Friendship, as to make no Apology for the Trouble I give you by Incloseing a Memorial to Congress,[2] and a State[ment?] of the Account it refers to, and in my next will venture to forward to you a State[ment?] of my Son's Affairs, for Wages &c.[3] I will say Nothing about my other Son,[4] but that I presume he would prefer Lisbon if the Appointment for that place is among the first. Otherwise he will go to France, Holland, or Spain. He loves France but I am Jealous least some kind of Subordination may take place there. Sweden is Cold and disagreable. I have lately received Letters from him. He desires his respectful Compliments to you. [*He*] did not write because he supposed you was at Congress. Mrs. Warren Joins me in every Wish for your Health and Happiness. I am sincerely Yours

J. Warren

E. Gerry Esqr.[5]

ALS, EG Collection of Elsie O. and Philip D. Sang, on deposit at Southern Illinois University Library, Carbondale; and photographic copy EG Papers, Library of Congress.

1. This letter by EG has not been located.
2. JW's memorial, dated Boston November 23, 1784, sought "an allowance of depreciation" on an account with the Commercial Committee in the years 1777 and 1778; see *JCC*, 28:35.
3. Lieutenant of Marines James Warren, Jr.
4. Winslow Warren, then in Europe.
5. This letter is docketed "ansd Decr 7th." That reply by EG has not been located. The docketing also suggests that MW had written to EG on December 1st another letter which has not been located.

§

EG had spent the summer and autumn recess of Congress in Massachusetts, dividing his time between Marblehead and Boston. Although reelected to Congress for the ensuing year, EG was initially uncertain about serving. On October 25, he wrote the Massachusetts authorities, "the situation of my private concerns prevents me at present from leaving the state and renders it necessary to request that my place be supplied by a new appointment." The state refused to accept the proferred resignation.[1]

Congress lacked a quorum until November 30, by which time EG, having succumbed to his desire to serve, was en route to Trenton, the seventh site for Congress. EG had served in all of them. The short interval before the December 24 adjournment paved the way for yet another shift of scene, this time to New York City.[2] In foreign affairs, meanwhile, EG helped to draw up instructions for our minister to Spain.

JW and wife were at Milton those closing weeks of 1784. Crippled James was with them but tubercular Charles had shipped to Hispaniola to avoid the rigors of the New England winter.[3]

1. Austin, *EG*, 1:438–40, 447–49, 460, 463, 467.
2. George Partridge to EG, Trenton, November 24, 1784, EG Collection of Elsie O. and Philip D. Sang, on deposit at Southern Illinois University Library, Carbondale; and *JCC*, 27:649, 661–710 *passim*.
3. Anthony, *First Lady*, 141.

Elbridge Gerry to James Warren

·   ·

Trenton, December 23, 1784.

My dear Sir,

It is fortunate that we arrived here as we did, for otherwise congress would by this time have been in Philadelphia and the treasury in such hands as you and I could not approve.

There was a stronger party formed against us than I remember to have seen, but I think it will subside and matters be in a good train again. We have carried two great points to-day by passing an ordinance, 1st. to appoint three commissioners to lay out a district on the branch of either side of the Delaware, within eight miles of this place, to purchase the soil and enter into contracts for erecting suitable buildings.

2dly. To adjourn to New-York and reside there until suitable buildings are prepared. This I consider a fortunate affair in every respect but one. It is so disagreeable to our worthy secretary that there is reason to apprehend he will resign his appointment.[1]

We have been so happy also as to remove some objections on the part of Mr. Jay to the acceptance of his office, and he yesterday took the oaths and entered on the business of his department. A report is now before congress for arranging the war office, and I think general Knox will be appointed secretary of War.[2] Be assured I am on every occasion, Your's sincerely,

E. Gerry.

Austin, *EG*, 1:469–70.

1. Charles Thomson (1729–1824) served as secretary to Congress until 1789.
2. Henry Knox (1750–1806), a florid 300-pounder often given to profanity, had fought in the Revolution from Bunker Hill to Yorktown. In 1785 he did become Secretary of War.

§

Congress reconvened on January 11 in New York, the city in which the future Mrs. Gerry resided. Although the journal does not mention him until the thirteenth, there is reason to believe EG was on hand when the session opened. At that time the Massachusetts delegation counted, in New York, Samuel Holten, Rufus King (1755–1827), George Partridge, and EG.[1]

1. *JCC*, 28:1, 3; and *LCC*, 8:lxxxvii–lxxxviii.

James Warren to Elbridge Gerry

· ·

Milton, January 11th, 1785

My dear Sir.

I Yesterday received yours of the 23d Ultimo. I always thought your going to Congress at this Time Important; and the Events have fully Justified the Sentiment and shewn that it was fortunate to the Country. It was Indeed a Crisis, and I am Exceedingly pleased with the Conduct of Congress so far. The points gained are great, and I hope ⟨by⟩ from the present Appearances, that others will follow equally agreable.

I do not recollect that any thing worthy your Notice has taken place here since you left us. The Scarcity of of Money ⟨which has taken place⟩ in Consequence of our excessive and extravagant Importations of British frippery has occassioned Stagnation of Trade, stopping discounts at the Bank, and other Embarrassments, and Confusions. This Country seems to be ⟨verging to⟩ in danger of ruin, which Nothing can prevent but a reformation of Manners, and an Establishment of frugality, in the room of that general profusion which has prevailed. But when and how that is to be Effected is a question difficult to be decided. The Coin is gone, and no Staples yet Established to restore it, and yet the Infatuation subsists. I don't see but that we must look to Necessity for those Effects, which every good Man might wish should be the Consequences of Virtue and Reason, ⟨and⟩ rather than fatal Experience.

⟨When you was here, I forgot to Enquire into the origin and reason of the policy, of reducing the Salaries of our Ministers Abroad. Was it right? I Inclose you a Certificate which may Enable you to recover my Son's half pay.[1] If any thing further be necessary, the Attempt in this way will discover it, and in that Case you will preserve the Certificate. I know your Goodness will Excuse the Trouble I give you, on so many occasions. Will any Consuls be Appointed soon?[2] And how long shall you remain at Congress?[3] Mrs. Warren desires her Compliments to Mr. Gerry. You will give mine to all Friends, and⟩ Accept the sincerest professions of Friendship from Your

J. Warren

E. Gerry Esqr.

ALS, Gerry II Papers, Massachusetts Historical Society; and Austin, *EG*, 1:470–71.

1. There is no record of congressional action relative to James Warren, Jr. in 1785, but, on March 11 of that year, Massachusetts took the following action: "on the representation of John Lucas, Commissary of Continental Pensioners, in behalf of

James Warren, jun., Lieutenant of Marines, who lost one of his legs by a wound he received in an engagement on board the "Alliance," Frigate: Resolved, That the said James Warren, jun., be allowed one half his pay as Lieutenant of Marines, from the first day of November, 1781, being the time of his discharge." See Mass., *A&R 1784–85*, 384.

2. This question could not be answered at this time. As early as January 17, 1785, EG was named to a committee "to revise the plan of a Convention for regulating the powers and privileges of consuls, vice consuls and agents," and as late as August 9 he was moving "That the Secretary for foreign affairs, report the number of Consuls and Vice Consuls necessary to be appointed by Congress, and the foreign ports in which they should respectively reside," which report was not forthcoming from Jay until September 20. See *JCC*, 28:7 and 29:621, 722–24.

3. In 1785, EG attended Congress from January 13 to March 1 and from July 12 to November 4.

§

In New York EG drew his share of assignments, among them continuing service on the committee concerned with the general regulation of trade by the United States. He it was who moved that the records of the Postmaster General, the Secretary of War, and of the Treasury be moved to New York on or before March 21.[1]

JW, meanwhile, continued to survey the world from his Milton Hill acreage. He was more favorably inclined toward the trend of national affairs, especially since Robert Morris, whom he considered a near king and a corrupting influence, was no longer Superintendent of Finance. Affairs in Massachusetts, however, he continued to view dimly. "In this place," he told the absent John Adams, "the System of Politics remains much as it has been; the same Imbecility, the same servility and the same Inattention still prevail and are likely to continue." Twenty-four hours later he might have expressed himself differently, thanks to the resignation of his *bête noir* John Hancock.[2]

1. *JCC*, 28:3–25 *passim*; and James Milligan to EG, Philadelphia, January 18, 1785, EG Collection of Elsie O. and Philip D. Sang, on deposit at Southern Illinois University Library, Carbondale.

2. *W-A Ltrs.*, 2:248–49.

James Warren to Elbridge Gerry

· ·

Milton, January 31st, 1785.

My Dear Sir,

It is now a long time since I have had the pleasure of a line from you. I want to know how you go on at New York, and whether it is a place agreable to you for the residence of Congress. I shall Certainly Consider it as a Misfortune to me, if your Letters should diminish in proportion to your Approach. I have scarcely heard any thing since you have made a Congress, and don't know what are the great National Objects that Occupy your present Attention. You began very well at Trenton, and I hope no Obstacles will Interrupt your Career at New York.

Every thing here has gone on in the Usual way till last Saturday, when a great political Phenomon made its Unexpected Appearance. Our first Magistrat made his resignation in form.[1] This I am well Informed is the Fact. I am not Philospher enough to Account for this strange Event, whether the *Gas* that has so long supported this political Balloon is Expended, or whatever other Cause has produced this singular Event, must be left to the Sagas of the airy regions of Caprice and Vanity to determine. For my part, I am satisfied with a Conviction that no Change can be for the worse. The last post Conveyed to you a letter from my Son.[2] I don't know the Contents but by his Letters to me, he wishes for the Appointment, and thinks it will be very Important to him. He seems to have fixed his residence at Lisbon, and to have formed his Expectations for that place. I have always thought the preference should be given to that place, but Circumstances which neither he nor I Can Judge of, must determine that matter, and we both are convinced it cannot be in more judicious, or friendly hands. My next shall be longer, at present can only add, after Mrs. Warren's Compliments that I am Your Assured and Sincere Friend

J. Warren

Honourable E. Gerry Esqr.[3]

ALS, EG Collection of Elsie O. and Philip D. Sang, on deposit at Southern Illinois University Library, Carbondale; and photographic copy, EG Papers, Library of Congress.

1. Governor John Hancock submitted his resignation from that post on January 29, impelled in part by an unusually painful attack of the gout. See Allan, *John Hancock*, 315.
2. Winslow Warren.
3. This letter is docketed "ansd 12th Feby 1785." That reply by EG has not been located.

§

EG served on the committee that recommended an *ad valorem* duty on goods brought into the United States after having originally been imported into Canada. In an effort to determine the size of the national debt and to provide for its discharge, EG moved that all persons having unliquidated claims against the United States be required to present them within twelve months, and that twelve months be allowed the commissioners in the various states to adjust accounts. In like fashion his desire to reduce the size of the standing army and his service on the committee concerned with reimbursing George Clinton for advances made in 1776 and 1777 identified him with economy and fiscal responsibility. He faced yet another fiscal issue in his service on the committee charged with settling accounts of expenses borne by Virginia in the occupation and defense of the western territory ceded by that state to the nation.

The western lands drew added attention from him while serving on the committee to consider "the best means to obtain possession of the Western and Northern Territory of these States and of the posts that it may be necessary to establish therein." The Post Office Department, loan officers, the appointment of a commissioner for the erection of federal buildings, the continued agitation that accompanied the Massachusetts claim to land held by New York, and the selection of John Adams as Minister to Great Britain helped make this a busy season for EG in New York.

Another old friend also counted on EG for an assist. When JW's memorial of November 23, 1784, referred to the Board of Treasury with an authorization calling for revision of his account, failed to receive prompt attention, EG authored a resolution concerning the matter.[1]

1. *JCC*, 28:23, 28–31, 35, 54, 59, 85, 88–89, 93–94, 98, 102, 105–110, 113, 117–18.

James Warren to Elbridge Gerry

· ·

Milton, March 13th, 1785

My dear Sir,

I have received your favours of the 12th and 21st Ultimo[1] and am much Obliged for your Attention to my Affairs. You do not mention what the Report of the Committee on my Memorial was, and why it was necessary to refer it to the Board of Treasury. If the depreciation was right Cast it seems to be so simple a demand on the Justice of Congress as to require but little hesitation. However if a further reference was necessary I think you have placed it in the most preferable Hands, and Can't doubt the Success, if their report should be made while you are in Congress. If you should return first, the Success may be more doubtful, Certainly longer delayed. When the Board of Treasury will meet, Can't be foretold here. Mr. Osgood tells me he will not Accept under the present regulations. He was going on when he was Informed, that ⟨now⟩ he was required to give Bonds, and in such a way too, as would make him responsible for the doings of others. I do not Understand enough of the matter to Judge of the propriety of giveing Bonds at all. It should seem to me the Nature of the Establishment did not require any, and Certainly it is enough for a Man to answer for his own Sins. If it is a political Maneuvre to get rid of the Measure it may be Cunning but not Wonderful. His difficulty is why you did not Inform him of it. I am glad the residence of Congress is so Agreable to you. The Appointment of a Minister to the Court of Britain is a New Measure, and if necessary I think your whole Arrangement is Judicious. If I was a Member of Congress I should Nominate Mr. Gerry for the Court of Spain. As I am not I will hope that some Body else will.

The Matters you mention now before Congress are Important, require great Judgment, and some of them must be touched with a delicate hand. The Appointments of Consuls Appears to me quite necessary, and that it has been delayed long enough where there are Commercial Treaties. Nor do I see the Impropriety of doing it to places where we have a great and Constant Trade even if no Treaty is made. I can't doubt that a Consul would be received in some of them, and perhaps such a Circumstance might facilitate a Treaty, ⟨but wh⟩ and the doing it would take but little Time, and Consequently Cause but little Interruption to other Matters. But why are these Treaties delayed? It is a long Time since Mr. Jefferson met his Colleagues, and yet we don't hear of one ⟨made⟩; is every other to give place to that with Britain; and to depend on the Malicious Caprice, and delay of that Nation; or are there other Obstacles that do not reach the Comprehension of ordinary men?

The Great and most general ⟨sp⟩ political Speculation and Enquiry here is on who is to be our next first magistrate. All the Efforts and Influence of the late Governor are in favour of Cushing, and some People think he will Effect it. His policy is to keep the place open to himself whenever he shall Choose to re-sume the Chair, and at the same Time to Gratify his resentment against Others in Nomination, all of whom are obnoxious to him. Mr. Bowdoin, General Lincoln, Mr. Dalton and some few have Named another Friend of yours,[2] which has brought on me a Most wanton abuse in the Papers, and certainly Unprovoked be-cause I never Named Myself for that or any other post. Time must satisfy the prevailing Curiosity. It is probable no one will be Chose by the People, and it is said Mr. H[ancock] intends to be a Member for Boston, and will by that means have it in his power to Influence the Election in the Assembly. The Caucussing part of the Town Talk of Mr. Bowdoin and Mr. Samuel Adams for Governor and Lieutenant Governor. It would be Laughable if Mr. C[ushing] Aspireing to the first, should oust himself of both places, and if Ambition should produce the same Beneficial Event, that the great Principle of a Rotation should do.[3]

It is reported here that all the States have come into the Measure of a General Impost, and put an End to any further questions on that subject. I wish it may End better than my

Fears. Our House had a Bill before them brought in by Mr. Bacon,[4] to lay a duty of 25 per cent on all Articles Imported from those states that had not acceded to the Measure. Moderate Men would have thought this a Violent measure, and Judicious ones might suppose it would produce violent Effects, if the Union was Composed of frangible Materials. I am with great Esteem Yours Sincerely

J. Warren

My Compliments to Doctor Holton and Mr. King. Mr. Partridge I suppose is on his return.[5]

Mrs. Warren desires her Compliments to you, and Commits to you the Care of the Inclosed Letter supposeing any Negotiation with a Lady of Character Cannot be disagreable to Mr. Gerry.

E. Gerry Esqr.

ALS, Russell W. Knight—Gerry collection, Massachusetts Historical Society.

1. These letters by EG have not been located.
2. JW's modest reference to himself.
3. The victors were James Bowdoin, governor, and Thomas Cushing, lieutenant governor.
4. John Bacon of Stockbridge.
5. In 1785, George Partridge attended Congress from January 11 to February 28.

§

From early March to early July, EG absented himself from the seat of Congress, drawn to Massachusetts by private business and the feeling that the affairs of Congress were routine rather than critical. In Boston, on March 4, he reported to the legislature concerning the foreign and domestic issues before the Congress at the time of his departure. Letters to Rufus King, for whom EG had developed considerable affection and respect in a short time, informed that delegate of the state of affairs in Massachusetts. In return, King regularly reported the problems and prospects in Congress to EG.[1]

Ailing Charles Warren, returned from his winter in the Caribbean, looked stronger and healthier to many that spring. His brother James hopefully anticipated the half-pay allowance for which he had applied. Their father, occupied with the seasonal labors of the farmer, was chided by letter by John Adams. "When shall I have the Pleasure to hear of my Friend Warren in public?" Before the same month, May, had passed, JW had lost a contest for the governorship to James Bowdoin. Of their common friend, Adams wrote, "I promise myself from Mr. Gerry's Attendance in Congress all those changes for the better in the Management of the general Affairs of the Union, which I have often seen proceed from the Clearness of his Head and the goodness of his heart. I know of scarcely any Man of more Address, more Industry or Perseverance. He never appeared in Congress without a great Influence."[2]

EG was back in New York, attending Congress, as the heat of July set in. He urged a revision of the regulations of the treasury department "without delay;" and in order to "derive the advantages which may result from the joint wisdom of the whole," he moved that the Secretary of Congress apply to the executives of the several states for copies of their legislative acts since September 1774. Among the domestic issues to which he gave close attention was the charge "to enquire fully into the proceedings of the department of war." In the foreign arena EG was intimately concerned with United States-Spanish relations in particular and our consular activities in general.[3]

At a time when the United States was striving to attain dignity at home and abroad, EG was especially solicitous of the Congress. Shortly after moving "That good carpets, mohogany arm chairs and tables be provided for the hall of Congress," along with a daily supply of writing materials, his motion, "That each Member of Congress shall take Rank of every officer of the U. States," promoted the creation of yet another committee on which he was called to serve.[4]

1. EG to R. King, variously from Boston and Marblehead, March 14 and 18, April 3, May 9 and 30, and June 16, EG Papers, Library of Congress; *LCC,* 8:71–72, 78–80, 87, 98–99, 104, 107–9, 113–14, 121, 123–24; Charles R. King (ed.), *The Life and Correspondence of Rufus King* . . . . (6 vols., New York, 1894), 1:73–109 *passim*; and Austin, *EG,* 1:492–95.
2. *W-A Ltrs.,* 2:256.
3. *JCC,* 29:520, 525, 559–64, 582–83, 619, 621.
4. *Ibid.,* 625, 649.

James Warren to Elbridge Gerry

.   .

Milton, August 31st, 1785

My dear Sir

I received your favour of the 8th Instant.[1] It is true that I *could* not Visit my Friend while at Marblehead, and was so *Unhappy* as to be gone from Home when he was so kind as to Visit me at Milton. If polite pursuits, dissipation or pleasure had been the Object, I should not have regretted the Event as a misfortune, or Expressed any surprise on the occasion. A Man that has taste, and Understanding enough to relish, and wish for the Acquaintance of my Friend Gerry must have Nobler Objects in Veiw. He should be polite, and if he dissipates, it should be in mental Enjoyments, and his pleasures those which ⟨f⟩ are derived from reason, Virtue, and social Conversation.

When I Condemned the policy of our State I did not mean that which relates to Britain. No retaliation can be too severe with regard to them. But why should we involve other Nations, who have treated us with Commercial Liberalities in the Consequences of our resentment to them, or why should we be guilty of the great Absurdity of Taxing the Necessaries of Life with more severity than those of the Extreemest and most Contemptible Luxury, Nails for Instance higher than feathers for Girls' Caps &c &c. I am Convinced of the necessity of placing the regulation of Commerce under a Single direction, and that the direction should of Course be in Congress. All my difficulty is to Guard this disposal. If they have it in their power to Lay duties for the purpose of a revenue and have the disposition of those Revenues, what security have we for our Liberties? Experience shews the futility of annual Elections in all Instances that have occurred. Even H[ancock] before his Capricious and silly resignation had it in his power, especially if United in the same Veiw with the C[ushin]g Family formidable by their Multiplied places of great Honour and Emoluments[2] to overturn this Constitution when he pleased. And no Goverment, or at least the public security of no People should depend on the Virtue of any Man, or set of Men. But is there no such thing as separateing the regulation of Trade from the raising a Revenue? I beleive there is Wisdom enough in Congress to do this even if duties are necessary Appendages to it, more especially under our peculiar Circumstances. You know I am an Enemy to all Imposts, Excises &c and I have a Sentiment perhaps peculiar to myself that if those Measures had not been adopted by the European Nations they would neither have been in Debt or Inslaved, and England might at this Time have preserved her Controul over America, without any Impediment from a Debt of [£]280,000,000 on her Shoulders. You ask me what I think of the policy of the Legislature in proposeing a Convention &c. I answer at once I think it ill Judged and very dangerous. I am glad you have Conducted with more Judgment and Wisdom.

With regard to the situation of my Commercial Negotiations ⟨they⟩ it is indeed *peculiar*. Mr. Osgood has promised to forward me such an account from the Treasury Books as you recommend.[3] I wait with Impatience for it, and flatter myself when I see it, I shall be able to Clear up all the difficulties. I Certainly must be Charged with goods I never received, or not Credited for what I have delivered. We have nothing New. Will you make my Compliments to Mr. Holton and Mr. King—and beleive me to be Yours Sincerely[4]

J. Warren

Honourable E: Gerry Esqr.

ALS, EG Collection of Elsie O. and Philip D. Sang, on deposit at Southern Illinois University Library, Carbondale; and photographic copy, EG Papers, Library of Congress.

1. This letter by EG has not been located.

2. In the period of Hancock's governorship in the early 1780's, Thomas Cushing had served continuously as lieutenant governor of Massachusetts.

3. Samuel Osgood, after serving in the Congress between 1780 and 1784, was elected one of the three Commissioners of the Treasury on January 25, 1785.

4. This letter is docketed "ansd Sept. 7, 1785." EG's reply has not been located.

§

It was not, the Massachusetts delegation concluded, the opportune moment to press for fundamental revision of the Articles of Confederation. In mid-September, EG was immersed in the tangled affairs of the continental loan offices.[1] Some of his absences from session might then have been related to the social life which was destined to wed him to a belle of Manhattan in the near future.

Meanwhile, for Mercy and JW, it was a season of waiting—for letters from Lisbon-based Winslow, for the adjustment of crippled James Jr. to teaching duties at Hingham, for declining health and approaching chill to dictate foreign travel again for tubercular Charles, and for Mercy's own return to health.

1. *LCC*, 8:206–12; and *JCC*, 29:674, 678, 695–720 *passim*.

James Warren to Elbridge Gerry

• •

Milton, September 18th, 1785

My dear Sir

I have had the pleasure of receiving yours of the 7th Instant.[1] You may be assured that I should be perfectly satisfied with possessing the power of describeing the qualifycations and Virtues of my worthy Friend, without Attempting that of any Addition to them. He will I hope at the same time permit me to admire the Ingenuity and delicacy of his strain of Compliments without making a fruitless Effort to Imitate ⟨th⟩it.

I am glad to see the French and Dutch Ministers are attempting to rectify the Measures taken by this State which are Injurious both to their Nations and to ourselves.[2] This may probably, at least in Conjunction with their own more mature Reflections produce some Amendments. I will Call on the Governor,[3] and see if I can [. . .] your Letter when Opportunity presents. He is now gone to Princetown. It might be happy for him if he should receive the Letter there, and derive some of the sage reflections of an old, and wise Counsellor on the subject.

Major Osgood has handed me a Transcrip ⟨of⟩ of my Account in the Treasury Books with regard to Goods received and delivered, which has greatly releived my Mind. It must appear at first Veiw that there is at least £1000 sterling in my favour. However all I wish is to have it Ballanced as it ought to have been Years ago. I think it can no longer operate as an Obsticle to their reporting favourably on my Memorial referred to them. I have stated the whole matter to him on Paper, which I wish you to see.

My Curiosity with regard to the Audience is Excited, and I hope will be gratified in proper Time. We have not a word of News. Will you make my Compliments to Mr. Holton, Mr. King and Doctor Lee. Mrs. Warren desires her Compliments to Mr. Gerry will thank him if he will Enquire of Mr. King if he received a Letter from her Incloseing one to Mrs. Montgomery.[4] I am Sincerely Your Friend &c

J. Warren

Honourable E. Gerry Esqr.[5]

ALS, Gerry II Papers, Massachusetts Historical Society.

1. This letter has not been located.
2. The reference is to the practice whereby the several states levied their own individual duties; see *JCC*, 29:202–5, 863 in regard to the Netherlands.
3. James Bowdoin had been elected governor late in May.
4. Apparently the reference is to Janet Livingston Montgomery, daughter of Robert R. Livingston and widow of General Richard Montgomery, a casualty of the Battle of Quebec. On November 30, 1785 the long-awaited arrival of a monument of Montgomery was announced in Congress; see *JCC*, 29:895.
5. This letter is docketed "ansd 27th." That letter by EG has not been located.

§

Even as he opposed successive amendments to the requisition for 1785, EG, conscious of the dignity of the government and of the signal services of certain men during the Revolution, entertained and advocated expenditures that many found unpalatable. His effort to raise the appropriation for federal buildings from $30,000 to $100,000 was rebuffed; and his willingness to authorize the payment of $15,000 to Baron von Steuben and $7,000 to Thomas Paine also suffered defeat.

Foreign affairs found EG concerned with the prospects attending a commercial treaty with Great Britain; and Jay's report indicated that a consul general for Portugal and Madeira, to whom the anticipated trade in the Mediterranean area would also be assigned, would be appointed to reside in Lisbon. The significance of such a post precluded the possibility of Winslow Warren's being named to fill it.

As November 4 and the end of EG's term approached, and a changed outlook in the Massachusetts delegation loomed on the horizon, the man from Marblehead redoubled his efforts to block the Society of the Cincinnati.[1]

1. Samuel Adams to EG, Boston, September 19, 1785, EG Papers, Library of Congress; *LCC*, 8:224; and *JCC*, 29:722–24, 734, 737–42, 771–75, 796.

James Warren to Elbridge Gerry

.   .

Milton, October 4th, 1785

My Dear Sir,

The Time approaches when you must leave Congress,[1] however Contrary it may be to the Interest and wishes of your Constituents. When your Successors arrive at Congress, especially if H[ancock] is one of them, and more especially if he obtains the presidency, there will probably be an End of Winslow's Expectations.[2] It always appeared to me a singular Resolution, that no Consuls should be appointed where there were no Commercial Treaties; and if it can be supported as a good general Rule, it should like other general rules be subject to some Exceptions, and Consuls appointed where the Trade was large, and the National disposition favourable. This is now the Case of Portugal, and besides we can hear of no kind of Obstacle to a Treaty, and yet none is made. It is a matter of Speculation here, why in the Course of more than 12 Months since Mr. Jefferson's Arrival, not one such Treaty has been made, especially when every Body is willing. Mr. Adams is gone to Britain. Mr. Jefferson remains at the Court of France. Dr. Franklin is returned to America.[3] Who is now to compleat this great Business, is another question that I am not able to answer, and if it is never done, are no Consuls to be appointed? Winslow would be much obliged by a Line from you, and I dare say frequent Opportunities present from New York. Mr. Low corresponds with him, and will forward it without any trouble to you. I have not a word of News, not even Tittle Tattle to give you. H[ancock] has got the Gout; whether it is a political, or natural fit, I don't know. If the former, he may have some reason to despair of the Presidency, and may wrap up in Baze, as a preparatory to a resignation when the Court meets. If every Body loved him as I do, they would save him that trouble, and excuse without the Expence of a single peice of Baze. I suppose by this Time Mr. Temple[4] may be with you. He is now decidedly the Servant of the British King, and should be allowed to pursue his Interest. I hope prudence will direct him to pursue it smoothly and softly, without any disagreable Altercations with Congress, or any of the United States, or with any foreign Consuls or Ministers. So shall his days be long in the Land of his Nativity. Will you make my regards to your two Brethren, to your President[5] and to my Friend Doctor Lee, and beleive me to be Yours sincerely,

J. Warren

I think a very singular Character is sent here to settle the marine Accounts. He is dark, reserved, disgusts every Body, affronts or ill treats all, is abused in return, and bears it as a dull Horse does a whip. His whole Time seems to be spent in finding, or makeing difficulties where there are none, and his motive, if I can trace it, is to continue in office. You may rely on it he will not finish this Business this six Years to come in the way he is in, and a Man of Abilities well disposed might do it in 3 Months. I suspect by way of Apology for himse[lf] he will represent our Accounts as irregular and Incompleat; but I can shew they are as much to the Contrary as the nature of things could admit off.

W-A Ltrs., 2:264–66.

1. EG's term expired on the first Monday of November 1785 and, thanks to Article V of the Articles of Confederation, he was ineligible for reelection to Congress.

2. Winslow's expectations were dashed before EG was replaced in the Massachusetts delegation to Congress. Hancock had been elected for the year beginning with the first Monday in November 1785 but uncertainty attended his filling the post. On November 23, 1785, despite his absence, Hancock was elected President of the Congress. See *JCC*, 29:876, 883, and *LCC*, 8:259.

3. Jefferson remained in France as United States minister until 1789; and Adams continued as the American minister to the Court of St. James until 1788. Meanwhile Franklin, becoming involved in politics at the state level, assumed the governorship of Pennsylvania in 1785.

4. Sir John Temple had been appointed British Consul General to the United States. Questions related to his reception by the American authorities arose after EG's departure from Congress; see *JCC*, 29:886–87, 894.

5. The "Brethren" were EG's colleagues from Massachusetts, Samuel Holten and Rufus King; the "President" was Richard Henry Lee of Virginia, then president of the Congress.

§

For no member of his family—himself, his sons or anyone else—did JW ever make the kind of effort he now dedicated to Winslow's desire to win the consular post at Lisbon. A flurry of letters went off from Milton Hill in the direction of New York, Paris, and London. Believing that Jefferson would control the Lisbon appointment, JW wrote John Adams, soliciting his help in that quarter. He added, "if Winslow succeeds it will be the only reward to and the only place at present held or expected by any of the family."[1]

Meanwhile, even as ailing Charles boarded ship en route to reunion with Winslow in Lisbon, Winslow, far from abreast of developments beyond the Atlantic and weary of that Portuguese city, had packed for his return to Massachusetts.

1. *W-A Ltrs.*, 2:266, 267.

James Warren to Elbridge Gerry

·   ·

Milton, October 9th, 1785
My Dear Sir,
    Since my last which went by the Monday's Post, I am honoured by your Friendly and polite favour of the 27th Ultimo[1] by

which I learn that Congress are in a way to adopt a Mode for the Appointment of Consuls. Whether the Mode be so consistent with propriety, or dignity, as a direct one by themselves, is a subject out of the reach of a Plebean, occupied in the manureing and culture of the Field, but I think a Ploughmam may discern that it is better than none, and therefore I hope it will succeed. I have taken your advice and wrote to Mr. Jefferson,[2] and have engaged some of my Friends here to do it. I request my Friend Gerry to interest himself in the same way; he is always the first on my List. My Opinion of his Abilities and Generosity have placed him there, and if that Situation gives him much Trouble, it at the same time gives me much confidence and pleasure. If the President, and any other Gentleman of Congress, will write in Winslow's favour, they would oblige me. I asked the favour of the G[overnor],[3] the only favour I ever did, or will ask of one. He replied that he wished it to succeed, but that he had never corresponded. I dare say this is all true, but yet it was a strange Answer from a Man whose rank Intitled him to write to any Body, but it is characteristic. How much is a Man's Friendship to be Coveted, or his Enmity dreaded, who does not feel that Ardent Animating Glow, unrestrained by Timid Cautious Moderation, which will force him, as it were Mechanically to stretch out his Arm to serve a Friend, or blast an Enemy.

I think the Exchange you mention, will be a good one, but I am intirely in your sentiment with regard to the residence of foreign Ministers here. The Addresses you mention, and the Anecdotes are Curiosities I wish to see. My Compliments to all my Friends. I am Yours most Assuredly,

J. Warren

W-A Ltrs., 2:267–68.

1. EG's letter of September 27, 1785 has not been located.
2. The letter to Jefferson was written this very day; see Julian P. Boyd (ed.), *The Papers of Thomas Jefferson*, 8:599–600.
3. James Bowdoin.

James Warren to Elbridge Gerry

. .

Milton, October 16th, 1785

My dear Sir,

It is necessary that I should retract or apoligize for one paragraph in my last Letter. Whether it proceeds from the Solemnity of the day, or whatever other Cause operates, I feel some Inclination to do it by way of a Sermon regularly and Mechanically Composed. My Text should be taken from Mathew 21st Chapter and the 29th Verse, "He answered and said I will not, but afterward he repented and went." This was the Conduct of the first Son stated in this Parable, that of the other was directly the reverse. In those days of Simplicity the question that followed, which of the Twain did the will of his Father, seems to ⟨have easily⟩ have been easily decided in favour of the first without a Metaphysical discussion. In our more polished days, in and on the Courtly principles of Modern politeness it would be determined in favour of the last. As I am neither a Courtier or a polite Man you will suppose I am satisfied with the original Answer. If I had the Vanity of most young Preachers, to suppose it possible that I could Edify my Auditory I might proceed and arrange my discourse into Doctrines, divisions, subdivisions, and applications, if the last as it properly might be refered to myself. But as it is I will stop short, and tell you a fact to which all the rest may serve as an Introduction. The Governor has sent me a very polite Letter to Mr. Jefferson, Expressed in the friendly, and Nervous Terms which are Congenial to my own feelings.[1] Your return is so soon Expected that I shall make a short Letter of this and refer every thing else to a long Conversation which I shall Expect with pleasure on Milton Hill. I am with Compliments to our Friends Yours sincerely

J. Warren

E: Gerry Esqr.

ALS, Russell W. Knight—Gerry collection, Massachusetts Historical Society.

1. Bowdoin's letter to Jefferson, dated October 10, 1785, includes this paragraph: "A friend of yours in this neighbourhood, and a distinguished one in the American Cause, General Warren of Milton, has a Son at Lisbon, Mr. Winslow Warren, whom I take the liberty of recommending to your friendship." See Boyd (ed.), *The Papers of Thomas Jefferson*, 8:601.

§

In October, 1785, EG was attentive, in foreign affairs, to Jay's report concerning consular representation. On the home front his awareness of the fiscal pinch led him to move that the states meet their quotas without delay. The first Monday of November closed out EG's service in the Congress.[1]

Instead of returning immediately to Massachusetts, to the seat in the legislature to which he had been elected, EG remained in New York City until mid-March 1786. There, on January 12, the forty-one-year-old bachelor from Marblehead married Ann, the beautiful and accomplished daughter of New York merchant James Thompson. When spring beckoned, EG took his bride north to Massachusetts. Disengaging himself from the business interests which had always been based in Marblehead, he established himself in the Boston area, thereby increasing his personal contacts with JW and reducing the volume of correspondence between them.

On June 17, 1786, EG was one of the quartet named to represent Massachusetts at Annapolis "for the purpose of considering the trade of the United States."[2] However, he insisted that the purpose of the Annapolis meeting was too narrow and refused to attend it. During the summer of 1786, EG purchased Elmwood, a 100-acre estate in Cambridge.[3]

Meanwhile misfortune continued her visits to the Warrens. Charles had died in San Lucar, Spain and Winslow had returned home from Lisbon, disappointed. In the spring of 1786 JW lamented the extreme scarcity of specie, insisting, "No Debts can be paid, or Taxes collected." His pessimism extended to politics with the words, "Our General Court sets often and long, do little and give no satisfaction to their Constituents."[4]

In the autumn of 1786, when 450 militiamen were required to protect the Supreme Court at Taunton from the enraged debtor-farmers led by Daniel Shays, JW insisted, "We are now in a State of Anarchy and Confusion bordering on a Civil War." Seven months later, he confided to John Adams, "the Town of Milton have honoured me with an Election to represent them. I feel myself embarrassed at a loss what Measures should be adopted in our present Situation." Shays' rebellion, more than anything else, had not only thrust JW back into the legislature but into the chair of Speaker once more.[5]

Meanwhile, in March 1787, Massachusetts elected EG and four others to represent the state at the convention called for Philadelphia to revise the Articles of Confederation. Early and late, in the course of demonstrating his customary political vigor, EG brought to the discussion of a new formula of national government views which combined the anti-democratic and the anti-tyrannical. Recent ills in Massachusetts he considered the result of an excess of democracy but, even as he opposed popular elections, he wanted, the better to avoid the prospect of tyranny, the annual election of the lower house of the national legislature and an enumeration of the powers of the national government.[6]

1. *JCC*, 29:823–24, 831, 845–46, 850–51, 855, 861.

2. Mass., *A&R 1786–87*, 296–97.

3. EG to Artemas Ward, Cambridge, September 26, 1786, EG Collection of Elsie O. and Philip D. Sang, on deposit at Southern Illinois University Library, Carbondale.

4. *W-A Ltrs.*, 2:272, 273.

5. *Ibid.*, 278, 279, 293; and Mass., *A&R 1786–87*, 664, 706, 784, 861.

6. EG to Ann Gerry, Philadelphia, May 10, 1787, EG Collection of Elsie O. and Philip D. Sang, on deposit at Southern Illinois University Library, Carbondale; *DFC*, liii–lv, 21, 32, 33, 59, 62, 71–72, 91, 221, 286, 323, 328, 330; and Mass., *A&R 1786–87*, 517.

Mercy Warren to Ann Gerry

· ·

Milton, July 28, 1787

[*Dear Madam*]

Had I attened to the dictates of my own heart—as well as to the rules of propriety and politness, I should certainly have wrote my friend Mrs. Gerry before this. But as I love neither appologies nor the necessity therefor I wave them at once, only exclaiming *procrastination*—not only thief but murderer of time.

I have seen Cambridge but once since you left it,[1] and then only rode through on my way to the retirement of my dear languishing and beloved Mrs. Russel.[2] I fear the slow Hectic is doing its fatal work, and that her useful life will close long before it reaches the meridian apportioned to the date of Man.

I know this is an interesting subject to you, therefore I shall dwell a little longer thereon; and tell you she appears at times so much better as to flatter many of her friends with new hope. But I must own I have never seen any simptom that appeared to me the promise of recovering health. Yet perhaps as I have painfully watched the the languide steps of one very dear to me[3] (who for two or three years trod the same path of patient suffering under complaints exactly similar to hers, and at last yealed in the bloom of youth to the relentless hand of Death) I may be too apprehensive—I hope I am. God grant I may be mistaken with regard to this amiable woman.

I am very glad you have had neither disappointment nor interruption in the pleasure you justly expected from your visit to New York. I wish it had been in my power to have met you there, but as Mr. Warren has at present no perticular call to that quarter I should not think of going there or any where else without such a Friend and Guard. Yet I should have been delighted to have made an excurssion to Philadelphia this season, not only from the novelty of the journey but from the pleasure resulting from an interview with many old acquaintance I might have met, and the many new characters I might have seen. Thus you will observe I have made a kind of acknowledgment that novelty has its charms even to the latest period, and indeed I think the mind must be little quallified either for observation or improvment who denys it.

The powers of the soul are apt to languish under a continual samness of place or company unless it is peculiarly fited for the contemplation of the various objects of nature—or can find its resources in conversing with ⟨with⟩ those who have long since bid adieu to the amusements and occupations of time. But as you my Friend are doubtless in too gay a circle to philosophize much, let us inquire a little of the Taste and Etiquette of the smaller officers [?] of the day, or if you please, of the great political movements in the southern hemisphere[4]—or, is all yet locked up in silence and secrecy? Be it so—some of us who have lived long enough not to expect every thing great, good, and excellent from so imperfect a creature as Man can patiently wait till the best systems of the wisest of them are sufficiently ripened for the inspection of the vulgar eye.

I hasten from the scene least from connexion with the actors on the political Theatre and from long habits of attention I should be led to say more than may be thought becoming in my sex.

If you have an opportunity you will most respectfully offer the regards of Esteem and Friendship on my behalf to General Washington and his lady if there. We flatter ourselves with some expectation that he will once more visit Boston and its environs.

I will not begin to chatter to Mr. Gerry if I do I must ⟨beg⟩ open another page. Therefore only remind him of his Friends at Milton who both unite in regards to him, to your parents and sister, and every complimentary salutation you may think due to others who may inquire after the welfare of Your sincere and affectionate friend

M. Warren

ALS, Gerry II Papers, Massachusetts Historical Society; and LC, Mercy Warren Letterbook, 471–72, Massachusetts Historical Society.

1. Apparently Ann Thompson Gerry and her infant daughter had accompanied EG as far as New York on his way to the Philadelphia convention.
2. Mrs. Sarah Sever Russell (1757–87), wife of Thomas Russell, died of tuberculosis.
3. Here Mercy refers to her own son Charles.
4. A reference by a stay-at-home citizen of Massachusetts to Philadelphia and the convention.

James Warren to Elbridge Gerry

. .

Milton, August 5th, 1787

My dear Sir,

We hear that you have brought the great Business of the Convention nearly to a Conclusion.[1] I wish it may be a happy one. We are told it will make us ⟨hap⟩ happy if it be not our own faults. But every Curiosity is raised to know the result in detail. Every pen is held ready for Action and perhaps it will be as thoroughly Scaned out doors, as it has been in Convention. Some from one principle and design, and some from others, will be lavish in their Applauses, or severe in their Criticisms. The upright Member will disregard both. A dead Calm, and perfect Tranquility prevails here at present. We have neither News or Events to Communicate. You have undoubtedly ⟨to⟩ seen the List of our Members of Congress, which I think I forgot to mention when I wrote last. I must dispose of my Farm soon at least of that part for which Mr. Ferguson was in treaty with me.[2] He offered me £2000 sterling. I have laid out some hundreds upon it since. However I would sell it for the same sum or less, even for ⟨£1900⟩ £1600 sterling if I can get no more, only reserving five acres for a house lot which will not incommode but be rather an advantage to the rest. It has occurred to me that probably you may see some Gentleman of fortune who would like to purchase such a place as you Can describe this. If you should you will very much Oblige Your Friend and Humble Servant

J. Warren

My regards to Mrs. Gerry
Honourable E. Gerry Esqr.

ALS, EG Collection of Elsie O. and Philip D. Sang, on deposit at Southern Illinois University Library, Carbondale; and photographic copy, EG Papers, Library of Congress.

1. At this time the convention was still six weeks from its conclusion on September 17.

2. Despite his desire and financial pressures, JW was not able to sell the Milton Hill farm until 1791.

§

In Philadelphia EG expressed concern lest numerically small quorums result in domination of the legislature by a minority of the states. His desire to exempt from publication in the journals of the Senate materials related to military operations and treaties was defeated. To forestall the prospect of foreign influence in American legislative circles, he expressed the hope that only natives would be eligible for such service. Insisting that taxation and representation were strongly associated in the public mind, he urged that the House of Representatives, the immediate representatives of the public, alone have the right to originate money bills.[1]

1. EG to Ann Gerry, Philadelphia, August 9 and 10, 1787, EG Collection of Elsie O. and Philip D. Sang, on deposit at Southern Illinois University Library, Carbondale; and *DFC*, 377, 380, 384, 391.

Elbridge Gerry to James Warren

· ·

Philadelphia, August 13, 1787.

My Dear Sir,

It is out of my power in return for the information you have given me to inform you of our proceedings in convention, but I think they will be complete in a month or six weeks, perhaps sooner. Whenever they shall be matured I sincerely hope they will be such as you and I can approve, and then they will not be engrafted with principles of mutability, corruption or despotism, principles which some, you and I know, would not dislike to find in our national constitution. I wish you had accepted a seat in congress, for the next year will be important.

Adieu my dear sir. Make my respects, &c. Your sincere friend,

E. Gerry.

Honourable J. Warren

Austin, *EG*, 2:36; and excerpt, Farrand, *Records*, 3:69.

§

During the closing month of the Philadelphia convention EG's opposition to the trend of the proceedings evidenced itself in debate and correspondence. To his wife, he wrote, "I do not expect to give my voice to the measures." Five days later he confided to her, "I am ... apprehensive, and almost sure they will if not altered materially lay the foundation of a civil War. I never was more sick of any thing than I am of Conventioneering. Had I known what would have happened, nothing would have induced me to have come." At the close of August he informed Ann, "I have been a spectator for some time; for I am very different in political principles from my colleagues. I am very well but sick of being here." At the beginning of September he wrote her, "Indeed I would not remain here two hours, was I not under a necessity of staying to prevent my colleagues from saying that I broke up the representation."[1]

EG's formal repudiation of the new document came on September 17 when he, along with George Mason (1725–92) and Edmund Randolph (1753–1813) of Virginia, refused to sign the Constitution. Two days earlier in the convention he had spelled out eleven objections to the emerging document. One of the most active men at the Philadelphia meeting, EG had addressed the convention a total of 119 times, a number exceeded by only five others.

A month later, and about to leave New York for Massachusetts, he wrote the Senate and House of Representatives of that state—the letter going to his old friends Samuel Adams and James Warren who were President of the Senate and Speaker of the House respectively—and enumerated his seven principal objections to the Constitution. Meanwhile, during the first month following the close of the Philadelphia convention, the war of words had shifted to the columns of the newspapers and the pages of pamphlets, the heaviest blasts coming from Federalist pens.[2]

EG had returned to Massachusetts when, on November 3, the *Massachusetts Centinel* first published the objections he had written to Adams and Warren two weeks earlier. In succeeding exchanges between Federalists and anti-Federalists, in Massachusetts and throughout the nation, personal abuse and scurrilous assaults became so routine that the employment of pseudonyms became the natural refuge of virtually all who expressed themselves in print.

Between November 5, 1787 and March 24, 1788, Oliver Ellsworth

(1745–1807), one of Connecticut's signers of the Constitution, published more than a dozen pieces in support of the new form of government. Departing from the impersonal tone which characterized most of his writing, Ellsworth named and criticized EG by name in items 4, 5, 6, and 8. Indeed the last-mentioned piece, dated December 24, 1787, was addressed "To the Hon. Elbridge Gerry, Esquire." Charging EG with untruthfulness and duplicity, Ellsworth insisted that the opposition generated in Massachusetts by EG derived "from motives most pitifully selfish and despicable." EG made two unsigned, public replies to Ellsworth, the first in a Boston paper of January 5, 1788, early enough to have impact in Massachusetts circles, and the other, on April 30, 1788, in a New York paper—after the Massachusetts convention had settled the issue there but before it had been decided in New York.[3]

During the election of the delegates to the state convention to consider the ratification of the Constitution, Massachusetts politics mounted a crescendo that included more than one anti-Federalist handbill thought to have been penned by JW, who, along with James Winthrop, was labeled "abettors of anarchy and confusion." In December, JW expressed his anti-Federalist outlook in two series of letters which appeared over the signatures "Helvidius Priscus" and "A Republican Federalist." Vituperation came his way in successive waves of denunciation by Federalists.[4]

Neither JW nor EG won a seat in the convention called to ratify the constitution in Massachusetts but EG, nonetheless, played for a few days a special role for that body. Because of his presence in the Philadelphia convention, he was invited to be present in order that he might answer questions put to him about the Philadelphia proceedings. However, EG heard things that prompted him to move from the role of consultant to that of participant and he quickly became *persona non grata*, blasted by Francis Dana and Rufus King in the exchange that led to his permanent withdrawal.[5]

On February 6, 1788, by a vote of 187 to 168, the Massachusetts convention ratified the Constitution. Accompanying that narrow margin of victory, however, was a list of recommended amendments which included point after point which had been advocated by EG, JW and other anti-Federalists. Massachusetts, although the sixth state to ratify the Constitution, was the first state to question seriously the adequacy of that document.[6]

In February, 1788, the nineteen-page pamphlet *Observations on the New Constitution, and on the Federal and State Conventions*, authored by "A Columbian Patriot," appeared in Boston. Mistakenly attributed to EG for considerably more than a century, this title should be assigned to MW, who easily matched the anti-federal outlook of JW and EG, but in a literary style all her own. Indeed, inasmuch as she enumerates eighteen objections to the Constitution, her opposition might be said to exceed that of either her husband or her friend. Too late to affect Massachusetts, this publication played a significant role in framing public opinion in New York where, in addition to being reprinted in the *New York Journal*, 1630 copies of the pamphlet circulated among the county committees of that state.[7]

Even as he fought over national issues, JW also tried to put his own affairs in order. To Samuel Alleyne Otis, younger brother of MW and one of the Massachusetts delegation to the dying Congress in New York, JW had turned for assistance in settling his old accounts with the Board of Treasury. Otis wrote JW, "I will very chearfully attend the settlement and if in my power effect it. As for the recovery of your depreciation I see no great prospect of it."[8]

After seven years at Milton Hill, during which he had received from his sons no significant assistance in his farming operation, JW, troubled by gout, had left the unsold Milton property and returned with Mercy to the old homestead in Plymouth.

1. EG to Ann Gerry, Philadelphia, August 21, 26, 29, and September 1, 1787, EG Collection of Elsie O. and Philip D. Sang, on deposit at Southern Illinois University Library, Carbondale; and *DFC*, 395–583 *passim*.

2. *Ibid.*, 576–77; Austin, *EG*, 2:42–45; Farrand, *Records*, 3:128–29; Charles Warren, *The Making of the Constitution* (Cambridge, 1947), 125; Charles Warren, "Elbridge Gerry, James Warren, Mercy Warren and the Ratification of the Federal Constitution in Massachusetts," Massachusetts Historical Society *Proceedings*, LXIV (October, 1930—June, 1932), 147; Ford, *Essays*, 5–10, 247–59, 283–91, 327–28, 333–36, and Ford, *Pamphlets*, 27–86, 155–61, 259–76, 279–325, 329–32.

3. Ford, *Essays, passim*; and Ford, *Pamphlets, passim*.

4. Charles Warren, "Elbridge Gerry, James Warren, Mercy Warren and the Ratification of the Federal Constitution in Massachusetts," Massachusetts Historical Society *Proceedings*, LXIV (October, 1930—June, 1932), 149, 155–56.

5. Massachusetts, *Debates and Proceedings in the Convention of the Commonwealth of Massachusetts, Held in the Year 1788* (Boston, 1856), 55–56, 57, 58, 63–64, 71–75; and Robert Allen Rutland, *The Ordeal of the Constitution; the Antifederalists and the Ratification Struggle of 1787–1788* (Norman, [1965]), 66–67, 96–97, 99–101, 103.

6. *DFC*. 651–53; Forrest McDonald, *We the People; the Economic Origins of the*

Constitution (Chicago, 1958), 182–202; and Jackson Turner Main, *The Antifederalists; Critics of the Constitution 1781–1788* (Chapel Hill, 1961), 288.

7. Charles Warren, "Elbridge Gerry, James Warren, Mercy Warren and the Ratification of the Federal Constitution in Massachusetts," Massachusetts Historical Society *Proceedings*, LXIV (October, 1930—June, 1932), 143–45, 157–64; and Anthony, *First Lady*, 156–58.

8. Massachusetts Historical Society *Proceedings*, XLV (October, 1911—June, 1912), 336.

Elbridge Gerry to James Warren

· ·

Cambridge,[1] June 28, 1788.

My Dear Sir,

I wish you would so order your arrangements as to favour us with a part of your time, although the alarm of our being together might be such as to station sentries at Charlestown bridge, and the fortifications for the defence of the federalists in Boston.

It is diverting to hear the manner in which these people amuse themselves at our expense. They suggest that I shall not be able to keep this place; and should it be true, I tell them I hope to find purchasers out of Boston. Others say I am much affected by political events, and disposed to grow melancholy, and so long as this is attended with a *mens conscia recti*, they may think as they please; for melancholy is like madness, which has a pleasure none but madmen know.

The convention of New-York will, I am well informed, annex a bill of rights to a conditional ratification, which will remove all our objections, and it is believed Virginia will do the same.[2] Patrick Henry has been brilliant in that convention, and very severe on [. . .][3] who is reprobated for his duplicity and versatility. I know not what judgment to form with respect to the final event, but trust in Providence for protection from the thraldom, which may be apprehended, unless the new constitution shall be modified and amended. Do not let [. . .][4] be deterred from visiting us, for fear that she and [. . .]⁵ may be again distinguished in Boston by the appellation of the anti-federal ladies.

Your's in great friendship,

E. Gerry.

Austin, *EG*, 2:84–85.

1. The Gerrys had returned to their Massachusetts residence.
2. Virginia, ratifying the Constitution on June 26, recommended a Bill of Rights touching twenty matters and an equal number of amendments. On July 26 the ratification by New York included a lengthy and unnumbered list of rights and amendments which that state advocated. See *DFC*, 659–73.
3. In this period EG's mail was tampered with very frequently. Accordingly, when the meaning was obvious to his correspondent and he wanted to escape the embarrassment of mentioning individuals by name, he left blank spaces in his letters. In this instance, EG referred to Edmund Randolph, who had moved from the anti-Federal to the Federal camp since leaving the convention in Philadelphia.
4. Mercy Warren.
5. Ann Gerry.

§

During the bitter verbal battles over the ratification of the Constitution that cost both of them friends and multiplied their enemies, EG and JW reinvigorated their long-standing friendship. In part it might have been a case of misery loving company; but much of it derived from firm allegiance to common outlook.

JW, defeated by Benjamin Lincoln in the contest for the office of lieutenant-governor, was close to calling it a day as far as his personal participation in politics was concerned. For EG, on the other hand, it was but a breathing spell in his political career, albeit a troubled one as he suffered defeat at the hands of that perennial favorite John Hancock in the race for the governorship.

James Warren to Elbridge Gerry

. .

Plymouth, July 20th, 1788

My Dear Sir

Neither the stationing of Centries, or the malicious wishes and Obliquy of the federals will ever prevent my visiting my friend at Cambridge when it is in my power. No Man, or at least very few, can at this day possess that invaluable Treasure *mens conscia recti* as I firmly beleive you do without being marked by ⟨allerch⟩ detraction and Ill nature. I have myself a large share of malicious Slander which I never deserved from this Country. I heartily despise it. My spirits shall never be affected by it, and among the numerous resources of Consolation it certainly is no inconsiderable one to be associated with a Man who I so much Esteem and with whom I have been associated in the most zealous and faithful services to this Country. They now wish us to be Bankrupt, and despondent, or they would not spread such ill founded rumours. They they gratify their Malice instead of exercising ⟨that⟩ those feelings which pity, if not gratitude should Excite on such an occasion if true. No Man was ever persecuted with such inveterate Malice as I am. It follows me in every step I take. An Instance has lately occurred in which the public certainly had no Concern, but more Noise has been made about my takeing of a few Locks from Milton House, than would have been made if another Man had burned it.[1] It is so in every thing, and I suppose will be so for the same reason it has been so. I will quit this subject after giveing you one anecdote, which I think sufficient to silence Malevolence itself. I went to his Agent and Informed him that there were a variety of Articles which would be very Convenient to Mr. Lee, that he should have the preference at a moderate price if he Inclined to have them, and afterwards received this surly answer, that he would not lay out a Shilling there, and now Complains that they are taken away.

We are now to see the Operation of the New Constitution with all its splendid advantages. You must prepare yourself for takeing a part in the Execution in one House or the other. Policy will prevail over Malevolence, and make your Election certain,[2] and your Acceptance ⟨for⟩ I think must be as certain as your Election, and will be a Choice only of the least evil. I have much to say to you on this and other subjects, which I design to do ere long *viva voce.* In the mean time give my great regards to the federal Lady and beleive me to be your Friend &c &c.

J. Warren

Honourable Mr. Gerry

ALS, EG Collection of Elsie O. and Philip D. Sang, on deposit at Southern Illinois University Library, Carbondale; and photographic copy, EG Papers, Library of Congress.

1. Advertised for sale and unoccupied, Milton Hill continued to be a source of worry for JW until he effected its sale in 1791.
2. Time proved JW a good prophet.

§

As Massachusetts and the nation moved from ratification to implementation of the new idea of government, EG's name once more buzzed in political circles of the Bay State. "Unwilling to expose him to the mortification of defeat," those friends who wanted his voice in the new Senate refrained from initiating his candidacy in that direction. Instead his name went before the electors of Middlesex in the race for the United States House of Representatives. When the balloting did not resolve the issue, and a second contest, between EG and Nathaniel Gorham, a strong Federalist, became necessary, the opportunity for EG's further airing his beliefs and stating his position presented itself.[1]

To an unnamed correspondent EG wrote, in mid-January, 1789, "I am now as I ever have been since the Commencement of our Independence anxious for an efficient federal Government, with every power for promoting the Welfare, and sufficient *checks* for securing the liberties of the people. this *latter* is what I have contended for, and those who wish to prey on the people by means of a corrupt government are loading me and every one else who opposed them with anathemas for urging Amendments. I consider myself bound by the voice of a majority whether in favour of the Constitution as it now stands or of amendments, but wish not for a seat in the federal Legislature and make this communication for your own satisfaction and not to answer any purpose of electioneering.''[2] However, the fact that Massachusetts, along with a majority of the states that ratified the Constitution, had recommended numerous amendments now made EG's position more acceptable. On January 29, 1789, he was elected to Congress.

1. Austin, *EG*, 2:88–89, 90–91.
2. EG to [?], Cambridge, January 12, 1789, EG Collection of Elsie O. and Philip D. Sang, on deposit at Southern Illinois University Library, Carbondale.

James Warren to Elbridge Gerry

. .

Plymouth, February 1st, 1789
My Dear Sir
    I think it is in Sicily a Man Can't Travel with any Security against the pillage and Murder of the Banditti without confideing his Person and property to one of them. Your Letter of the 22d January came by the hands of Mr. Lothrop, and it came safe.[1] You may write me again in the same way, and give me the same pleasure, but Winslow or George[2] can Convey Letters safely by Federals or antis who will deliver them on the principles of honour of some description ⟨if however⟩ or other. It has been long very Apparent that the design of the prevailing party was to "hunt down all who were Attached to Revolution principles." Hancock has been supported by a Coincidence of Strange Circumstances, and lately [b]y an Influence that he should before now have [s]uspected. The Object of their views was to delay his fall ⟨for⟩ till their own purposes were Compleated and then to pitch him down into the Mud ⟨with the rest of us⟩. The Time of Execution is arrived, and he must have an Accession of Strength from a natural resource, or Share the same fate with the rest of us.[3]
    Whether the proposition made to you is founded on his At-

tachment to the whig Interest, on liberal and Extended principles, or on personal views cunninly Concocted your sagacity will soon determine, and your prudence will direct your Conduct accordingly. I say this because I am perfectly acquainted with both your Understanding, and Judgment. I have had too much Experience to be without suspicion of him or his Agent, especially at such a Crisis. However I would open both arms to Embrace them on proper principles. I think an Union of the old Whigg Interest an Object of very great Importance. They may yet be strong enough to Correct the prevailing Sentiments, and to Crush the Influence of the Tories and that of the self Created Nobility which have become really intolerable to the feelings of the sensible and independent. But such an Union should not be shackled with prejudices and little piques. It should be Extensive and Compleatly Confidential as it used to be. For my own part I am so intirely neglected by one Party, and ill treated by the other, that I Expect no propositions from either.[4] You are the only Confidential Friend I have.[5] I have always thought and frequently said, that the most effectual way of counteracting the designs of the present order would be the Institution of Another, of at least equal pretensions. I therefore highly Approve your plan which so perfectly Coincides with my own Sentiments. I don't know but that the general Outlines are as well drawn as the Nature of things will admit of, and the bounds as accurately and properly designated. It is in good hands. I know your resolution, your patience, and perseverance. These with your extensive Acquaintance and Experience promise success, but you must expect to have your resolution and patience brought to the Test on this occasion. You will be Embarrassed by the deceitfulness of false Brethren, by the Lukewarm[ness?] of timid and Moderate Men, by the rancour of Enemies, by the Intrigues of unprincipled, designing Men, and they may all abuse you in the Licientious way some of them have done, without damping ⟨their⟩ your Ardor till you grow as Callous to their ill nature as I have done, but I shall without reserve wish you success.

I am perfectly of your Opinion with regard to a Seat in Congress. For the sake of the Country I wish you may be a Member, for your own I wish you may not be. My best regards always attend Mrs. Gerry. I hope the sweet little Girl and Boy[6] are well. Mrs. Warren will write her by this or the next Oppertunity. I am very sincerely your Friend &c.[7]

J. Warren

Honourable E: Gerry Esqr.

ALS, EG Collection of Elsie O. and Philip D. Sang, on deposit at Southern Illinois University Library, Carbondale; and photographic copy, EG Papers, Library of Congress.

1. EG's letter of this date has not been located. Apparently the bearer was Isaac Lothrop of Plymouth.

2. Twenty-nine-year-old Winslow, the wanderer, was in Boston, having known a restless sojourn in Maine since his return from Portugal. George, after readying himself for the law only to find little or no business in Milton, had gone, at age twenty-one, to a tract of land on the Kennebec River in Maine in which JW had invested.

3. JW misread Hancock's future prospects. When death came to John Hancock, on October 8, 1793, he was in the midst of his eleventh term as governor of Massachusetts, which office he had held without interruption since 1787.

4. Correct in the assessment of his own political prospects, JW was unsuccessful in his pursuit of public office until 1792.

5. John Adams, returned from Europe and Federalist in outlook, was no longer the bosom friend of days past.

6. EG's son died in the autumn of 1789.

7. The letter is docketed "ansd 14th 1789," which apparently refers to EG's letter of February 15, *q.v.*

Elbridge Gerry to James Warren

·   ·

Cambridge, February 15, 1789.

My Dear Sir,

I suspect you will consider me as manifesting a disposition to change my principles, or of a want of resolution to adhere to them, when I tell you it is probable I shall go to congress. Indeed if this be your opinion, you will alter it when I assure you of all political events in which I have been interested, my election I consider as most unfortunate to myself. I had not, during its pendency, the most remote idea of acceptance, but thought of it with horror.

I now think the measure one of all others that threatens destruction to my peace, interest and welfare, and yet such has been the torrent of abuse against me, that no person here will listen to my declining; my best friends say they shall be sacrificed by my refusal, and that I myself shall be considered as an obstinate opposer of the government, which is an opinion that has recently been much circulated.

Should I decline then, I am to be considered as a non-juror in Great Britain, or an Irish Catholic, and sooner than so live, I would quit the continent. In accepting, I see nothing but two years of extreme disagreeables. To gratify my friends, and to avoid the consequences menaced, I have selected a certain positive evil; whether it be the least of the two, I am yet to learn.[1]

Austin, *EG*, 2:95–96.

1. Inasmuch as this letter is available only through Austin, it is not known whether any deletions have occurred.

Apparently JW made prompt reply to this letter late in February, to which EG, in turn, replied on March 2. Neither letter has been located; indeed that of March 2 never reached JW's hands.

§

During the weeks of uncertainty attending the election and acceptance by EG of a seat in the first Congress under the Constitution, the sentiments of his admirers and supporters contributed to the ultimate outcome. From New York, Samuel Osgood, late Commissioner of the Treasury and future Postmaster-general, wrote him an encouraging and challenging letter. From westernmost Massachusetts, John Bacon of Stockbridge wrote, "I most sincerely congratulate you on your Election to a Seat in the Congress of the United States. It will check the sanguine views of our violent Constitutionalists, and add strength and importance to the sober friends of Liberty & Government."[1]

In this same period MW, one eye on her developing history of the Revolution and the other on current events, was exchanging letters with John Adams, soon to become Mr. Vice President.[2]

1. S. Osgood to EG, New York, February 19, 1789, and J. Bacon to EG, Stock-bridge, February 26, 1789, EG Collection of Elsie O. and Philip D. Sang, on deposit at Southern Illinois University Library, Carbondale.
2. *W-A Ltrs.*, 2:305.

James Warren to Elbridge Gerry

· ·

Plymouth, March 3d, 1789

My Dear Sir

You have really taken yourself of to New York in a Tangent, and perhaps arrived there before I could have supposed you had left Cambridge.[1] I did wish to have had a few hours Conversation with you before you left us. In the mutability of Man, in the versatility of his Conduct, and the uncertainty of Friendship that so generally prevails, I could have given you some Instances, that might even now astonish by their singularity, and be of some service to you. But they must not be committed to paper. I must be contented to suffer in silence, without giveing a Lesson of Caution to a Freind. Ambition when *great* is a passion violent in its nature and when accompanied as it always is, by Credulity, distrust, and Jealousy, excludes those of a more laudable kind. I thank God I never forgot an old Friend or easily beleived any thing to his disadvantage.

I suppose you are now just launching into the ocean of Politics, an ocean always turbulent, perhaps now more tempestuous than usual. I wish your habits and Experience may preserve you from Seasickness, while the uniformity of your Conduct, and the rectitude of your Mind may lead you to stem the rolling Billows. Your situation may be singular, but you may as well oppose the Billows as run with an easy Sail before them. Your antifederal Sins will never be forgiven by a Party who while they wish you to support their System, are malignant enough to represent you as puerile and unsteady in your own, that is they report that you was greatly elated with your Election, and had become the highest federal in the Country. All this and much more would be too contemptible to be mentioned for any other purpose than to shew the Temper of the Party. I often reflect on your situation, and think where you will fix your Confidence. A Man that has been used to act with the old Patriots will feel a defect in modern Sentiments, and modern views which even considerable Abilities will not supply the place of. While you are directing the reins of Goverment, I will follow the plough; and in spite of all the persecution that I have suffered for Years I could be very happy in this Employ if I could have common Justice done me. I have a demand for 15 or £1600 for my Services and while at the Navy Board.[2] I have stated my Account to the Commissioner Colonel Walker. He complains of our Books. Mr. Henderson kept them and says they are regular. I always thought so. He was always reputed a good accountant if not he was the best because the only one we could obtain. And you know from the Magnitude of our Business it could not be supposed we could keep them ourselves. You know my Assiduity and fidelity in public Employment and the ⟨diff⟩ very great difficulty attending that at the Navy Board at the Time we were there. Colonel Walker objects to my private account because he says I have charged £900 instead of £450 per annum. It is very true I have done that from October 31, 1778 when Congress resolved "That the Commissioners in the Navy Boards in the eastern and middle departments be allowed a Salary of three thousand dollars per annum each in Consideration of the extensive Business of their Departments." This appeared to me a clear and regular Establishment, and never to my knowledge was reversed. I staid there upon the faith of it which I should not have done without it, because the Business was very great and embarrassing, and the Expence of liveing in Boston nearly equl to the first Establishment. I want Advice and influential assistance. I have presumed to trouble you with this matter because it is important to me, and because I know your readiness to serve me. You will most certainly add a new Obligation by paying some Attention to it. With regard to

our general Accounting I am able to shew by our original Instructions and by subsequent Letters that nothing more was
required of us than a Cash Accounting. We nevertheless kept
many others. If they should not be perfectly regular they may be
better than none. If they do no good they do no hurt. We are yet
to learn whether Mrs. Gerry went with you. If she did please to
assure her of the joint regards of Mrs. Warren and me to you both.
I am sincerely Your Friend &c

J. Warren

Honourable Mr. Gerry

P.S. If General Washington should think it worth while to
enquire after a Man neglected and persecuted as I have been,
I beg you to make my respectful regards to him, and to assure
him that I am the same Man I was when he honoured me with
some share of his Confidence at Cambridge.[3]

ALS, Rare Book Dept., Boston Public Library.

1. Contributing to the rapidity of EG's movement on this occasion was the very
brief interval between the date of his election and that of the opening of the Congress.

2. To the fact that JW's claims had not been settled by the Congress under the
Articles of Confederation and the added fact that the transition to the government
under the Constitution logically called for a restatement of the pending claims should
be added the truth that the stubborn man of Plymouth was in desperate financial
straits at this time. Needless to say, EG's presence in the first Congress accentuated the
timeliness of JW's move.

3. JW's desire to be remembered to Washington might simply have been a polite
social gesture; but, on the other hand, he might have hoped also for executive favor
regarding his unsettled claims or some call to service by Washington.

§

On Wednesday, March 4, the day appointed for the opening of the
first Congress, EG and three of his Massachusetts colleagues were in
their seats but the lack of a quorum forced adjournment. While EG, unable to initiate his new duty, lingered in New York, the thoughts of his
friend MW also turned to that place. "I think," she wrote Henry Knox,
"I should like to look into the Federal City once in the course of my
perigrinations, though not that I sigh for the splendour of Courts. I love
my old Friends, many of whom are collected at New York."[1]

1. *AC*, 1:99; and *W-A Ltrs.*, 2:306–7.

Elbridge Gerry to James Warren

· ·

New York, 22d March, 1789

My dear Sir

I am favoured with yours of the 3d, and assure you that my Situation here, is as I conceived it would be very awkard. I foresaw it was impossible for me to feel easy in a branch of the federal legislature, where I had few or no connections and friends, whilst these were in the same body but politically sequestred.[1] Whatever the State of my case upon republican principles may be, I cannot Seperate from my mind the idea of a degradation, when I reflect that the flower of my life has been spent in the arduous business and see a preference to those who have endured very few of the toils of the revolution. But we both know that republican governments never were remarkable and probably never will be for gratitude, and therefore private life is the System which we ought to pursue for happiness: whilst the road to preferment is thro the maizes of intrigue Servility and corruption, and there is no great prospect of attaining it if we mean to preserve a "reverence for ourselves."

I have had so much of politics as to feel an aversion to them, and should be happy to bid a final adieu to them, more especially to legislatures,[2] whether State or Federal, as a measure that would most contribute to my own and my family's happiness: and therefore I fear not any mortification from my enemies, but from my friends I experience it, by their urging me to places which are neither pleasant lucrative or honorable. These measures of the *latter* have put me in trammels; and had I declined them, the consequences must have been ⟨been⟩ injurious to *them* as well as to myself, by giving an opportunity to my enemies to represent me as an enemy to a federal government, and to reproach my friends for supporting my election when I would not attend Congress to procure those amendments which I had so warmly urged.[3] Whilst I only thot that there was a probability of misconsequences from my declining the appointment, I was determined on that line of conduct, but when I found from all quarters that my resolution had actually produced that effect; I found that I must either leave the State in order to seek a more agreable place of residence; which I could not do without giving away a great part of my real property, or submit to a temporary mortification in order to counteract the malignity of inveterate foes and therefore I concluded on the latter, altho I think it not very probable that I shall continue in the office till the expiration of my commission.

I wanted exceedingly to have seen you before we left Cambridge, but after I had determined to accept, it was necessary to be off without delay, for there was no possibility of conveying my family in february to New York[4] either by water or on wheels, and the Slaying broke up the night after our arrival: apprehensive of this I left many of my arrangements for leaving home incompleat 'till after my arrival here. I want much to have the anecdotes you hint at, but the delay of them will not make me less cautious for there are very few to whom I shall commit myself. Notwithstanding the Scurrility which I have experienced, I cannot but be highly diverted at the arts or folly for I know not which is the true cause, of the federalists in representing me as being elated with my late appointment, when I consider it truly, or at least the acceptance of it as ⟨the⟩ an act of the highest injustice to myself. A federalist I always was, but not in their Sense of the word, for I abhor now as much as ever the corrupt parts of the constitution, but am bound on honor to Support a government ratified by the majority untill it can be amended, for to oppose it would be to sow the seeds of a civil War and to lay the foundation of a military tyranny. I shall however be a Spectator till I can form Some adequate idea of men and measures.[5]

I have not had an oppertunity yet of seeing Colonel Walker, but be assured I will make your case my own, and do every thing in my power to[6]

ALS, photographic copy, EG Papers, Library of Congress; and excerpt, Austin, *EG*, 2:96–97.

1. What was true of the Massachusetts delegation, wherein fewer than 50 per cent of EG's colleagues had seen service in the Continental Congress, was generally true throughout the first Congress. EG's uneasiness was accentuated further by the fact that the overwhelming majority of those he knew well, Federalists as they were, viewed him with considerable suspicion and hostility.

2. In the light of this statement it is noteworthy that once EG withdrew from legislative halls, in 1793, the remainder of his career never returned him to them as law-maker.

3. This exact sentiment had been expressed by Samuel Osgood in his letter to EG from New York on February 19.

4. The happy coincidence that New York was both the seat of Congress and the hometown of Mrs. Gerry made logical this move to Manhattan.

5. For almost four weeks, between April 1 and 27, EG was an interested spectator rather than an active participant in the affairs of Congress.

6. The letter is incomplete.

§

Scarcely had John Adams assumed office as vice president when MW sought favors from him. Among other things, she jogged Adams' mind in reference to her son Winslow, still an unsuccessful pursuer of political favor. Despite the common outlook shared by MW and JW, she, in writing to the vice president, had swallowed a measure of pride, or had attained a degree of reconciliation which JW, in his refusal to correspond with John Adams in this period, could not match.

Beyond being named to the Rules Committee of the newly organized House, EG spent the opening weeks there listening to the debate concerning import duties and in assessing the mind and the membership of his branch of Congress.[1]

1. *W-A Ltrs.*, 2:308–10; and *AC*, 1:101–77.

James Warren to Elbridge Gerry

·   ·

Plymouth, April 19th, 1789

My Dear Sir

I had the pleasure a few days ago of receiving yours of the 31st of March, but fortune always Capricious has niggardly deprived me of another Boon, and suffered yours of the 2d of that month[1] to fall into the hands of some federal Pirate who has never yet restored to me the Contents his Curiosity or Malevolence had made prize off. As the Case is Circumstanced, I can only hope the Contents were of such a Nature as not to gratify both those passions, especially the last, and to suggest the necessity of have-ing recourse to the Mercantile Mode of Covering Goods in Neutral Bottoms that your own Apprehensions may not deprive me of that unreserved, Confidential Communication I have been used to, and which I now Expect from no other quarter.

Our Spirit of Electioneering has been as high or higher than it ever was, when the prize was much more Important. It is over for the Year, and probably Hancock and Adams have succeeded.[2] Bowdoin ⟨and Lin⟩ may be Mortified. Lincoln Certainly is, and must wish he had never been in, unless the predicament he is now placed in may make him more an Object of Attention in the General Goverment, and secure him a place there, to Effect which I suppose resentment and Compassion will Unite their forces.[3]

With regard to our Affairs in general, they are much in the State you left them. All Eyes are looking up to Congress for the restoration of the Golden Age. Dazzled with the Splendor and Magnificence of the begining of your Career, they have no other Ideas. Perhaps history cannot furnish an Instance when simplici-ty, and frugal Manners have so suddenly Changed to Pomp and Expensive parade, and republican habits and Sentiments Changed to ⟨those that⟩ monarchical. As the Taste and Manners of the People give the Tone to Goverment, I expect to see our political Hemisphere Illuminated by radiant Establishments to support that Splendor which every Body seems reconciled to, and most people Consider as naturally Connected with the new Goverment, and necessary to put us on a footing with others.

I am much obliged to you for your attention to my affairs, and for your kind offer to prosecute the matter further, in order to which [sic] you permit me to Obviate the Objections Mr. Walker makes, more especially as it is very Important to me to have the account settled before Mr. Walker's Commission Expires. The principal thing is the Salary. I do not know that any Words in the English Language could have been Chosen more full and Expressive for fixing my Salary at £900 than those in the Resolve, and I would presume that Congress did not design to deceive their Servants, as I certainly should be if it is not allowed me as 450£ ⟨usu⟩ was no Object with me to remain there at a great *Expence* when I could have made much more money with half the trouble. And if I recollect right you was acquainted with my design, and that I made an actual attempt to resign as it was. Those you know were days for geting money and I got nothing by being in that Business even at 900£. Besides, I sacrificed every other Advantage to serve the public there. I refused going to Congress. I refused the Election of Lieutenant Governor, and it would be now peculiarly hard to be deprived of a fair Contract on the part of Goverment Explicitly made in their Resolve. With regard to the account Mr. Walker shews, when a settlement was made with Mr. Vernon, signed by me it may have been done inaccurately and without proper Attention, but the true design was this, and I think it should be Considered as a very Generous, and disinterested one. When the Navy Board was dissolved, there were large Sums due to many poor Tradesmen whose familys were suffering, and no way to raise sufficient Monies to pay them and ourselves. We therefore paid ourselves up to the first Establishment that they might have a part of theirs, and took our Chances for the remainder. Disinterestedness is so rare a Virtue that I should not wonder if he suspected it, but Certainly it should not operate against a Man. But supposeing a Case the strongest of all, that we had been stupid enough to have forgot the resolve for 900£ and made a mistake. Should it not in all Conscience be rectified?

With regard to the 80,000 dollars deficiency, I am sorry Colonel Walker should mention that as an Objection. The very Individual Bills are now in my Custody. They were offered to Mr. Pennell when at Boston. He did not Choose to take them then. I have more than once desired Colonel Walker to send forward an order properly authenticated to rid me of the

Incumbrance, and perticularly by Major Haual last Fall. After that they should never be mentioned but in such an order.

I never could consider it necessary for me to be at the great Expence of Money and Time to go to New York for the purpose of settleing my private Account. If any Illucidations of the public Accounts are wanted provision should be made for paying us for going on which has never been done. On the Contrary we have been told not to Expect it. Mr. Vernon dare not go on Account of the Small Pox. I was not so Conversant in the Accounts, as in other Lines of the department, and therefore could not perhaps give the necessary Information without Mr. Henderson and it could not be Expected that he would go at his own Expence, and I certainly cannot afford it. We all attended Mr. Pennell at Boston and would have done the same to Mr. Walker without pay or reward and there the accounts should have been settled, on every principle and view of the matter.

I am ashamed to give you so much trouble, or even to make an Apology. You must set me at Work on your Farm. I will plough and hoe as much as you please.

Upon the whole I can't help flattering myself that Colonel Walker upon a Cool reveiw of this matter will not make any further difficulty in settling my account as Exhibited. He has indeed signified to me that some of the articles were not admissiable. I do not know or can Conjecture which. However I had rather loose £100 or £150, than not have it settled provided he will specify the articles deducted. I have therefore upon that presumption Inclosed an order to pay the securities or other Ballance to you. I only wish that if it should be done that it may be in several securities, that I may if I have Occasion Negotiate a part, and reserve the rest. I go upon the supposition that the Ballance must be paid in securities, though Cash would be preferred. I Conceive no Vouchers can be wanted, Except Mr. Henderson's receipt for £75—paid him, and Mr. Paine's Bill for about £15, both [*of*] which Mr. Otis has. If mislaid I will give any Engagement to supply them. Mrs. Warren Joins me in Sincere regards to you, Mrs. Gerry, to Mr. and Mrs. Thomson[4] and the young Ladies, will write Mrs. Gerry soon. Believe me to be on all Occasions Your Sincere Friend &c[5]

J. Warren

Honourable E. Gerry Esqr.

ALS, EG Collection of Elsie O. and Philip D. Sang, on deposit at Southern Illinois University Library, Carbondale; and photographic copy, EG Papers, Library of Congress.

1. Neither EG's letter of March 2 nor that of March 31 has been located.
3. John Hancock and Samuel Adams were elected to the offices of governor and lieutenant-governor respectively.
3. General Benjamin Lincoln, having put down Shays' rebellion in 1787 and having served as lieutenant-governor the following year, was soon named federal negotiator with the Creek Indians.
4. Mr. and Mrs. James Thompson, Mrs. Gerry's parents.
5. The letter is docketed "ansd 9 May." That letter by EG has not been located.

§

In time both his knowledge of and interest in commerce and finance drew EG into debate. On April 27, he spoke twice about import duties. A third speech followed the next day and on the twenty-ninth he was one of three named to a committee "to prepare and report an estimate of the supplies requisite for the present year, and of the net produce of the impost as agreed to by the House." The committee report sparked a week of debate, during which EG spoke no fewer than five times on the subject of duties on imports. When the issue came to a vote, EG, reminiscent of earlier days, called for the yeas and nays. This act, approved July 4, 1789, became the first revenue measure of the infant government.[1]

When debate turned to the establishment of the executive departments, EG was again a leading spokesman. He likewise served on the committee charged with the preparation of bills providing for the creation of the Departments of Foreign Affairs, Treasury and War, three areas in which he drew upon more than a decade of experience.[2]

More committee service came EG's way on May 25 when he was named to the committee to consider the subject of compensation for both the executive and legislative officers of the new national government. Twenty-four hours after the subject of western lands was introduced on the floor of the House of Representatives EG, on May 29, successfully moved the appointment of a sub-committee "to consider the state of the unappropriated lands in the Western territory."[3]

Despite his contention that the Constitution needed amendment, and despite his advocacy of amendments, EG, when the issue of amendment first arose, insisted upon giving other matters priority. "The people know we are employed in the organization of the Government," he declared, "and cannot expect that we should forego this business for any other."[4] However faulty EG considered the federal ship of state, he certainly felt that the changes he desired in its rigging should come after its successful launching.

This same spring MW, seeking the help from the powerful that might result in a political plum for a son, had appealed to John Adams only to be rebuffed by him.[5]

1. *AC,* 1:217, 219–21, 239–41, 302–3, 327–28, 345–49, 355, 364–65, 369, 370 and 2:2183–86.
2. *Ibid.,* 1:395–96, 399, 400–404, 406, 406–7, 409, 411, 411–12.
3. *Ibid.,* 412–25, 431, 432.
4. *Ibid.,* 440–41, 462, 466.
5. *W-A Ltrs.,* 2:310–14.

Mercy Warren to Elbridge Gerry

.   .

Boston, June 11th, 1789

My Dear Sir

At Boston on a short Visit, I made a little excurssion to Cambridge and visited your neighbour Fayerweather on Monday last. They very much regret the absence of your family. Indeed the place had a Gloomy appearance to me who so lately enjoyed it with a high relish in the Company of my friends. It is a painful Circumstance that those we most esteem in that Character should be removed to so Great a distance, but convinced it is for the benefit of the public, we must acquiesce. Mr. Warren is not with me, as he is much engaged in building a new house on *Clifford Farm* which he visits every pleasant morning but you will hear from him soon as he told me he should improve the first leisure hour of my absence to write you.

You seem to go on very harmoniously in all public affairs,

which I hope is a happy presage for our Country. It appears to us at this ⟨quarter⟩ distance that all appointments will be made at head quarters and I am requested by a young friend of yours to mention the name of Major Henry Warren[1] to the president as Collector of the Customs for the port of Plimouth and Duxborough,[2] and that you would back the application with your own influence. I wish it might be successful as I have a great desire that he may find some tie in an eligible mode of bussiness to fix him at Plimouth as so much of the happiness of his parents depends on his continuance near them for the residue of their lives.

We are not used to make applications to the *Great* for offices and place—and believe if ever it has been done in any instance it has been rather awkwardly as I now feel though to a Gentleman in whom I have more Confidence than in any other of the nominal or real friends we have at or about the Court. I have no doubt Mr. Dalton, Mr. Langdon, Mr. Strong and others of the Senate[3] may be spoken to with advantage on the subject. R. H. Lee I know to be a friend of Mr. Warren's, and I cannot say the Vice President would not be willing to serve him,[4] but you would be astonished were you to know all the little underground acts that have been used by the malignant to prejudice his mind and break his attachment to G[eneral] Warren. I never knew the one half of them myself till this Visit to Braintree, Boston and Cambridge, but the meanness and passion of a little—a very little man in office at Cambridge—the malignancy of a *Fortunate.* [?] I have lived long enough to see that is the bane of peace. Yet I will observe that I have wished to see you in the Chair of Government because I think you deserve it—and if you could be happier in the elevated station, I wish to see it yet. But in such an event, whenever the day of retreat arrives, I hope you will retire with the blessings, and not the execration, of the people.

You see, Sir, that though my pen is not so often taken up as formerly, yet the old habits of fredom and Confidence remain; and when they cannot be indulged, I wish no further Correspondence.

I have been long used to write to presidents, ambassadors, negotiators and Great men—yet I have always felt as if they were but men. My heart has been too proud for adulation but it is always the receptacle of friendship, but when rebuffed by ingratitude and neglect.

These feelings are recipprocal in the breasts of both your friends at Plimouth who have formerly been gratifyed by many of your confidential epistles.

They still would feel the same enjoyment both from personal and literary intercourse.

We have both bid adieu to the pursuit of pleasure or amusement abroad, but the door of hospitallity is still open to receive the friend, or to bid the stranger wellcome. Nor are there any persons of any class, rank, or description who would be more cordially received than Mr. and Mrs. Gerry, both by Gen. Warren and myself, who with usual esteem [*and*] respect subscribes your Friend

Mercy Warren

ALS, photographic copy, EG Papers, Library of Congress.

1. Twenty-five-year-old Henry, fourth son of the Warrens, was then living in Plymouth, at which place his parents were eager to keep him. On June 2 the House of Representatives had designated Plymouth a port of entry for the collection of duties; see *AC*, 1:434.

2. I.e. Plymouth and Duxbury.

3. Tristram Dalton (1738–1817) and Caleb Strong (1745–1819) represented Massachusetts in the Senate. John Langdon (1741–1819), one of the senators from New Hampshire, and president pro tem of the Senate in opening days of this session of 1789, had known the Warrens since the first Continental Congresses and his stint as navy agent in 1776.

4. Richard Henry Lee's friendship with JW dated from 1775. In view of John Adams' letter of May 29, MW is somewhat presumptuous regarding his support; see *W-A Ltrs.*, 2:313–14.

§

In the mid-June search for constitutionality and efficiency, EG was one who spoke repeatedly about the appointive powers of the president. "It appears very clear to me," he said on June 16, "that however this power may be distributed by the constitution, the House of Representatives have nothing to do with it. Why then should we interfere in the business? Are we afraid that the President and Senate are not sufficiently informed to know their respective duties?"[1] As one of many looking for the bright dawn of a new day, EG relied on experience, logic, a healthy skepticism, and much more that had come his way in the course of two decades of concern about public issues.

1. *AC*, 1:491, 498–532.

James Warren to Elbridge Gerry

.   .

Plymouth, June 17th, 1789

My Dear Sir

I have lately been very unwell or should have not failed to Acknowledge before now the receipt of yours of the 9th May,[1] and to Express my Obligations for the Attention you have paid to my Affairs.

Mr. Walker in his Statement has drawn a Curious picture of our Books which if well founded must make us, and our Bookeeper, very ridiculous indeed. I am Inclined to suppose, and I should not wonder if there were some Inaccuracies in our Books (tho' Mr. Henderson will not admit such a Supposition at all) but the Statement he has given is not in some Instances founded in facts. He may in the Course of such a large Transaction, Conducted in a hurry, pick out some Instances where his Observations may Apply. But I am Certain they will be few, and of trifling Consequence. The Cash Account his Querulous and Captious predecessor acknowledged was Compleat, and well vouched by a receipt for every Article of Charge, and I think I am certain it is so. The Truth is, this is a remnant of the Persecution I have suffered for some time. Not satisfied with its operation here, it is extended to New York, and is virulent enough to follow me to every quarter of the Globe. Thus situated I must submit while others have had no difficulty in Obtaining settlements, and paid much larger Ballances than I have any reason to suppose due to them.

You seem to go on smoothly with your revenue System and if

practice coincides with Theory will soon have a revenue sufficient for every purpose. Time will shew the success. We are all submission to the Wisdom of Congress, and perfectly acquiescent to every Measure without a Murmur or a Groan. This is certainly the Golden Age returned to Bless the Western Hemisphere, when every Man setting under his Vine, and fig tree can read the History of your proceedings without any Emotions or feelings but those of Curiosity or Amusement. No Body can say that the Constitution has not full Scope to Operate on its principles. Federals and antifederals are agreed in their Wishes that it may take its range. My Curiosity is Excited to see the Nature and Effect of Mr. Maddison's [*Madison's*] plan for amendments.[2] I suppose we shall soon have the one, and be in some measure able to Judge of the Other. I wish to know in the mean time how you Calculate the amount of your proposed revenue, and that of your Expenditure, and whether it is supposed that your Impost and Lands will be sufficient without takeing the Excise. You say that your Stile is Courtly. I ⟨am⟩ certainly think it is. Republican principles and Virtue have a Trial which While I regret, I can easily beleive you feel as sensibly as any Man in your Body. Are you on Terms of Confidence with the Vice President[3] or—or—or it is dangerous to ask questions, and more so to make Observations? I shall reserve both till I see you when I shall do both without hazard or reserve. You will make my regards to your good Lady, and all her Friends and beleive me to be your sincere Friend &c.[4]

                                                        J. Warren

E. Gerry Esqr.

ALS, Gerry II Papers, Massachusetts Historical Society.

1. EG's letter of May 9 has not been located.

2. On June 8 James Madison had urged the House of Representatives to resolve itself into a committee of the whole to consider amendments. JW's awareness of this move indicates that however removed he was from active politics, he was abreast of the proceedings in the Congress.

3. This query about EG's relations with John Adams is added proof of the continuing estrangement between JW and the vice president. Meanwhile, despite the fact that JW nursed and possibly magnified his differences with his former friend, MW continued her correspondence with him; see *W-A Ltrs.*, 2:308–14.

4. This letter is docketed "ansd 10th July 1789." That letter by EG has not been located.

§

EG was often on his feet, expressing his ideas at length. In successive roll-call votes he was never alone, within the Massachusetts delegation, in his position. When the bill providing for the creation of the Department of Foreign Affairs, read for the third time, was voted upon favorably, 29 to 22, EG was in the camp of the numerous opposition. Continuing his opposition to cabinet officers, he said, while the Treasury Department was under consideration, "If the doctrine of having prime and great ministers of state was once well established, he did not doubt but we should soon see them distinguished by a green or red ribbon, or other insignia of court favor and patronage."[1]

On occasion EG's views on the nature and powers of the executive branch circulated outside the halls of Congress. Late in June, this word came from Boston, "Your argument as printed in Childs paper is unanswerable. I have given it to Edes with an introduction to print tomorrow."[2]

EG's adamant stand in reference to the structuring of the national government did not blind him to the fiscal realities of the moment. On July 1, voting with the majority, he supported the bill which imposed a duty on American shipping tonnage. That same day he reported a bill "for the establishment and support of light-houses, beacons, and buoys." A law covering this subject was approved on August 7.[3]

Meanwhile MW, dedicated to obtaining federal appointments for her sons, had shifted her New York-directed correspondence from Vice President Adams to Secretary of War Henry Knox. Beginning one letter to Knox with a request that her son Henry be named collector of customs at Plymouth, she quickly continued by nominating Winslow for some post in the military establishment. Inasmuch as General Knox was not personally acquainted with 30-year-old Winslow Warren, MW added, "General Lincoln is undoubtedly his friend. He was his first aid de camp in the successful expedition against the insurgents of the western counties."[4]

1. *AC*, 1:555–58, 596, 599–600, 603, 606, 608, 614, 624.
2. James Sullivan to EG, Boston June 28, 1789, EG Collection of Elsie O. and Philip D. Sang, on deposit at Southern Illinois University Library, Carbondale.
3. *AC*, 1:643 and 2:2215–16.
4. *W-A Ltrs.*, 2:315.

James Warren to Elbridge Gerry

. .

Plymouth, July 2d, 1789

My Dear Sir

Mrs. Warren has shewn me your obliging Letter to her.[1] There are several things Expressed in it that I wish for time to reply to. I could tell you how much I want to see you at Plymouth, how much pleasure and advantage I could derive from a ramble over my Farm, &c &c but the Bearer can't wait, and I must only Attend to the Exigency of the Moment. If there is a predilection in favour of the old officers, their Characters should be Understood, the Collector of Impost and Excise, and the Naval office for the Port referred to. The Character of the first I don't wish to say more of than that he is an ordinary Man, who got the place first by accident, and has kept it by the prevalence of Party and prejudice against me. My Son has been chosen several times by a large Vote of the House, and been defeated by a negative which the Senate gained from the foolish simplicity of a Concession of a Former House. He has therefore only remained in office for two or three Years without an Election, and I think against both Law and Constitution, which I think renders his being in office of no validity, and at least sets ⟨his⟩ the pretensions of his Antagonist upon as fair a footing. The last is a Man of no kind of respectability. He is too little and mean to avoid the Contempt of every Body, and too disgusting in his Manners, and Conduct to avoid the detestation of Men of discernment and honour, and besides is a Bankrupt. His being first in place I reckon among my political Sins, which I heartily repent off. My regards to Mrs. Gerry and Connections. I am in haste Your Sincere Friend &c &c[2]

J. Warren

E: Gerry Esqr.

ALS, EG Papers 1772–1882 (gift of Samuel Eliot Morison), Massachusetts Historical Society.

1. Apparently bearing a date of late June and replying to MW's letter of June 11 (*q.v.*), this letter by EG has not been located.
2. The letter is docketed "ansd 29th 1789." That letter by EG has not been located.

§

On the subject of amendments, few members matched the number of times EG was on his feet expressing himself. However he was not the voice of Massachusetts on the committee to which prospective amendments were referred, and very often his demands for altered phrasing were voted down.[1]

When the idea of a Home Department invited discussion, EG opposed the proposition on both fiscal and political grounds. Interest in finance led him, successfully, to advocate the appointment of a Committee of Ways and Means. Continuing concern about revenue led EG to introduce a bill that called for registering and clearing vessels, ascertaining their tonnage and regulating the coasting trade. On August 7, he was named to the three-man committee to bring in bills "for the further encouragement of the commerce and navigation of the United States."[2]

A germinal idea related to the future Library of Congress was voiced by EG on August 6 when he "moved that a committee be appointed to report a catalogue of books necessary for the use of Congress, with an estimate of the expense, and the best mode of procuring them." Late in the session he enumerated "the debts, taxes, and burthens of the people" as he buttressed his arguments for economy.[3] In the free-for-all that included the consideration of sites on the Delaware, Susquehanna, and Potomac Rivers, and in Delaware for a permanent seat of the government, he strongly preferred the northernmost.[4]

Meanwhile an appeal to General Knox by MW had elicited a cooperative response. He detailed the precise kind of letters and support that could best serve son Henry's prospect of obtaining the customs post in Plymouth. But even as he lifted the hopes of one young Warren, the cabinet officer dashed those of another when he wrote, "As the military establishment will not probably be augmented, at present no new appointments can take place." In August, however, Henry's dream exploded when William Watson was appointed Collector for the port of Plymouth.[5]

1. *AC*, 1:687–91, 732–808 *passim*.
2. *Ibid.*, 694, 696, 697, 710, and 2:2217–31.

3. *Ibid.*, 1:705, 826, 935; and W. Dawson Johnston to Elbridge Thomas Gerry, Washington, October 21, 1901, EG Papers, Library of Congress.
4. *AC*, 1:915–20, 957, 958, 962.
5. *W-A Ltrs.*, 2:315n, 316–17; and *AC*, 2:2187–2214.

James Warren to Elbridge Gerry

· ·

Plymouth, August 23d, 1789

My dear Sir

It is high time to Acknowledge your favours of the 10th and 18th July[1] the first of which has been but lately received. When I mentioned that you went on smoothly with your revenue system, I did not suppose it would fully answer federal Expectation but I must own I thought it would be much more productive than it now appears to be. Where the resources to supply so large a deficiency can be found, and at the same time to avoid one of the Alternatives you mention is a question I shall not undertake to decide. The next step I suppose will be to take the Excises, nor do I see how it can be avoided, however Embarrassing the measure may be to the State Goverments. You have indeed a Choice of difficulties, and you are placed in full view of those Mortifications which your own sagacity foresaw as the Natural Consequences of impolitic Combinations of power. I hope you will frequently recollect the shrewd old preacher's Observations, and not let one or the Other prey on your Constitution. I know this to be a hard lesson to a Man of your sentiments, and Temper but you must adopt it, and reserve your Energy for more hopeful prospects. The question you mention would in the same hands have formerly been differently decided "Sed Tempora mutantur, and ille mutatur in illis."[2] When we meet in your back parlour or mine we shall be at Liberty to Compare former with more modern Times, old principles and sentiments with New ones, and Men with themselves without Incurring the Imputation of Treason.

I can easily Conceive the Time is approaching, and not far distant when others beside the Man you mention will awake from their Golden Dreams, and perhaps make the same Conclusions, which may be just in another view if a Monarchy should be Established. It is a Curious instance of the versatility of Mankind to see (as you and I have) a whole Country within the short period of ten years struggling with energy to get rid of Monarchy, and the same Country makeing every effort to fix another. We did not make the world. We should not have mended it if we had. The dispensations of Providence must be submitted to, if they are greivous it is a Consolation to be able to Lament them, and to be distinguished from that unmeaning folly which equally rejoices in Good and Evil.

The Appointment of revenue officers is made. The Man I gave you a true, tho' not a Compleat Character of in my last has this. If all others, and ⟨p⟩ doubtless some are like this, it would be necessary for a new Committee of supplies to form a New Estimate of the revenue. A fixed rule has been talked of, that is the Continuing the old officers, a Bad one if Adhered to. But this rule has in many Instances been dispensed with, but not in my favour. I find my antifederal Sin in once thinking the Constitution not infinitely wise, just, and politic, is not to be forgiven or forgotten, and what is still more is like Father Adam's to descend to posterity. I suppose Russel's influence with Morris in favour of this new Connection has Carried it. If a vacant Head, with a total want of Ability to Connect a very few scattered Ideas to form a Judgment with a Badness of Heart equal to the weakness of the Head, joined to an insuperable Indolence can form a revenue Officer they certainly can add no respectability to Goverment. We have no News. Mrs. Warren joins me in sincere regards to you, Mrs. Gerry and your Friends. I am with sincerity your Friend &c

J. Warren

Will you please to Inform me in your next if there be now in being a Commissioner for settleing Marine Accounts. Mr.

Henderson and I have serious thoughts of going to New York to Combat the horrid Charges made against us by the last Commissioner, but I should Choose that should be during a Session of Congress.

E: Gerry Esqr.

ALS, Russell W. Knight—Gerry collection, Massachusetts Historical Society.

1. These letters by EG have not been located.

2. Quite possibly JW intended the quotation from Harrison's "Description of England" (1577), which reads, "Tempora mutantur, nos et mutamur in illis."

James Warren to Elbridge Gerry

. .

Plymouth, August 27th, 1789

My dear Sir

When I wrote to you a few days ago I wrote in a hurry, and what frequently happens to those who do things in a hurry, in that Instance happened to me. I paid no attention to that part of my subject which had really made the strongest impression on my mind. You will recollect the zeal and fervour with which I adopted the plan you proposed last winter. My Temper which is not Fabian in its Constitution has been impatient of delays. I wish to see it Compleated. No time is to be lost to Check the rapid Career of Insolence which pervades every Town and Hamlet and marks ⟨ev⟩ almost every department of office, and grows with Time, with favourable Circumstances, and strengthens with our delays. Let us strike at once and beleive what is often true, that Fortune with all her Caprices will favour the Resolute. You shall have the Honor of being the Father of the Institution and shall have as you deserve my Vote for the first President. Permit me to Christen it, to Call it the order of *Sydney*, and to affix to it his Celebrated Motto, "Manus haec inimica Tyrannis, petit placidam sub Libertate quietem."[1] Let the Constitution and the object be of a peice with the Motto, and let it be pursued with an ardor equal to the importance of the object.

I live in a world of Changes, but you know I am as little subject to them as any Man. I feel the same independency of Spirit I used to. I detest as much as ever the prevailing servility and Insolence. They are inseperable Companions. If one is suffered to Exist, the other will shew its shameless front. It has been your Business and mine, and should be again to efface every trait of both. You know my opinion of the proposed plan if it be not the only one, I think it the best. Your prudence and discretion in the Conduct of it, will insure success.

God prosper you, and beleive me to be your sincere Friend[2] &c

J. Warren

E: Gerry Esqr.

ALS, Russell W. Knight—Gerry collection, Massachusetts Historical Society.

1. When Algernon Sidney first wrote these words in an album in Copenhagen, they read:

> "Manus haec inimica tyrannis
> Ense petit placidam sub libertate quietem."

2. The docketing reads, "ansd Sepr 19." That letter by EG has not been located.

§

When Secretary of Treasury Hamilton indicated his readiness to submit a plan for the support of the public credit, EG eagerly anticipated it. In a lengthy speech, EG repeatedly insisted that no distinction be made between the foreign and domestic debts. Continuing to demonstrate his belief "that Public Credit is the main pillar on which this Government is to stand," he next insisted at even greater length, on February 18, that there be no discrimination between the original and assigned holders of public securities. As winter gave way to spring, EG was a vigorous and leading advocate of the assumption of the state debts by the national government.[1]

Although he conceived the fiscal affairs of the new government to be its most pressing business, EG also desired "to see measures pursued by every nation, to wipe off the indelible stain which the slave trade had brought upon all who were concerned with it."[2]

As a member of Congress, EG was asked repeatedly to render special services. From the town of Charlestown, Massachusetts came an ill-timed request that compensation be made for property losses of June 17, 1775.[3]

Yet another correspondent and supplicant, MW, while addressing herself to Congressman EG and Secretary of War Henry Knox, had also employed another tack to win official favor. Under date of March 20, 1790, she dedicated her *Poems, Dramatic and Miscellaneous* (Boston, 1790), to President Washington. In the same period the distaff member of the Warren household, advancing her history of the Revolution, was pleased to learn from General Benjamin Lincoln, "My public papers are at your command."[4]

1. *AC*, 1:1080, 1081, 1136, 1216–20 and 2:1325–33, 1345–1644 *passim.*
2. *Ibid.*, 1:1231.
3. EG to Gentlemen of Charlestown, Massachusetts, New York, April 19, 1790, EG Collection of Elsie O. and Philip D. Sang, on deposit at Southern Illinois University Library, Carbondale.
4. *W-A Ltrs.*, 2:317–18, 323.

Mercy Warren to Elbridge Gerry

·   ·

Plimouth, May 24, 1790

Sir

Though we have neither of us receved a a line from you since Mr. Warren's return from New York[1] I have not a doubt but it will give you pleasure to hear from your Plimouth friend, more especially as I can now inform you my dear partner is nearly recovered from a very dangerous Illness. His very fatiguing journey in the late inclement season produced complaints of an ⟨unna⟩ alarming nature and threatened a speedy period to his useful life, but a fit of the Gout though an unwelcome visitor is sometimes a salutary friend ⟨to us⟩, gives us hopes that he will kick away with one foot those appearances that have greatly alarmed my mind, as he does with the other the unmerited abuse to the unjust detention of his property that would wound the feelings of any man of less philosophy and Conscious virtue than himself.

You who have witnessed his long services and sufferings in the Cause of his Country, who have seen his exertions and his labours through the best period of his life—when he sacrificed health, ease, and convenience without reward—will suffer me to complain a little. Nor will you wonder if you should discover some risings of indignation when the claims of common justice have been denied and the small pittance of hard earned wages rather cruelly withheld.

But I could despise all pecuniary considerations, notwithstanding the equity of the demands, had not his sacrifice of time and property in the public cause have put it out of his power to assist effectually a family of sons ⟨eddu⟩ educated and quallified for any bussiness[2] who from these Circumstances and the malignancy of party yet stand unemployed while those who can claim nothing, either from thier own or the merit of their ancestors are amply provided for.

But I forbear after asking why the plums of Gratitude are all directed to the military line. Were not the patriots in the legislature and other departments as indefatigable, as necessary, as meritorious and as much endangered as those in the field—and if a Warren sacrificed the happiness of Domestic life and relinquished various private departments in bussiness (that gave an income sufficient to answer the convenience and to gratify the Ambition of his family, from the principles of advancing the Fredom of his Country and the liberties of mankind,[)] is he not as much entitled to the Consideration of his Country and the Gratitude of his fellow Citizens as a *Steuben*[3] or any other soldier of fortune or foreign nobleman?

But we do not ask a stipend or liberal donation. We only request our own—a *property* advanced for the public weal—and the scanty pittance of wages due for laborious duty—for the payment of which the public Honour and equity was plegeed, and which every honest man in Government must blush to see with-held from a faithful servant of the United States.

You will, Sir, pardon my emotion when you contemplate not only the feelings of the wife and the mother, but the woman who has suffered much in the great struggle for American liberty, both in her repose, in her connexions, in her health and her for-tune. But in every situation in life beleive me, Sir, to be Sincerely your friend and Humble Servant

M. Warren

Mr. Warren desires me to tell you, after his best regards, that as soon as health is a little more confirmed, he shall write you him-self and thank you for your late strenuous exertions that justice might be done him, as well as for every other Instance of friend-ship.[4]

ALS, photographic copy, EG Papers, Library of Congress.

1. On March 25, 1790, JW had gone to New York to settle his accounts as a member of the Navy Board between 1776 and 1781. Secretary of Treasury Hamilton's report to the Speaker of the House of Representatives, dated April 12, concerning the memorial presented by JW insisted, "That when an account has been adjusted, and a balance discharged, no claim for depreciation ought afterwards to be admitted." See Syrett, *P-AH*, 6:309, 362–64.

2. On March 24, 1790 Benjamin Lincoln, writing to Hamilton, had recommended young Henry Warren for "an office in the revenue." See *ibid.*, 309.

3. For some time considerable attention had attended official handling of the claims and memorial of Baron von Steuben. On May 10, the House had voted an annuity of $2400 to him, a sum later raised to $2500. In addition to the fact that a foreign military man (von Steuben) received consideration that a native civilian (JW) did not receive, it possibly irked MW that EG had so actively and successfully backed the claims of the general. See Syrett, *P-AH*, 5:212–15 and 6:310–27; *AC*, 2:1572, 1584, 1602, 1605, 1609–10; and John McAuley Palmer, *General von Steuben* (New Haven, 1937), 321, 324–25, 327, 331.

4. The docketing reads: "ansd June 11, 1790." This reply by EG has not been located.

§

A number of issues, including the public debt, amendments, the general post office and the seat of government, occupied EG and his colleagues.

John Adams informed EG, on July 24, that he planned to recommend the congressman's brother Samuel Russell Gerry for the office of Collector for the port of Marblehead. It pleased EG that his brother, "a man of strict honor and integrity and assiduous in his undertakings," should be so rewarded. The former commissary official, naval officer and collector of excise not only had a public record to which he could point with pride, but also a large family and pressing needs.[1]

1. *AC*, 2:1724, 1728, 1735–38, 2293–94; and EG to John Adams, New York, July 26, 1790, EG Papers, Library of Congress.

James Warren to Elbridge Gerry

Plymouth, September 20th: 1790[1]

My Dear Sir

I Congratulate you, and Mrs. Gerry on your return to your peaceful, pleasant and Elegant Seat at Cambridge.[2]

If the Gratitude of your Country is too Negligent, or too feeble to Call you again into public Life, on the Approaching Election, I hope you will Enjoy private Life, in all the Gise of a Phylosophic Farmer.

If their Understanding should again be sufficient to Elect you, I hope you will again leave all the Charms of Cambridge with the dignity of a Patriot, but I suppose both the Gratitude, and good Sense of your Country, will have Cunning Intrigue and Misrepresentation to Combat, if they finally Succeed. At all Events I flatter myself with the pleasing hopes of seeing you at Plymouth and shall Endeavour to make you a Visit at Cambridge before you return to Congress. Mrs. Warren joins in the most sincere regards to you and to Mrs. Gerry. I am Sincerely Your Friend &c &c[3]

J. Warren

E: Gerry Esqr.

ALS, Miscellaneous Manuscripts, Gen. James Warren, The New-York Historical Society.

1. Courtesy of The New-York Historical Society, New York City.

2. Congress had adjourned in New York on August 12, to resume its work the first Monday of December in Philadelphia.

3. Docketed "ansd 7th Oct." That letter by EG has not been located.

§

In this period Henry Warren, ill, returned to Plymouth from Boston where he had served briefly as Benjamin Lincoln's clerk. Mercy busied herself sending complimentary copies of her book *Poems, Dramatic and Miscellaneous* to such powerfully placed persons as the Vice-President and the Secretary of War.

EG, meanwhile, spent some of his time, between sessions in Boston, studying the Acts and Resolves of Massachusetts in order to buttress his case for assumption of the state debts by the national government. One indication of EG's position in Massachusetts politics that autumn was his endorsement, on October 1, by the *Herald of Freedom*, a Boston newspaper, for the governorship.[1]

1. *W-A Ltrs.*, 2:321–23; Jos. Ward to EG, Boston, September 25, 1790, EG Collection of Elsie O. and Philip D. Sang, on deposit at Southern Illinois University Library, Carbondale; and item 7357, Marblehead Historical Society.

Ann Gerry to Mercy Warren

. .

Cambridge, 9th December, 1790

My dear Madam

I suppose you have heard before this, of Mr. Gerry's departure for Philadelphia, at which place he expected to arrive last Tuesday.[1] You may well conceive how lonely I feel,[2] knowing as you do, how constant a companion he was ⟨of⟩ by the now solitary fire-side, for tho' his time was much taken up in writing, which was a bar to Conversation, yet I could never feel alone, and I could see that he was well; but now I can scarcely beguile the long evenings with all my invention. The mind grows fatigued by a long application to a Book especially without the pleasing relief of having a kind Companion occasionally to make a remark to, or guide an opinion which you wish perfected. He was so much at home that I feel it more than if it were otherwise, and to add to the tediousness of the time we are likely to have a very long winter. I hope I shall have the pleasure of hearing from our good friends at Plymouth frequently, that I may not feel forgotten, as well as forsaken, by all I value, for next to their society, a letter from our friends produces the most pleasing sensations.

I am very sorry to inform you of the ill success of our second trial in the wheel of fortune.[3] I enclose the ticket that you may at least have the consolation of looking at the Number, and with my best respects to the General and Miss Catharine's[4] love to Uncle and Aunt Warren I remain dear Madam yours sincerely

Ann Gerry

ALS, Mellen Chamberlain Collection, Rare Book Dept., Boston Public Library.

1. If EG reached Philadelphia on Tuesday, December 7, he did so too late to take his seat that day. He was there, however, the following morning. See *AC*, 2:1833–34.

2. Now that Congress no longer sat in New York, the home of her parents, Mrs. Gerry, with her children in Cambridge, was destined to a long separation from EG.

3. Numerous in America for years, lotteries were approaching a peak of popularity at this time. It is impossible to identify the one referred to but it quite possibly was the Semi-Annual State Lottery of Massachusetts, which had started earlier in 1790, its 25,000 chances selling at $5.00 each. See John Samuel Ezell, *Fortune's Merry Wheel: the Lottery in America* (Cambridge, 1960), 178–79.

4. The first of EG's offspring, this daughter was named for her maternal grandmother.

§

As he took his place in the Massachusetts delegation for the third session of the first Congress, EG's mind was occupied with and continued to be concerned about loved ones left behind in Cambridge. In letters to his wife, whom he generally addressed as "my dearest love" or "my dearest girl," he poured out the loneliness and affection which also conveyed his concern about her health and that of his two daughters, one approaching her fourth birthday and the other an infant of less than six months of age.[1]

1. EG to Ann Gerry, Philadelphia, January 25 and February 4, 1791, EG Collection of Elsie O. and Philip D. Sang, on deposit at Southern Illinois University Library, Carbondale; and W. C. Ford (ed.), "Letters of Elbridge Gerry," *The New-England Historical and Genealogical Register*, XLIX (October, 1895), 435–36.

Mercy Warren to Elbridge Gerry

· ·

Plimouth, February 6th, 1791

[*Sir*]

I know you sir will permit me to address a short letter to you
though neither Mr. Warren nor myself have been favoured with
a line from you since you left this state. But I preclude your
apology by a reflection on the magnitude of bussiness that must be
before you and the whirl of amusement, company, and inteligence
in the great capital of America. We hear indeed little but what
the public papers contain though for myself I must say I had
rather read one letter from a *Friend* than all the medly of weekly
papers that have come to hand this winter. That pleasure I have
had two or three times under the signature of a lady at Cambridge[1] and were it not for the dreary season I should certainly
call on her in your absence.

Now sir if you will excuse the curiosity of an author you will
permit me to inquire if you have heard anything of a certain
volume of Dramatics &c in Philadelphia. I should like to know
if Mr. Hamilton[2] and General Knox ever received one of the
copys designed as a compliment to them. Some other great
character have very politly acknowledged the reception of a
volume. This makes me doubtful if some accident did not prevent
the others from reaching as directed. Yet I should not be willing
they should know I had this curiosity.

Your friend hear is in very good health, longing for the return
of spring to indulge in his favorite and philosophic [?] amusement, observation on the beauties of nature the innocuous the
pleasure and the advantages of agriculture. On the back of this
Hobby Horse he rides over all political Theory, and looks down on
the bustle of contending Nations.

Did I not promise a short letter. I did. Therefore to maintain
my veracity, not in compliance with inclination I must hasten
to subscribe the name of your Friend and humble servant

M. Warren

ALS, Russell W. Knight—Gerry collection, Massachusetts Historical Society.

1. Ann Gerry.
2. Concerning Hamilton, see Syrett, *P-AH*, 8:522–23.

§

During the short session that adjourned on March 3, 1791, EG's greatest activity centered upon two issues related to successful administration, the amendment of the new revenue bill and the establishment of the Bank of the United States. On occasion he expounded some of his general views on government, asserting that "no form [*of government*] is stationary, they are always verging either to Democracy or Monarchy, or to Aristocracy and Despotism."[1]

A stanch supporter of the idea of the Bank of the United States, EG believed the Bank had the following objectives: "to render the fiscal administration successful, to give facility to loans on sudden emergencies, and to benefit trade and industry in general." His longest speech in Congress was a massive denunciation of Madison's insistence upon the narrow construction of the Constitution which would preclude establishment of the bank. Soon after the act incorporating the Bank of the United States was approved, EG acquired thirty shares of the Bank.[2]

Matching EG's eagerness to bring the session to a conclusion was MW's desire to win favor at the seat of the national government. Copy after copy of her new book of poems had gone to John Adams, resulting in an exchange of letters which further repaired the breach between the Warrens and the Adamses. Still more of Mercy's ungenerous view of the men operating the national government must have dissipated when, on March 4, 1791 Winslow Warren was appointed to a lieutenancy in the Second Regiment of the United States Army. However, before Winslow could don uniform, he was subjected to sackcloth and ashes. Cornered by creditors whom his father could not satisfy, bankrupt Winslow first had to serve a debtor's prison sentence in Boston.[3]

1. *AC*, 2:1926.
2. *Ibid.*, 1997, 2003; and EG to Ann Gerry, Philadelphia, February 4, 1791, EG Collection of Elsie O. and Philip D. Sang, on deposit at Southern Illinois University Library, Carbondale.
3. *W-A Ltrs.*, 2:324–26; *AC*, 2:1830, 2415–18; and Anthony, *First Lady*, 174–78.

Mercy Warren to Elbridge Gerry

.   .

Plimouth, March 24, 1791

Secret and *Confidential*

I thank you, my Esteemed friend, for yours dated Philadelphia, February 24.[1] Observations on the Contents more perticularly the latter part thereof I shall postpone untill I have the pleasure of seeing you.

⟨I came⟩ It is my purpose Sir at the Conclussion of a certain Historical and biographical Work[2] to make a few strictures on the origin, the nature, and the probable consequences of the new Goverment. [*I*] should therefore like to know a little more of the real character of some who have arisen and figured in our times than I have yet had an oppertunity that will justify a sketch from my pen, perticularly the *great* Financier Mr. R. Morris, James Wilson[3] &c.

Is Patrick Henry a good or a bad man?[4] What is become of Mr. Laurens, Gadsden,[5] and many others of the best patriots of '75, are they sunk into oblivion by their own choice or by the neglect and ingratitude of their Country, while some others that might thus have been hidden in the *pine* barrens (like some of our nighbours who thus found Saningbourgh [?] Wood a place of Security) have come forward with Effrontery and impatience and are rewarded with places, honours, and emmoluments with no merits that I have ever heard off but their Suppleness, Servillity, and Capacity for Speculation and land jobbing.

If in your leasure moments you would furnish your friend with anything relative to Negotiation and Character national or personal, anent influances or opperative principles that have produced great consequences, and that have not yet been recorded by other historians yet are proper to be transmited to posterity, or the loan of any manuscripts that you think might be useful, the Seal of discretion shall be placed on the Communication. The work alluded to is brought forward to the treaty of peace.

Did Dana do any thing in ⟨in⟩ Russia[6] either great or honorable to himself or Country? Was he a man of address, penetration, knowledge of Courts or of the human heart sufficient for an envoy to so great a power? From the irritibility of his nerves I should judge his mind was too often disturbed by little passions and prejudices to command and retain the respect of great ⟨Statsmen⟩ Statsmen and polititians, or even of the common observers of human Character. He is undoubtedly a man of understanding and professional knowledge and if I name him at all[7] I wish to lay asside my own prejudices and to do him justice.

You may think Sir the bussiness I am upon is a bold undertakeing. It was begun for the amusement of myself continued ⟨wit⟩ with a veiw of conveying to my Children the Causses of the Struggle and an information of the Conduct and Characters of the principle actors in the beginning of the revolution and I wish to finish it in a manner that may be useful to them and entertaining to *thier* friends. My *own* I have out lived except Mr. and Mrs. Gerry and three or four others. Perhaps this circumstance has given me a better opportunity of seing the human Character and the Conduct of human life in a more just and proper light than if I had been a favorite of fortune.

Had your Plimouth friends been always dandled in the lap of prosperity they would certainly have had many flatterers who would have arrogated the honorable appellation due only to the name of *friend*, yet perhaps might have been as tottally destitute of friendship as they now appear.

If you receive this letter in Silence I shall think you mean to convey by that a delicate intimation that I have gone out of my line. If you note the Contents as requested I shall go on with Spirit. In either Case I shall think you mean nothing unfriendly to Your Respectful Humble Servant

M. Warren

My best regards to Mrs. Gerry.

The favour I ask of you Sir I mean not to confine within the limits of the last year or too of the War. I shall if I live revise the whole therefore for any hint or information from you from your first being a member of Congress may be useful.

ALS, EG Papers 1772–1882 (gift of Samuel Eliot Morison), Massachusetts Historical Society.

1. EG's letter of February 24 has not been located.

2. The reference is to the long-term project that became her three-volume *History of the Rise, Progress and Termination of the American Revolution, Interspersed with Biographical and Moral Observations* (Boston, 1805).

3. At this time Robert Morris (1734–1806) was one of Pennsylvania's U.S. Senators; he had declined the post of Secretary of the Treasury in Washington's cabinet. James Wilson (1742–98), at the moment of Mercy's query, was sitting as an Associate Justice of the U.S. Supreme Court.

4. EG's answer to this question, if it were available, might prove interesting, especially inasmuch as the paths of the two men had seldom crossed since their service together in the Continental Congress of 1776. During the Washington administration, Henry declined a succession of political posts, the first of which had been that of Chief Justice of the U.S. Supreme Court.

5. Henry Laurens, after signing the peace treaty with Great Britain, had retired to his plantation near Charleston, South Carolina. Declining a number of political positions at both the state and national level, he persisted in his withdrawal from public life until his death in 1792. Christopher Gadsden (1724–1805) a fellow South Carolinian who had served in both the Continental Congress and the Continental Army, had occupied his last political office in 1780.

6. Our first minister to Russia, Francis Dana had filled that diplomatic post between 1780 and 1783.

7. Rarely today does a general account of the Revolution mention Dana.

§

Even as he departed from Philadelphia at the close of the first Congress, EG knew, having been reelected, that he would return there in the autumn of 1791. What he did not appreciate fully at that time, however, were the influences that would come to bear upon him in the intervening months. The half-year between March and October sharpened EG's awareness of the following: the hardening of party lines, lines that accentuated his minority position, lessened his capacity to achieve his objectives, and dampened his enthusiasm for the political arena; the well-being of his young and growing family that required more attention to his properties and investments; and the increased tugs of a household that counted youngsters who needed the presence and guiding hand of their father and a loving wife whose indifferent health underscored the desirability of his remaining at her side.

Speaking more infrequently than in the previous session, EG remained characteristically adamant once he made up his mind regarding an issue. On the subject of the ratio of inhabitants per congressman, he stanchly supported the 30,000 to 1 proposition. In the field of financial policy, he "urged the propriety of doing equal justice to every class of the public creditors."[1]

Several facets of the operation of the post office department drew his attention. He fortified his insistence that "the power to establish post roads was coeval with that of establishing post offices," with the query "why the commercial interest only should be accommodated, and the inland inhabitants excluded from the advantages of post roads?" Opposing a tax on newspapers, he declared, "That wherever information is freely circulated, there slavery cannot exist; or if it does, it will vanish as soon as information has been generally diffused," a sentiment that led him to report out of committee a bill for the reduction of postal rates on newspapers.[2]

When the inhabitants of Northumberland County, Pennsylvania laid a petition concerning distilled spirits before the House, EG, objecting because it sought repeal of legislation, verbally castigated the people of the western counties for non-payment of taxes. The Whiskey Rebellion was then but a cloud on the political horizon, but EG was vigorously supporting the position of the national government. Another regional matter with national implications, the fisheries bill so dear to the hearts of New Englanders, found him stanchly and successfully backing the measure. A sense of history, combined with the incomplete and prejudiced reporting that then characterized the coverage of congressional activity, led the ex-Marbleheader to propose "a full and impartial publication of the debates of that House."[3]

The May-to-November period between sessions of Congress in 1792 further demonstrated, in the diminution of his correspondence, EG's slackened identification with politics. Meanwhile his purchase, on June 4, of land in Cambridge emphasized the primacy of his personal interests at the time.[4]

The four-month second session of the second Congress (November 5, 1792—March 2, 1793) found EG's interest and participation in the business of government almost in eclipse, despite attention accorded the

recent expedition led by General St. Clair, the interest rate of government loans, claims against the United States, the pay of the late army,
and the public debt.[5]

While EG was moving closer to retirement from Congress, additional
misery and grief fell to the lot of Mercy and JW. However humiliating to
his parents, Winslow's incarceration in debtors' prison had evoked a
manliness and moral courage in him that had never previously been in
evidence. In mid-1791 he made his way west via Pittsburgh to join
General St. Clair at Fort Washington. North from that place 2nd
Lieutenant Warren moved with the army of 1400 that the Indians
ambushed on November 4. Among the casualties that day was Winslow
Warren, dead. Mercy's grief fed her irritation with the government that
was slow to inquire into the fiasco.[6]

1. *AC*, 3:168–69, 190–92, 243, 267–68, 273–74, 331, 531–32.

2. *Ibid.*, 236, 289, 308, 436, 1333–42.

3. *Ibid.*, 299–300, 375–78, 401, 563–65, 1329–32.

4. Deed, June 4, 1792, Gerry-Townsend Land Papers, 1675–1846, Manuscript
Division, New York Public Library.

5. *AC*, 3:669, 682–83, 687, 700–701, 706, 756–57, 759, 805–7, 812, 823.

6. Anthony, *First Lady*, 174–85; and *W-A Ltrs.*, 2:327–28.

On April 3, 1791 MW addressed to EG a one sentence note in which she expressed
apprehension about her letter of March 24 to him. That note, not reproduced here, is
docketed "ansd April 11, 1791," That reply by EG has not been located.

James Warren to Elbridge Gerry

. .

Plymouth, December 18, 1792

My dear Sir

I frequently regret the loss of that intercourse with you which
I used to enjoy for so long a course of years. I now seldom see your
name but in the debates, motions, or Committees of Congress.
This is not my fault, because there is no subject in this barren
quarter worth your attention.[1] And the same reason may excul-
pate you from a fault, when you drop a correspondence from
which you can derive neither pleasure nor advantage. The
elections have engrossed our attention. Before you recieve this

you will have seen in our papers the lists of those already made, and be able to judge of the complexion of the whole; however not exactly perhaps; because some have obtained their elections by the inattention of the people, and some by art and management. If the poll had been kept open to the usual hour in Boston, neither Ames or Cobb[2] had been chosen; and on another trial the latter would never get a quarter of the votes. If we are to judge of the votes to the Southward by those here for Vice-President, his political character must stand higher than was expected, and he must enjoy a much greater unanimity than I believe he could hope for. I want much to know how the political machine operates in other parts of the continent, and what is [*it*] that so alarms the Aristocrats for the safety of the *best* of governments.

I have lately trod the sacred ground of Concord, where the noble resolution was taken to raise an army to oppose the mighty power of Britain. I visited with a degree of veneration the room where the Committee set. A thousand recollections, and a thousand reflections filled my mind. I saw but few of the old hands, and little of that noble spirit, and as little of those comprehensive views and sentiments which dignified those times. Thus I have lived long enough to feel pains too great for me to describe.

I have been so used to call on your friendship, that I think I will make no apology for enclosing to you a power to obtain for my son the arrearages of his pension.[3] He will certainly feel himself exceedingly obliged to you for your attention to this matter, which is of some importance to him.

I congratulate you on the fine prospects and appearances in France. You must give my best regards, and love if you please to Mrs. Gerry—to her Sister and her precious little girls. Mrs. Warren joins in my best wishes for health, happiness, and the blessings of Heaven to you all.

I am Sincerely, as I ever have been, Your friend and humble Servant[4]

J. Warren

Honourable Elbridge Gerry Esqr.

LS, EG Collection of Elsie O. and Philip D. Sang, on deposit at Southern Illinois University Library, Carbondale; and photographic copy, EG Papers, Library of Congress.

1. Despite his dedication to farming and his removal, in Plymouth, from the political winds of Boston, JW obviously followed the affairs of Congress closely in the press.

2. Fisher Ames (1758–1808) a Federalist, served as a Representative from Massachusetts during the first four congresses. Meanwhile David Cobb (1748–1830) was elected Representative in 1792 to the third Congress, the only one in which he served.

3. James Warren, Jr.

4. This letter is not in JW's hand, but the signature is his. The shakiness in that signature indicates, when compared with his handwriting in letters of the late 1780's, that JW had suffered noteworthy physical deterioration. The docketing reads, "ansd 7th Jany 1793," which letter by EG has not been located.

EPILOGUE

. .

WHEN, in the Christmas season of 1792, James Warren told Elbridge Gerry, "I have lately trod the sacred ground of Concord . . . with a degree of veneration . . . and a thousand reflections filled my mind," he spoke of more than a personal pilgrimage, for it was the closing of an era.

All of the revolutionary and dissenting trio, Elbridge, Mercy and James, lived on for years and years, some in the limelight of public affairs, but with the firm establishment of both state and national government, the political era that had opened in 1776 had closed.[1]

James Warren

Destined to live sixteen years after his pilgrimage to Concord, James Warren was a weary 66-year-old man in 1792. The aging that was evident in his shaky signature made writing difficult and in truth he wrote few letters during the remaining years. Politically his few allies still found him stanch and unyielding. His political foes preferred to term him querulous, stubborn and sour.

For three years, 1792–94, he served in the governor's council but that, for JW, was a lesser arena than the one he had liked best, the Massachusetts House of Representatives. In 1804, reduced to playing a bit part in the passing political drama, he was named one of the presidential electors for Massachusetts. Death came during the night of November 27–28, 1808.

Mercy Warren

Two years younger than her husband, and destined to outlive him by six years, Mercy Warren was vigorously keen most of the years that remained

---

1. For comment on the unity of the constructive political era between 1776 and 1791, see Samuel Eliot Morison, *By Land and By Sea; Essays and Addresses* (New York, 1953), 13.

to her. As the demands of her thinning family permitted, she spent more and more time with her major prose project, her history of the Revolution. The dramatist in her nature had departed and her poetic urge, with rare exceptions such as the marking of the death of her son George, subsided.

Even as she borrowed the public papers of some significant figures and picked the memories of others for facts and opinions, MW surely discussed many of her conclusions with her husband as she recorded them in her growing manuscript. Finally the project that had busied her intermittently for a quarter of a century emerged, in 1805, in three hefty volumes under the title *History of the Rise Progress and Termination of the American Revolution, interspersed with Biographical Political and Moral Observations*. Frequently subjected to scholarly study and historiographical assessment in subsequent years,[2] the work sparked more than one furor upon publication.

When John Adams found himself depicted as "a statesman of penetration and ability, whose passions and prejudices were sometimes too strong for his sagacity and judgment,"[3] he inaugurated a flow of letters of furious protest. Mercy's rapid replies were in kind. Their heated correspondence climaxed the coolness that had marked Warren-Adams relations since the late 1780's.

Only in 1813, five years after the death of James Warren and almost within the shadow of the grave that embraced both Mercy and Elbridge Gerry did the latter effect a reconciliation between the literary lady of Plymouth and the ex-president.

At the age of eighty-six, MW expired, American womankind's most generous gift to the era of the American Revolution.

Elbridge Gerry

When Elbridge read James Warren's statement of his pilgrimage to the past, he was himself completing the final months of his service in the national House of Representatives. There, in February, 1793, he served on a three-man committee "to bring in a bill to establish fees in the Treasury Department, for the transfer of public securities." However,

---

2. One fine historiographical assessment is in Maud Macdonald Hutcheson, "Mercy Warren, 1728–1814," *The William and Mary Quarterly*, X (July, 1953), 396–400.

3. Mercy Warren, *History of the Rise Progress and Termination of the American Revolution. . . .* (3 vols., Boston, 1805), III, 392.

when the committee introduced the product of its labors, Gerry "objected to the bill on general principles."[4]

Despite such obstructionist tendencies on occasion, EG had nonetheless cast his votes—for bills, resolutions, amendments, and so forth, with the majority more than 73 per cent of the time that last session of his service in Congress. Perhaps the joys of family were calling him but at the same time, however he disliked the cleavage of parties, he was not unalterably opposed to the pattern of ideas that moved the new government along those formative first years.

Of the remaining twenty-one years of his life, EG spent the first four with his family, diminishing his correspondence and recoiling from the world of active politics. In 1797, as a presidential elector, he helped John Adams into the presidency. Adams, in turn, named him to the unforgettable XYZ mission which still tends to heap anathema upon EG.[5] After four successive and unsuccessful races for the governorship of Massachusetts at the turn of the century, he again withdrew from the political arena. During the interval 1804–10 his most important political activity found him serving as a presidential elector in 1804, on which occasion he cast a vote for Thomas Jefferson.

In April, 1810, in his sixty-sixth year, he won the first of two successive one-year terms as governor of Massachusetts. While in that post, in February, 1812, he was a party to the gerrymander that indelibly etched his name into American political science. Narrowly defeated for a third term as governor, EG was nominated in June, 1812 as the vice-presidential running mate of James Madison.

Vigorous in his conduct of the business of the Senate and in his pursuit of society in Washington, EG was en route to his office and his work when he was stricken in his carriage. Death came quickly on the morning of November 23, 1814, a scant five weeks after the burial of Mercy Warren.

The youngest and most significant of these three revolutionaries and dissenters, EG was the last to go. Admittedly a secondary figure, EG has not been accorded the stature he deserves in the Revolutionary era. Casual students and textbooks historians alike tend to depreciate him on three counts: 1) the man who refused to sign the Constitution, they infer, had to be unbalanced; 2) the man who lingered in France in 1798 must have been a questionable character; and 3) the man who connived to

---

4. *AC*, 3:868, 879.

5. In an effort to combat this negative assessment of EG, Russell W. Knight has published *Elbridge Gerry's Letterbook: Paris 1797–1798* (Salem, 1966).

secure party dominance must be distrusted. Only when more breadth and less single-mindedness is indulged—when more secondary figures are appraised and fewer historical spotlights are turned solely on the giants in the drama will EG receive his just desserts.

In 1776 James and Mercy Warren and Elbridge Gerry were dissenters, opposing the rule of Britain. For that successful dissent they, like many others, are now acclaimed as exponents of political wisdom. In the 1780's, on the other hand, as they fought certain patterns of thought and political trends, the same trio emerged in the losing camp. Winners in the military struggle, they are approved; losers in the political struggle, they are belittled—despite the relationship between their dissent and the first ten amendments to the federal constitution.

Close study of such successful-unsuccessful revolutionaries can validate the necessity, the indispensability of dissent in the early political as well as military moments of our nation. For this reason a perspective on the Warrens and Gerry serves a useful purpose today.

As we move into what promises to be a prolonged period of bicentennial celebrations, it would be well if that "veneration of 'The Founding Fathers' whose words and deeds, like the beads of a rosary, keep believers in touch with their faith"[6] could embrace more of the secondary figures and the dissenting ideas. If that can be achieved, the need for dissent demonstrated by James and Mercy and Elbridge may help contribute, in our time, to a perspective that enhances the dignity of dissent.

---

6. Adrienne Koch (ed.), *Notes of Debates in the Federal Convention of 1787 reported by James Madison* (Athens, Ohio, 1966), vii.

Index

Adams, Abigail: letters from, 21, 53, 81; meets EG, 45; letters to, 46, 67; complaints by, 67; mentioned, 48n6

Adams, John: letters to, xxvi, xxvii, xxix, 10, 14, 16, 23n1, 30, 34n5, 49, 53, 54, 55, 61, 64, 67, 71–72, 75, 81, 90, 95, 117, 122, 137, 153, 154, 156, 164, 168, 172, 183, 196, 199, 221, 226; elected to Continental Congress, 3; activities of, 13n2; letters from, 14, 21, 23n2, 24, 34ns3, 7, 44, 46, 61–63, 70, 92, 140, 170, 189; regarding fortifications, 14; discusses fire ships, 30; named commissioner to France, 99; in France, 115n2; praise for, 170–71; minister to Great Britain, 185, 196n3; recommendation by, 240–41; copy of book for, 245; characterization of, 254; mentioned, 4n1, 19, 25, 37, 45, 49, 83, 93, 105n1, 138, 139n4, 174, 214n5, 227

Adams, Samuel: influence of, xxx; letters to, xxx, 111, 115, 128, 134, 148, 205; elected to Continental Congress, 3, 49; letters from, 61–63, 70, 71, 118, 122, 124–25, 128; serves on committee, 118; mentioned, 4n1, 44–45, 83, 93, 105n1, 114, 115n5, 130, 133, 148, 222

The Adulateur: MW's play, xxviii

Aid: by French, 33, 52, 125

Albany, New York: mentioned, 59

"Alexander" (brigantine): cargo of, 69; commanded by Capt. John Williamson, 73

"Alliance" (frigate): commanded by Pierre Landais, 124n3; confusion aboard, 146–47

Alliances: EG regarding, 26

"America" (sloop): Plymouth-owned, 119

American Academy of Arts and Sciences: EG elected to, xx

Ames, Fisher: elected to Congress, 251; identified, 252n2

Andrews, Capt.: at Portsmouth, N. H., with ship, 76

Annapolis, Maryland: EG in, xxi; praised, 178; mentioned, 170, 174

"Argo" (ship): arrival expected, 155; loss of, 157

Army: movements of, 13

Arnold, Benedict: assignment of, 120; identified, 121

Articles of Confederation: signed by EG, xix; formulation of, 56; consideration of, 77, 89; EG regarding, 89, 90; nearing completion, 92; completed, 94, 95–96; await action by Mass., 109; ratified by Mass., 112; revision of, 192, 200

Austin, James T.: editorial practices of, 52n3

Bacon, John: identified, 188n4; mentioned, 188, 215

Baltimore, Maryland: EG in, xviii, xix; conditions in, 53

Bennington, Battle of: mentioned, 79, 80n1

Berkshire County, Mass.: militia from, 59

Bernard, Sir Francis: Tory, 129; identified, 131n2

Beverly, Mass.: regiment at, 17

Biddle, Capt.: commands "Randolph," 89